INSPIRED SUSTAINABILITY

Ecology and Justice

An Orbis Series on Integral Ecology

Advisory Board Members
Mary Evelyn Tucker
John A. Grim
Leonardo Boff
Sean McDonagh

The Orbis Series on Integral Ecology publishes books seeking to integrate an understanding of Earth's interconnected life systems with sustainable social, political, and economic systems that enhance the Earth community. Books in the series concentrate on ways to

- Reexamine human-Earth relations in light of contemporary cosmological and ecological science.
- Develop visions of common life marked by ecological integrity and social justice.
- Expand on the work of those exploring such fields as integral ecology, climate justice, Earth law, ecofeminism, and animal protection.
- Promote inclusive participatory strategies that enhance the struggle of Earth's poor and oppressed for ecological justice.
- Deepen appreciation for dialogue within and among religious traditions on issues of ecology and justice.
- Encourage spiritual discipline, social engagement, and the transformation of religion and society toward these ends.

Viewing the present moment as a time for fresh creativity and inspired by the encyclical *Laudato Si'*, the series seeks authors who speak to ecojustice concerns and who bring into this dialogue perspectives from the Christian communities, from the world's religions, from secular and scientific circles, or from new paradigms of thought and action.

INSPIRED SUSTAINABILITY

Planting Seeds for Action

by

ERIN LOTHES BIVIANO

ORBIS BOOKS

Maryknoll, New York 10545

ORBIS BOOKS
Maryknoll, New York 10545

Fathers and Brothers
MARYKNOLL™
TOGETHER IN GOD'S MISSION OF MERCY

Founded in 1970, Orbis Books endeavors to publish works that enlighten the mind, nourish the spirit, and challenge the conscience. The publishing arm of the Maryknoll Fathers and Brothers, Orbis seeks to explore the global dimensions of the Christian faith and mission, to invite dialogue with diverse cultures and religious traditions, and to serve the cause of reconciliation and peace. The books published reflect the views of their authors and do not represent the official position of the Maryknoll Society. To learn more about Maryknoll and Orbis Books, please visit our website at www.maryknollsociety.org.

Sections of chapters 1 and 3 appeared in "Come with Me into the Fields: Inspiring Creation Ministry among Faith Communities," *New Theology Review*, March 2013, and "Worldviews on Fire: Understanding the Inspiration for Congregational Religious Environmentalism," *CrossCurrents*, December 2012. The author extends sincere thanks to the editors.

Manufactured in the United States of America.

Library of Congress Cataloging-in-Publication Data

Names: Lothes Biviano, Erin, author.
Title: Inspired sustainability : planting seeds for action / Erin Lothes Biviano.
Description: Maryknoll : Orbis Books, 2016. | Includes bibliographical references and index.
Identifiers: LCCN 2015039181 | ISBN 9781626981638 (pbk.)
Subjects: LCSH: Human ecology—Religious aspects—Christianity. | Ecotheology. | Human ecology—Religious aspects. | Sustainability.
Classification: LCC BT695.5 .L68 2016 | DDC 261.8/8—dc23 LC record available at http://lccn.loc.gov/2015039181

For my father, Peter Brink Lothes,
who taught us that if you take care of it,
it will last forever.

Contents

Acknowledgments

This book has been a great joy to research, and I am indebted to the persons who shared their time and insights as research participants. I would like to thank each of the research participants for their gifts of time, profound observations, and thoughtful engagement with the ideas raised in our focus group conversations. Most of all I celebrate their outstanding leadership as early pioneers in faith-based environmental advocacy. Their vision and dedication inspires and encourages me. All are acknowledged by first or full name, according to their preferences, in Appendix B.3.

This research was made possible by an Earth Institute Fellowship at Columbia University from 2007 to 2010. I extend very special thanks to Jeffrey Sachs, executive director of the Earth Institute, and to John Mutter, director of the Fellows Program, who included me in an extraordinary community of sustainability scientists as the fellowship program's first humanist and theologian. This was an unequaled opportunity for me to encounter the range and breadth of cutting-edge sustainability research and to grapple with the scale of the crisis we face. I also warmly thank Robert Pollack, whose Center for the Study of Science and Religion was a unique, novel, and hospitable home for exploring the moral dimensions of sustainability research and other critical questions at the nexus of religion and science. I am also deeply grateful to David Krantz and Sabine Marx of the Center for Research on Environmental Decisions (CRED) and other CRED and Earth Institute colleagues for the opportunity to participate in many conversations, seminars, and annual meetings, which occasioned an invaluable cross-fertilization of ideas about the dynamics of environmental decisions. This research and analysis would not have been possible without the dedicated and expert work of Bob Scott, Columbia Libraries, and my research assistant, Kara Kaminski.

I especially thank Rev. Fletcher Harper, executive director of GreenFaith, for introducing me to the original six New Jersey congregations and their sustainability committees. It has been a pleasure to share many subsequent collaborations with Fletcher and the many faith-based environmental leaders in the rapidly growing movement that GreenFaith has been instrumental in fostering. I would also like to thank John Jones for his early support of this project and his suggestion to broaden the research nationally, an immensely rewarding process that the Earth Institute Fellowship made possible. I could have conducted endless focus groups and express my gratitude to all those who introduced me to the other congregations nationwide, including the Catholic Rural Life Council, Roshan, and Daniel Rosen.

I warmly acknowledge the pleasure of many opportunities to converse and collaborate with Mary Evelyn Tucker and John Grim, the deans of the scholarly field of religion and ecology. My long-standing association with the Forum on Religion and Ecology at Yale has been intellectually and personally rewarding. My research continues to be enriched by the many colloquia, conversations, and publications supported by the Forum and all its outstanding colleagues and friends. My warmest gratitude to Elizabeth Johnson and Leo Lefebure for their friendship and visionary scholarship advancing the horizons of ecological theology and interreligious understanding. I especially thank the College of Saint Elizabeth for its commitment to faith, spirituality, and care for creation.

Many colleagues read drafts, and I am indebted to their insights, while all errors that remain are my own. Warm thanks go to Bede Bidlack, Julia Brumbaugh, Mark Caponegro, James Cornwell, Kathryn Lilla Cox, Mary Doak, Walter Grazer, Fletcher Harper, Linh Hoang, Jennie Javore, David Krantz, Leo Lefebure, Sabine Marx, Cynthia Peabody, Brian Robinette, Larry Troster, Julia Upton, Julianne Warren, and Nancy Wright. I am also grateful to family members who provided not only encouragement but critical reading as well: Angelo Biviano, Elspeth Lothes, Alison Lothes, Katherine Walker, and Edward Dabuzhsky.

I wish to thank Jim Keane and all at Orbis Books most sincerely for their wise editorial direction and support; it is a privilege and a pleasure to be part of the Orbis legacy of scholarship, which advances new horizons in theology and social justice.

The satisfactions, challenges, delights, and frustrations of the writing process were shared continually with Kathryn Lilla Cox, and I gratefully acknowledge the joys and support of our theological and personal friendship.

As always, every aspect of the work I love is encouraged, supported, and often proposed by my husband, Angelo Biviano, who truly inspires and sustains me.

This book is for Davey and for Matthew.

Preface

In my ancestral soul, I am a forest dweller. I meet the peace of God under the trees. If those forests are cut down, where will I and so many others find peace in the cool of the evening? And as deforestation destroys the lungs of the world, how will we breathe? At some point in the late 1990s, I began to see that the cause of the poor championed by my church and all religious traditions was gravely threatened by global warming, which was then still felt as a future possibility at most. If we were left with a world damaged by deforestation, climate change, desertification, and pollution, how could people live healthy lives, move out of poverty, breathe clean air, and find God in the beauty of the earth? This became an intensely existential and spiritual question for me in 1998, the hottest year on record.

That summer, as I drove from my job in Queens to visit my fiancé in New Jersey, over the traffic-choked miles of the Cross Bronx Expressway, mocked by the legend of American freedom of the car, blasting the air conditioning, cursing the greenhouse gases I was emitting that were making the planet all the hotter, heartbroken over the ranks of urban buildings and projects unrelieved by any visible green space to offer shade, let alone spiritual peace to their residents, it all came together for me. This has to stop. Why aren't we saving our own planet? This was a religious as well as a social-justice and an environmental question for me. I began to search for places where people with similar missions were at work. I found many.

I began with my home faith, the Catholic tradition. I cold-called the director of the Bishops' Office of Environmental Justice in Washington, DC, and the director of the New York Archdiocese's Catholic Charities office. I met with both to ask them about how they understood the church's mission for the environment and received different answers. I joined a much smaller group of Catholic scholars who met at a Minnesota retreat center to discuss theology and the environment, sponsored by the United States Conference of Catholic Bishops. That year, working with a local interfaith coalition, I participated in the planning of a state-wide conference on environmental justice in New Jersey. (Ironically, I learned five years later that one of my focus group participants had also attended this conference!) I found my way to a meeting of the United Nations Environmental Programme Interfaith Partnership in the United Nations complex in New York, attended by Jains, Sikhs, Christians, Jews, Buddhists, and many others. With several hundred others, I attended a large celebration of the tenth anniversary of the National Religious Partnership for the Environment in Washington, DC, a coalition of Catholics, mainline Protestants, evangelical Christians, and Jews.

I was inspired by the great energy of so many dedicated leaders, and fascinated by the capacity of religious concern to bridge and transcend the traditionally liberal interest in the environment with traditionally conservative values. I still remember a presentation image of the Amazon forest combined with a fetal ultrasound, with the river tributaries flowing into the umbilical cord. I began reading scores of articles on ecological theology and searching websites. This led me to the cutting-edge scholarship emerging in the new field of research fostered by the Forum on Religion and Ecology, and I attended many of their conferences as well, hearing from major scholars and creative activists of all backgrounds. Along the way, among other things, I ended up giving a presentation for a Unitarian-Universalist youth convention and sharing a college panel with a ground-breaking Orthodox Jewish woman who pioneered a movement for Orthodox environmental Torah living.

Through all of this I encountered a diversity of spiritualities, symbols, resources, statements, texts, interpretations, prayers, guidelines, and catechisms that would make a cultural anthropologist jump for joy. Everyone agreed—across all faiths—and issued official statements—that caring for the earth is a moral and religious obligation. There were many paths to this goal, a veritable splendor of eco-spiritualities and personal appropriations. In all these communities people were revisioning their faiths to put a verdant planet at the center, and all the while scientific evidence for the earth's degradation mounted.

So why wasn't more action evident? And among those who were active, were there any common factors that could be identified and thus supported?

My theological question thus turned of necessity to a social question requiring a systematic investigation into spiritual beliefs and moral motivations. I have Robert Pollack, director of the Center for the Study of Science and Religion at Columbia University and professor of biology, to thank for his vision and courage to support this investigation as a study in which ineffable notions become data that can and should be examined via methodical, repeatable analysis; in short, as a work of science.

For supporting this research, I am deeply grateful to Jeffrey Sachs, executive director of the Earth Institute, Columbia University, and John Mutter, director of the Earth Institute Fellows Program, for extending to me the opportunity to learn from world-class researchers who are redefining interdisciplinary sustainability research in the pursuit of a less poor and more just world.

From Ideally Green to Really Green

Madeleine: I appreciate your asking the question about faith because I think it really has in some way made me think more about what my faith means. I'm a poet and a writer and I've always felt this connection to nature and I've always felt that God is in nature. That really hasn't changed, but it's become refined with my consciousness about responsibility. I realize that I truly do believe in the Incarnation. It's God in us, but us means us ... as part of nature. So if God is going to work through us, it's not just people to people. It's also people to where we are and it's this gift. Our being is not just this body but it's also where we live.

You have a responsibility to not only love your neighbor as yourself, but loving your neighbor also includes loving where we live because that's part of life, too. I don't think I really thought about it too much until I had to start thinking about it. I keep coming back to this, but responsibility becomes overwhelming. It really does. As a budding activist, you're constantly overwhelmed with this responsibility. If you really believe that God is with us, if you believe in the Incarnation, you get this rush of peace that it will get done. You do have a part in it. You can't give up, but then you're more willing to do what you can do as part of your faith because you believe that God is in all of us.

> *Some people have this sense that we don't need to worry about the environment because God's going to take care of it. God's will be done. You need to pray and have a relationship with God, but it's going to be taken care of. When I began to talk about this, I realized, "Oh, my sense of the Incarnation is different, really different from theirs. I have to act. I can't just trust that God is with us and taking care of it all, that I have to be a good person but I don't have to worry about this." I suddenly realized, "I do."*
>
> *Charlie: That's the gap. How do you close that gap?*

Madeleine and Charlie spoke to me in the first focus group conversation I had with faith-based environmentalists in my quest to understand *what leads to action*. Religious environmentalism is a growing movement both globally and nationwide that is dedicated to protecting the environment. Aware of the real crises facing the planet, pastors, lay people, and national religious organizations are critically reappropriating traditional teachings in various and creative ways. Inspired by a sense of reverent obligation to care for creation and the people who suffer from environmental degradation, pastors and congregants are coming to this mission together.

Virtually every religious body in the United States has issued formal statements commending care of creation. Still, religious teachings do not necessarily translate into action. Environmentalists share the pew with people for whom climate change is not a burning issue. While many signs of green spirituality are hopeful and growing, it is not a virtual grassfire akin to a green "great awakening." Why does religiously expressed concern for the environment become an active passion within some individuals? Why do those who accept a responsibility to live sustainably often fail to act with the resolution they themselves admit is needed?

Inspired Sustainability is a search for the spark that drives spiritual Americans who feel the environmental crisis as a sacred loss, and who are reimagining their faith and life through environmental advocacy. *Inspired Sustainability* examines the actual dynamics of lifestyle conversion: what are the facts, feelings, and habits that make it possible for faith-based environmentalists to act. I had the opportunity to interview dozens of dynamic, inspiring people who spoke honestly about the struggles they experienced trying to see their faith and their love of creation come together. This book explores how they navigate the "green blues"—a mélange of ambiguity, conviction, discouragement, and persistence regarding sustainable living. This book shares the hopes and successes of American faith-based environmentalists who shared their thoughts with me during my research fellowship at the Earth Institute at Columbia University. I had the privilege to listen to their own words about *how* to live their inspired passion for creation. At the same time, I was hearing from cutting-edge climate scientists, hydro-engineers, soil scientists, about the intense challenges facing the earth.

Why listen to faith-based environmentalists? Certainly earth-denying religious traditions have been often criticized, with good reason, for their role in humanity's neglect of the earth. That criticism is very important and has been explored extensively elsewhere—but not here.

At the same time, without arguing that secular, technological culture has caused the environment crisis, it is certain that this technological culture has not solved it. According to Gus Speth, former head of the United Nations Development Programme, the years of professional environmental service since the Clean Air Act of 1971 have succeeded in narrowing the project of environmental defense to specialized litigation and policymaking. This approach has scored some major victories but also isolated the problems from the hearts and consciousness of the average citizen. The rise of the environmental expert has not seen the end of the crises but instead their multiplication in the years since the Clean Air Act. Inspired communities have successes to share, precisely in this necessary terrain of claiming hearts. Their stories show that conviction and passion can move mountains, when landslides of information leave people immobile.

Other reasons warrant attention to religious environmentalism, even outside of a personal interest in faith or theology. First, the United States remains a relatively religiously observant society. Eighty-five percent of Americans identify with some religious tradition. Religious communities, as the social context of personal faith, both shape and are shaped by these shifting currents in behavior and belief.

Langdon Gilkey, the ecumenical theologian, defined the theological task as concerned with two great questions. First, theology addresses questions of justice, liberation, and peace. The crises of poverty, inequality, and violence demand that theologians (and citizens) attend to ecological degradation. Second, theologians tackle the hermeneutic problem: "how traditional words, concepts and symbols are to be interpreted intelligibly in our cultural present."[1]

If the post-Enlightenment West once hoped that the modern secular culture would inevitably replace the old language and expression of religions, that expectation has not entirely come to pass. The assumption, as Gilkey puts it, was that the "accompanying cultural values of that scientific society—pragmatic openness; tolerance; freedom of inquiry, of belief and of decision; the democratic process; and self-control" would increase. Yet this expectation has been confounded by the rise of charismatic, mystical, sectarian, fundamentalist, ecstatic, and new age practices and communities. The failure of religions to "dissipate as an effective force in personal and social life alike" calls for a reexamination of what a "secular" understanding of religious really meant.

What does this say about the "secular" American experience of religious culture? Given the aforementioned fact that 85 percent of Americans identify with some religious tradition, it may be hard to pigeonhole which "seculars" are judging which religious persons.

Furthermore, religious authority is often recognized even by those who do not officially accept religious teachings. Though some observers may perceive a loss of moral credibility and many insiders bemoan loss of membership, American congregations retain a historic legacy of moral leadership. Thus, the historic legacy of moral leadership in American congregations is a boon for ecological justice, as global society often mimics American lifestyles, and thus American leadership for sustainable mores is crucial.

---

1. Langdon Gilkey, "Theologian for a 'Time of Troubles,'" *The Christian Century* 121, no. 25 (1981), 475.

Religious communities have led major social movements for abolition, civil rights, and peace. But the environmental crisis is a novel problem for churches. Norms are tricky to establish given the complexity of ecological/biochemical/atmospheric interactions. Theologians and pastors grapple with unfamiliar issues on the tilting ground of science: Should there be ethanol ethics? Church parking spaces reserved for hybrid cars? Earth images in the sanctuary? Despite these challenges, the signal contribution of faiths lies in their authority to define the religious obligation to nature against their strong traditions of moral teaching and ethics.

While much of this book discusses individual decisions and motivations, most of my research participants were engaged in advocacy for systemic change. Being personally engaged empowered them to engage others and enabled them to critique the resistance and motivations for sustainable living.

Political action for systemic change is essential. Sustainable policies on the necessary scale require systemic action. Nonetheless, personal behavior offers a test case for the spiritual struggle of conversion, of taking action—whether small acts or collective advocacy. Ironically, those who feel their own personal efforts aren't meaningful may feel "unworthy" to advocate for wider societal change. The persistent gaps point to an inner struggle, where *"Between the emotion / And the response / Falls the Shadow"* (T.S. Eliot, "The Hollow Men"). These are the "green blues." Bob expressed his "green blues" clearly in my conversation with his Unitarian-Universalist congregation.

> *Bob: Whether I am optimistic or pessimistic will depend a lot on the next election. And with this, I'm very pessimistic with our current policies, our current leadership and the way they approach things. And if they are mentioning it at all now, it's just lip service, it's certainly isn't set in real strong policy. I think that is our biggest need, to do anything else is to work to get the policies to change in this country. Whoever it is, Republican or Democrat, to get them to support the right policies.*

Second, as a richly diverse society, the United States' communal problems invite comment from a variety of religious authorities. The role of the American religious community is particularly important given the global influence (for good or ill) of American policies, economic and industrial systems, and patterns of consumption.

Theology today, especially theology of a globally shared experience such as the planetary threat, must be in dialogue. Persons of every tradition within contemporary American society share many social pressures and common experiences. By its very nature the problem invites comment from all faiths; by practical exigency persons working together meet with colleagues, neighbors, and citizens of all faiths. How each tradition interprets a call to responsibility illuminates how the wisdom of individual traditions can be brought to bear on this situation. Dialogue need not lead to a lowest-common-denominator recognition of general ecological goodwill, without the power and clarity of specific religious traditions and the insights of their founders and adherents, forged in particular cultural and historic experiences.

In fact, dialogue can lead to deeper understanding and appreciation of one's own tradition, while coming to respect and gratitude for the insights of the other. Perspective is a gift, best received with mutual hospitality. Dialogue enables those from various backgrounds to share and hone their own tools for interpretation and self-understanding. Each tradition offers unique categories with which to analyze motivation, values, behavior, and inspiration.

At the heart of this book is the question of how love and concern for the earth overflow into action, despite all the forces that make it so easy to do ... nothing. Many great thinkers, religious and otherwise, have long pondered why people choose the good or fail to choose the good, recognizing the inevitability of moral choice and the reality of moral failure. Paul accused himself, "that which I would do, I do not, and that which I would not do, that I do" (Romans 7:15). Augustine agonized over his conflicts and distilled from them a psychology of the free will that is precisely not free, but bound and caught by habits, pressures, and cravings. This psychology, infused by belief that our actions do matter to

God and others, underlies the Christian teaching of original sin. William James rightly diagnosed these men as "sin-sick souls," but nonetheless their scrupulosity produced clear insights into the reality that human persons do not easily or automatically do even that which they know is right. Central to this perspective is the recognition that knowing the good does not equate with doing the good. Much suffering exists not for lack of practical solutions but because of the willful pursuit of selfish aims. In other words, to paraphrase Gus Speth, technocracy is not the answer. Courage—the virtue of the heart—and inspiration are essential to get to green. This book explores how religious and philosophical insights can contribute to our understanding of humanity's moral response to the environmental crisis. It's crucial to understand how to support motivation because, as the Gallup poll concludes, "Americans don't care about climate change any more than they did in 1989."[2]

Although this book does not focus on secular environmental groups, this is not meant to leave any impression by omission that their impact and effectiveness is not intensely significant, valuable, and long-standing. In fact, faith-based environmentalism is the younger sister of a long tradition of "secular" environmental organizing that itself builds on a robust tradition of environmental philosophy, ethics, nature writing, and nature spirituality.

Inspiration to care for the earth is a part of a movement that is diffuse, widespread, secular, as well as faith based.

Paul Hawken describes this worldwide movement as a spontaneous greening, a natural, instinctive, "immune response" of the earth.[3] He describes the thousands of organizations, projects, and movements, large or small, that have sprung up organically worldwide. Through their advocacy, innovation, and creation of new lifestyles and food, energy, and transit systems, these organizations are healing the earth. These movements are clearly inspired by love

---

2. Philip Bump, "Americans Don't Care About Climate Change Any More Than They Did in 1989," *The Wire*, April 4, 2014, http://www.thewire.com.

3. Paul Hawken, *Blessed Unrest: How the Largest Social Movement in the World Is Restoring Grace, Beauty, and Justice* (New York: Penguin Books, 2007), 12.

of the earth and of all its communities of life. The impact of secular groups is indeed critical, and faith-based environmentalists are frequently partners and collaborators in their work. My question here simply relates to the underlying problem of motivation as analyzed with the data provided by faith-based environmentalists reflecting on their advocacy and struggles.

As a Christian theologian, my perspective, intellectual categories, and habits of faith discernment shape my perception and interpretation of environmental crises, causes, solutions, conflicts, and struggles to effect change. When listening to persons from Native American, Jain, or Muslim faith, I do not pretend to observe from a neutral stance. Nonetheless, while recognizing the impossibility of doing justice to their traditions, it is essential to include voices from all traditions in analyses of religious environmentalism, and I hope to highlight some of their unique insights through the words of their own adherents.

Even among those aware and concerned, there is a gap between knowing and acting that demands to be explored. The assumption that human behavior is rational can no longer explain our ecocidal behavior. Sociologist Jared Diamond identifies failed civilizations throughout history, such as the ironically named Easter Island, whose fatally unsustainable practices confirm that ecocide is not new.[4] But presumably those civilizations had fewer tools for assessing their race toward ecological degradation. The dynamics of self-conscious ecocide today raise even more pointed ethical questions. Somehow, like the well-fed rabbits silently coexisting with the shining wire snares in the novel *Watership Down*, society is able to persist in conscious folly, glamorize lethal lifestyles, and coopt discussion.

Free will and sin, or, more neutrally, spirituality and fallibility, are thus key terms to employ for understanding human behavior. How do people find the spirit and energy to make sustained, sustainable choices? What does the ecological crisis reveal about choosing or resisting the good? Does ecocide challenge a new interpretation

---

4. Jared Diamond, *Collapse: How Societies Choose to Fail or Succeed* (New York: Penguin Group, 2005).

of grace and sin, of "the free will bound?" The perennial limits of human frailty are cast in a darker shadow by the earth's losses we can already see. Somehow, society, satisfied with hiding, is content to resist challenging facts. The challenges and successes of those already engaged in advocacy can empower effective action and leadership in the future by faith communities trying to get to green.

Most traditions have developed doctrinal and ethical resources to guide practicing believers seeking a moral response to the environmental crisis. Much theological research has focused on the relationship of God to the world, correcting inappropriate interpretations of "dominion," offering spiritualities grounded in the cosmos, and expressing global solidarity.

This necessary but preliminary orientation to doctrine as the leading edge of a faith tradition's contact with the environmental crisis has driven much of recent scholarship attempting to revise and green theology. Unquestionably, religious teachings are essential to shaping people's understanding and commitment; theological statements carry forward the tradition and embody our communal vision of what we are as people, as religious communities, as part of the earth. Yet the cognitive and intellectual frame that holds theological statements addresses only one part of the human subject. Emotions and values and perhaps unconscious forces influence action at least as much as reason and intellectual ideas.

This book is not raising a new question about the God–world relationship, but asks: How do Americans come to awareness that they are complicit in and responsible for the environmental crisis? How they do they find ways to make appropriate sustainable changes in their behavior and consumption, through religious values, interpretations, and motivations? What are the dynamics of religiously inspired, evolving green self-understanding? How does love for the earth become strong enough to overcome the gaps in the way of creating a sustainable life?

We don't have to ask, Is it possible for our theologies to be greened? It is! They are! [5] Now, how action is *inspired* and *maintained* is

---

5. The "Lynn White" thesis sparked this debate about Christianity's green potential versus its anti-environmental bias in his now-classic article

the most critical question. Given the social power of institutional faith communities, it is productive to ask, How do faith communities inspire significant responses to the environmental crisis? What challenges do they face in the process?

Despite persistent denial among many American citizens and politicians, scientists are in consensus about the already evident changes in our planet. Global warming is occurring now; ecosystems are changing; and people, animals, plants, and the earth's fertility and beauty are being harmed as a result. Mary Evelyn Tucker, a pioneer in the scholarship of religion and ecology, calls up the shocking and painful image of the earth as under hospice care, in an extreme and irreversible state of species loss and the death of ecological vitality.[6] What further life survives is in our power to determine.

Even if scientific literacy was high and the case for changing behaviors and policies was perfectly clear to the general public, behavior change is a complex matter closely linked to fundamental

---

"The Historical Roots of Our Ecologic Crisis," *Science* 155, no. 3767 (1967): 1205. The roots of an ancient ambivalence toward nature are also explored by Donald Worster, who argues that nature was rejected by a defensive Christianity, deified by Romanticism, stripped of intrinsic value and coopted by modern science, and lastly, a lingering Arcadian innocence was jarred by the darkness of Darwin's vision; see Donald Worster, *Nature's Economy: The Roots of Ecology* (San Francisco: Sierra Club Books, 1977). Aldo Leopold also partly attributes our selfish lack of concern for the environment to a biblically based "Abrahamic concept" of the land. See *A Sand County Almanac* (New York: Ballantine Books, 1949), xviii, 240. For a critique of Leopold's views of the Bible, see Martin D. Yaffe, ed., *Judaism and Environmental Ethics: A Reader* (Lanham, MD: Lexington Books, 2001), 2-6. See also Ivone Gebara, *Longing for Running Water: Ecofeminism and Liberation*, trans., David Molineaux (Minneapolis: Fortress Press, 1999); Dieter T. Hessel and Rosemary Radford Ruether, ed., *Christianity and Ecology: Seeking the Well-Being of Earth and Humans*, Religions of the World and Ecology (Cambridge, MA: Harvard Center for the Study of World Religions, 2000); J. A. Passmore, *Man's Responsibility for Nature: Ecological Problems and Western Traditions* (New York: Scribner, 1974); and Larry Rasmussen, *Earth Community, Earth Ethics* (Maryknoll, NY: Orbis Books, 1996).

6. Mary Evelyn Tucker, "Religion Enters Its Ecological Phase," address given at the *25th Anniversary Celebration of Genesis Farm*, Genesis Farm, October 2005.

worldviews and morally ambiguous influence—both topics of great interest to religious interpretations of human nature. Religions have always recognized denial, delusion, and sheer selfishness as realities of human nature that affect right knowing and right acting.

Theological reflection on human nature accepts that irrational behavior is all too common, but psychological decision science often begins from the opposing assumption that behavior and decisions are rational and cognitive. As a result, the significant role of emotion and affect within human judgment and decision making has been overlooked. A similar presumption that the cognitive aspects of religious worldview are most influential has oriented much important theological attention to theological teachings and magisterial statements.

Furthermore, explicitly stated values and reformed eco-ideals do not necessarily lead to changed behaviors.[7] A disjuncture between values and actions often shifts environmental concern to last place. This disjuncture affects not only those basically uninterested in the environment and those too distracted to focus on it, but even concerned and knowledgeable people. Even such thoughtful citizens have conflicting needs for their time and effort and inadequate social options to enact their values.

The research presented in this book asks, then, What beliefs do make a difference? What does impel action? There is certainly no one influential or decisive teaching in any denomination, and certainly none shared across all faiths, though there are many commonalities in their teaching. People express a variety of motivations, from gratitude for earth's blessings, to concern for grandchildren, to guilt for global neighbors affected by overconsumption, to love for the earth and pain at its desecration.

One of the clearest results of focus groups to date is that most religious environmentalists recognize multiple levels of global interdependence (economic, ecological, political, and spiritual) and

---

7. Anna L. Peterson, "Talking the Walk: A Practice-Based Environmental Ethic as Grounds for Hope," in *Ecospirit: Religions and Philosophies for the Earth*, ed. Laurel Kearns and Catherine Keller (New York: Fordham University Press, 2007), 49.

their moral implications. Recognizing multiple interdependencies grounds their commitment to new forms of social justice. What was once my business, my purchase, my property and my pesticides is seen to be linked to the well-being of others. The earth is recognized as "the new poor." Physical and organic links become moral links. The stamp of the ecological footprint is clear, though the right steps forward remain unsure. As people of faith, they then seek to express a profound sense of being called to care for the earth, within their faith life and with their congregations. The ecological vocation appears, by its nature and spirit, to be a shared mission.

What my research has done is listen carefully to environmental leaders in their faith communities. The analysis of their comments here results in what could technically be called an ethnographic phenomenology, an analysis rooted in observation that seeks to answer the questions, How can we resolve the green blues, the sadness experienced for the earth's degradation? How do we move past conflicts of not knowing enough, not caring, and not acting? The technical description of my research strategy is outlined in the Methods; this section may be of more or less interest to some readers. Complementing the Methods are the Appendixes, which list the frequency of participant comments. I emphasize this is a qualitative study; it does not involve statistical analysis. Rather, it draws on the qualitative methods of ethnography, focus groups: in short, structured, organized, listening.

Chapter 1 describes observed patterns in the spirituality of American faith-based environmentalists. First, I describe how persons of faith actually live their spiritual-environmental practices, focusing on how tradition energizes their work or impels new thinking. I have spoken with Baptists, Buddhists, Catholics (both middle class and migrant workers), Episcopalians, megachurch evangelicals, Hindus, Jains, Jews, Native Americans (Navajo and Gwich'in), Reformed Christians, Presbyterians, and Unitarian-Universalists across the country. Through focus groups, I identify seven major patterns within ecological spiritualities.

Chapter 2 identifies obstacles in the way of "getting to green," and shows how gaps in knowledge, concern, and action are the key barriers. It clarifies the difference between the cognitive challenges we all share given how we process information, and the responses that call for determination, rather than information.

Chapter 3 shows how the power of communities energizes members of faith communities. Sharing values reinforces their ability to communicate and collaborate on new and unfamiliar issues such as climate change. Furthermore, through the regular opportunities for discussion, moral reflection, and celebration that faith communities offer, people gain the support and energy to develop new solutions. As part of society, however, congregations face the same challenges to "business as usual," and have the same ability to defer genuine confrontation with the moral dimensions of the environmental crisis. Thus, this chapter also examines the ways congregations are complicit in societal denial and disengagement.

Chapter 4 explores how a philosophical model of human fallibility sheds light on the persistent struggle to live green, which my research participants themselves name. This chapter proposes that human fallibility proceeds from the disproportion between finite ways of knowing, acting, and feeling and the inexhaustibility of the world presented to our choices. For my conversation partners, these disproportions emerge as a lack of certainty regarding the state of our planet and its future, the lack of proven road maps guiding action, and the competing loves that drain energy away from tackling our most urgent problems head-on.

Chapter 5 explores how traditional theological resources illuminate their ways of living out new concerns within received faith. Religious genius is no stranger to human conflicts and great aspirations for building just communities. This chapter creates a colloquium between Buddhist scholars, the ancient Christian monastic Evagrius, and Joseph Soloveitchik, the founder of modern Orthodox Judaism. Other voices chime in, including Pope Benedict XVI, Hussein Seyyed Nasr, and Thich Nhat Hanh, the Buddhist leader. Each offers religious practices that help the environmental pilgrim on her way.

Chapter 6 celebrates the emerging mission of environmental spirituality, justice, and sustainability springing up across faith traditions by suggesting a symbiosis between several key symbols:

sacrifice, *shalom*, and interexistence. A profound awareness of the unity of all lives enables this symbiosis, which makes compassionate giving possible.

My own catechism began botanically: by planting a bean in a cup with my neighbor and volunteer catechist in Brazil. Watching it grow, I saw how God's love brings forth life. Talking with so many new "neighbors" through this research has also been a powerful spiritual encounter with growing green faith. For example, Kathy grew up in Elizabeth, New Jersey, a city with lovely old neighborhoods but also chiefly recognizable to East Coast drivers as the site of apocalyptic energy plants pumping steam through an incomprehensible mazes of pipes above the New Jersey Turnpike. She shared how experiences in nature inspired her creation ministry during our focus group conversation at St. Mary's Church in central New Jersey.

> Kathy: *For myself, I was always very interested in nature. I grew up in an apartment house in the city, but there was a park across the street. I spent a lot of time there. I also wasn't really raised a Catholic. I wasn't really raised in any religion. So I had a lot of communing with God through nature long before any of this happened. When I did go to this conference, it was, there again, hitting stuff that I already knew and just awakening in me the sense that ... what was a personal experience for me should be a universal experience.*

> Q. How big was the park?

> Kathy: *It was three city blocks long, in New Jersey, in Elizabeth. Not a tiny park, but not a huge park either. There was another county park not too far away that I also loved. So I guess, you know, that's where it was for me.*

Hearing this struck me powerfully with a sense of the Spirit choosing Kathy to be a witness: that God in nature was seeking to be known, to be revealed, to be loved, in a small city park.

Latha, a participant in the Hindu focus group, brought the discussion to where the rubber meets the road. As she said, "It's very nice to sit and chat," but how are these ideals, no matter from what tradition, applied and brought to action? She recognized clearly that the road involves a learning process—and, a shared, interfaith learning process.

> *Latha: The scriptures speak very nicely about all the good stuff, the fact that we're in harmony, connected, mother earth and what not. It's very nice to sit and chat about it, but in the actual application, there are still lots of things that the mindful people are doing no matter which religion.... So it's a learning process for everyone. We are sharing this earth and we are recognizing it. And as long as we are getting that knowledge, we are all growing and we can help each other.*

Throughout this book, my aim will be to discover the "theologies that work"[8]—that is, the beliefs that actually motivate the people I speak with to make changes in their lives, and the kinds of inner or cultural resistance they experienced while putting these beliefs to work.

How did they get really green, not just ideally green? What are the obstacles on the road?

---

8. I am indebted to Rev. Fletcher Harper for the phrase "theologies that work."

CHAPTER ONE

Seven Patterns
in Green Spirituality

Kathy (Catholic): This earth is a gift from God, and as Catholics, as Christians, we're called to care for this gift that we've been given. So even if you don't want to do it for your grandchildren, or you don't have grandchildren, or whatever else, it's still . . . technically it's not an option. If this is your faith, then this is part of what we believe.

Meeting Kathy, and over one hundred religious environmentalists across the United States like her, was a tremendous experience of hope and encouragement. During more than twenty-five focus group discussions between 2007 and 2009, they gave voice to their hopes that our earth remain green and beautiful, with its abundant resources available for all. These leaders included Baptists, Buddhists, Catholics, Episcopalians, megachurch evangelicals, Hindus, Jains, Jews (Reconstructionist, Reform, and Conservative), Muslims, Native Americans (Navajo and Gwich'in), Reformed Christians, Presbyterians, Unitarian-Universalists, migrant workers, and urban environmental justice advocates.

While a rich diversity of religious values inspires them, they share a spirituality with perceptible patterns. Those who are taking action with their congregations have found sources of certainty in scientific literacy and religious teachings about the neighbor. They draw energy from their faith, reverent love of nature, and hope for justice. They feel free to act on their green inspiration and have a gift for building roads and bridges over the "gaps." These qualities

1

unite in a spirituality that is literally "grounded" and deeply aware of global interdependencies.

The convictions and insights of active environmentalists in faith-based contexts across the country present both a picture of success-ful green living, inspired by faith, and a deeper understanding of human nature. How do we persist in our highest goals, and what forms of self-contradiction and self-betrayal let us down? In other words, does the evident capacity for ecocide seen in today's society and the work of those seeking a better way teach us anything new about human weakness and strength? These are critical questions that I will address in later chapters, for only by attending to such profound questions can we as individuals and society make lasting progress in our efforts to build a more sustainable society. This is not a problem solved by superficial, Band-Aid fixes. In this chapter, I begin with the positive sources of energy and motivation. That is, where do faith-based environmentalists find inspiration and hope?

The first part of this chapter outlines seven features of green spirituality that emerged in the focus groups. The second part shows how influential information first ignites the spark of motiva-tion, and how local leaders inspire green conversion through their personal example and friendly persistence. The third part discusses the religious resources people have found to support their hope for the future of life on this planet in the face of dark realities.

Seven Patterns in Green Spirituality

Scientific Literacy

Scientific literacy is essential to the success of religious environmen-talism, and as such was an outstanding shared concern of religious environmentalists. In my conversations, statements about scientific knowledge comprised the largest category by far, and occurred independently more than any other single topic. Scientific literacy was discussed in virtually every conversation. It is an inescapable foundation of active concern for the environment.[1]

---

1. Though in a qualitative study such data by themselves do not carry weight, I provide them for comparison within this study. Scientific literacy

High literacy. Most of the participants are highly scientifically literate. They are deeply mindful of the diversity of life, the complexities of ecosystems, and have some scientific understanding of ecological interrelationships. This was especially true at one of the most radically sustainable congregations, the Unitarian-Universalist Congregation of Monmouth County in New Jersey. One congregant estimated that at one point one-third of the congregation was employed at Bell Labs. Many members were engineers and scientists, including a Nobel Laureate. One participant's spouse had worked on an early mathematical climate-modeling project involving raw climate data, which contributed to the unusually high level of awareness of the empirical reality of climate change.

Jim commented on how the presence of so many scientists within the congregation catalyzed a high level of awareness about the environment. He said, "We have had the benefit of a scientific elite here, which has been really extraordinary and which has livened my consciousness of what it means to a community to have so many people who are scientists."

The group's scientific literacy intensified as climate change information drew their moral attention to the climate crisis, and moral consciousness motivated ongoing education about climate change. A feedback loop connected the spiritual value of interrelatedness and a high level of scientific literacy. That high level of sophistication Jim noted prepared the community to understand and accept the reality of global environmental changes, incorporate that awareness into their spiritual interpretation of reality, and support their social concern for the harmful effects of ecological changes.

Roshan, another member, noted that the national Unitarian-Universalist Association of Congregations, the official organization of the Unitarian-Universalist congregations, formally adopted a seventh principle, which affirmed the interdependent web of all being in the 1980s. Roshan felt that his community accepted the new principle very readily. Roshan was raised as a Hindu, one of

---

was mentioned in 79 statements in 23 out of 29 conversations. The "knowledge gap" was mentioned 50 times in 16 conversations. See Appendix C.2.

the Eastern traditions that characteristically emphasize the inter-connection of all reality, so he was particularly sensitive to teach-ings about interdependence. But this same sensitivity permeated his Unitarian-Universalist congregation. As he saw it, this group of Unitarian-Universalists had always had a sense of mindfulness toward the world and other beings. Roshan perceived that "being related to the world around us was a part of the ethos of this par-ticular community and Unitarian-Universalism in general." The high scientific literacy of this Unitarian-Universalist congrega-tion seemed to be part of their spiritual mindfulness and prepared them to pursue their sustainability goals with particular focus. As Roshan said, the principle of relatedness "was a religious value which emerged more clearly in the '80s, but it seems to have existed before that, so there was a sense this is the right thing to do."

Having this value was fertile ground for the group's extraor-dinary mission to make their congregation into a "Green Sanctu-ary" and even encourage members to strive for carbon neutrality in their own homes. The group in fact completed the rigorous Green Sanctuary guidelines of the Unitarian-Universalist Association of Congregations, which one member compared to a LEED document (Leadership for Energy and Environmental Design, or LEED, is a guideline for green building developed by the U.S. Green Building Council.) After fulfilling all the steps, the congregation was recog-nized at the U-U national convention, an honor that gave them all a sense of pride and increased their motivation to do more.

I saw one cross in a church that I visited during one research trip that symbolized to me how scientific awareness could have a kind of spiritual meaning. Instead of a crucifix with a hanging body, the intersecting crossbars were circled by two golden rings. While no particular description or explanation of the symbolism was promi-nently displayed in the church, to me the circling rings suggested an idealized and beautiful representation of the atom. This image somehow captured an often ineffable awareness of scientific reality as a spiritually significant dimension of faith, an awareness that played into moral advocacy. Somehow, the deepest levels of scien-tific truth could be brought into harmony with the fundamental symbol of the Christian cross.

The knowledge gap. Participants in the focus groups also specifically discussed how they perceived a widespread lack of scientific literacy to be a major obstacle in motivating others in society to take climate change seriously and act accordingly. I am calling this extremely important concept the "knowledge gap." When asked to describe what they felt prevented greater action, participants felt that scientific illiteracy and denial about climate change played a major role. Denial of the very existence of a climate risk has unquestionably slowed responses to the problem. Denial has taken multiple forms and spawned various tactics for delaying, avoiding, and discrediting action.[2] On the other hand, my research participants' familiarity with information about consumption, greenhouse gases, and climate change allowed them to draw moral connections.

Without scientific awareness, moral connections between climate change and ethical responsibility were harder to make. Ralph, a Baptist geologist, succinctly connected scientific awareness, moral honesty, and responsible action.

Ralph (Baptist): I think we need a change of perspective, which I think is happening. The person who drives the Hummer at eight miles per gallon, and those who see that person, understand that that person isn't being greedy, that person isn't being wealthy, that person is shitting in our swimming pool, all of ours, his too. And, I'd say we have a great ability to be willfully blind to the consequence of our actions, to externalize costs, and now we see that we are affecting ourselves. I think the ability to change that is one of our great hopes.

Many participants agree that basic information is still needed by many in their congregations, neighborhoods, and society as a whole. One participant estimated that the number of people who in 2007 doubted that global warming is real was perhaps 60 percent. During the course of one discussion a participant (not a regular

---

2. Mary-Elena Carr and Madeleine Rubenstein, "Challenges to Authority; Understanding Critiques of the Intergovernmental Panel on Climate Change," *Union Seminary Quarterly Review* 63, nos. 1-2 (2011), 58.

member of the ecological committee) recognized that she had just learned "how we get light." This happened after Charlie recounted his day at a river clean-up with a local Muslim girls' club. He took the opportunity to educate them about electricity and enlightened a deacon in his church as well.

> *Charlie: I was trying to tell the students about the impacts of their work and I said, "Now just think now. We have electricity. Where does electricity come from?" Some of them said, "It just comes from a plug in a wall." I said, "It doesn't. It comes from a man shoveling coal into a furnace. All that coal's burning up. How many of you use a hair dryer every day?" Of course all the girls raise their hands. Just remember now when you plug it into the wall what happens to that and they are people who live in that community, and what happens to the pollution that that causes.*

> *Beth: I would just say, Charlie, you just simplified how we get light for me. I never really thought about it. Okay, it's somebody shoveling coal into.... Then I know the coal dust and all the people getting killed in the mines and all of that.... So if you depress a few people, you probably enlightened a lot more.*

Discussion in environmental committees can effectively raise awareness of climate change—precisely because the congregational group promotes the trust to listen, question, learn and rework beliefs. Let's face it: facts matter. And, through these discussions, which allow people to discuss and make sense of challenging new facts, the knowledge gap starts to close.

The special case of evangelicals and science. Northland, A Church Distributed, is an evangelical megachurch near Orlando, Florida. "Distributed" refers to its outreach through media connections and online worship. Members and worshipers at the same service may be "distributed" between the main sanctuary and living rooms far away where they are logged in. Northland's environmentally engaged Creation Care Task Force members emphasize the authority of the Bible and a desire to be obedient to a scriptural mandate to care for God's creation.[3] They do not overtly link this mandate to any particular crisis in the earth's ecosystems. As one member of the group, Raymond, said, "For a while I felt like I was able to avoid the issue because there seemed to be conflicting signs in the data." In fact, there is an expressed sense that their vocation to care for the earth is deeper and more enduring than the need to fix immediate problems. Because it is rooted in scripture, the vocation will endure despite the crises of the day.

> *Raymond: But then, once it was presented from a biblical perspective it was something we have to do. It sort of negates the issue from the scientific community; it doesn't matter whether the earth is pristine condition or horrible condition. We still have an obligation out of obedience and out of stewardship to do these things. So I think, for me, it wasn't necessarily that when I realized it was in trouble and I had to do something, that wasn't the motivation. It was more me recognizing, wow, this is a responsibility we have like taking care of the poor or the elderly, doing all these things that the church has been great at doing for hundreds and hundreds of years. It's not just recognizing that there's some trouble. It's sort of ... getting permission or acceptance that this is a biblical thing.*

The evangelical Christians with whom I spoke explicitly played down the authority and influence of scientific warnings as a factor in their concern for the earth.

> *Sarah: I would say in private, well yeah, I think global warming is happening. But I would never really want to frame the issue that way. I don't think that ... I completely agree with you guys, I don't think that's the point.*

---

3. This group has understandably received a fair amount of attention, and their pastor is a well-recognized public figure within evangelical circles. For further scholarly study of the Northland Creation Care Task Force and Raymond in particular, see Lucas F. Johnston, *Religion and Sustainability: Social Movements and the Politics of the Environment* (Bristol, CT: Equinox Publishing, 2013).

Sarah's confession that global warming is a fact to be acknowledged in private speaks volumes. This group did not feel that their faith rejected or contradicted science. Where conflicts appeared, they expected some further developments in scriptural interpretation or scientific understanding to clarify the conflict. The point of her comment is that science is not the determining authority that compels her environmental action; nor can science even be a public authority.

Still, ecological awareness in the group is also undeniably high. Their Creation Care Task Force includes a student concentrating in sustainable development; a management professional in a utility, energy, and water use company; the owner of an environmentally friendly cremation and burial service; an underwater filmmaker; and an employee of Florida's estuary protection agency. The environmental concerns that troubled them no doubt influenced their choices of careers. This concern for concrete environmental issues cannot be separated from their decisions to join a creation care task force, as if scientific information had no effect on their commitments, even if they declare that biblical authority is most influential. Yet this spiritual authority is also very important, as several of the group said they were not sure their two loves, earth and God, went together until they found it in the scriptures or heard it preached by their pastor. Both authorities matter; moral connections rooted in the authority of faith paved the way for acting on the authority of science.

Without question, their commitment to creation care is deeply nourished by the unique evangelical quality of their faith which lives its enthusiasm publicly and actively.

> *Sarah: My identity as a Christian is so connected with that, with environmentalism or with creation care I'd rather say, and helping the poor and all these kind of things—but I don't know if I would be that way if I wasn't Christian. As an individual I've always been so much more rational, logical, and pragmatic and just ... not necessarily that merciful, not necessarily that caring. If I wasn't a Christian I'd probably just say, we're just human beings, we're just animals, this is the*

way the world goes, we just need to make the best of it while
we're here. And it was really searching through scripture that
led me to the care that I have for creation.

As traditional definitions of morality shift and new concerns claim attention as a legitimate aspect of Christian social justice, issues that once were taboo are questioned. One evangelical Christian leader mused about how new questions about justice and the environment, even if not traditionally understood as part of Christian discipleship, claim his attention.

Ted: I've actually seen my perspective shift in that regard.
One reason is Pastor Joel and his teaching. Another one is
my kids. When I grow up I want to be like Sarah—so moti-
vated purely by compassion. That's the genuine perspective.
I think my compassion is growing. I've said that in five years,
do I want to be more right, or do I want to be more loving.

Ted demonstrated the paradox of simultaneously affirming the unshakeable primacy of gospel faith and recognizing that being more loving demanded a broader perspective—a perspective that included the suffering caused by the environmental crisis. Being "right" for an evangelical has to begin with the authority of scripture. At the same time, Ted wished to be more loving and express love by caring for the earth. Loving one's neighbor is clearly the core meaning of the gospel for him, but given the uncomfortable newness of environmental conscience and the traditional dislike of a liberal agenda, expressing love through care of creation still didn't quite seem "as right." Ted had the historical perspective to root this conflict in the divide between the evangelical and liberal churches in America. As he said,

If you go back to the split amongst the evangelicals and liber-
als, the evangelicals took the gospel side of the message, and
the liberals took the social side of the message. So there's this
embracing of the gospel and any deviation from that looks
like a compromise. I'm in ministry, and there are peers of
mine that still think it's the gospel, the gospel, or the gospel,

one of those three. And I don't disagree with them; I also see
a broader sense of responsibility in terms of stewardship.

In short, evangelicals are often in a difficult position regarding their comfort with publicly embracing scientific authority as a key reason for their concern for the environment. Paradoxically, though, they seem to be influenced by both authorities. While I do not claim to have a definitive interpretation of this paradox, and have not made it a focus of my analysis, the paradox of joint authority may be parsed as follows: scripture is the first authority, and science, because of the high level of literacy in this group, is a private authority.[4]

Scientific literacy and environmental justice. For minority communities disproportionately affected by pollution and environmental degradation, protesting environmental injustice was direct self-preservation. Often, especially in a city, the environment can appear to be "out there," a wilderness to preserve, a sacred sign of God in the spaces emptied of humanity. This form of wilderness protection has been criticized as the privileged concern of elites for nonhuman life. And, conversely, it is sometimes assumed that low-income urban residents can't identify with the destruction of nature. This is the classic view that they "can't be bothered about the polar bears." True, "nature" may seem invisible in the concrete city jungle. But education and awareness can clarify the impacts of environmental burdens in the city, on the reservation, and near the thousands of Superfund sites nationwide. With new clarity about the impact of toxic wastes, many people have seen the victim, and it is them. For victims of environmental injustice, scientific literacy means understanding the threats to their own health.

Environmental justice is the name given to the movement within environmental advocacy that demonstrates and protests the disproportionate burden of ecological degradation borne by vulnerable human communities. This link was first made in the landmark

---

4. See the Evangelical Environmental Network, "a ministry dedicated to the care of God's creation," at http://www.creationcare.org/websites, and Sojourners, Faith in Action for Social Justice, at http://sojo.net.

report "Toxic Wastes and Race in the United States," published by the United Church of Christ in 1987. The National Resources Defense Council credits the United Church of Christ's Commission for Racial Justice for releasing the first report to show that race is the most important factor in determining where toxic waste facilities are sited in the United States.[5] This document demonstrated the link between zip codes predominately populated by people of color and the disproportionate number of toxic-waste sites in their neighborhoods. Given these findings, the justice implications of the link between the destruction of the environment and the vulnerability of the poor cannot be understated. It is one of the most significant contributions of religious environmentalists to the ecological movement.

My research participants included members of different communities living in proximity to environmental hazards. Members of a Flagstaff, Arizona, Navajo reservation lived near coal and uranium mining waste. They were at risk for lung cancer from inhalation of radioactive particles, as well as bone cancer and impaired kidney function from exposure to radionuclides in drinking water.[6] Likewise, Episcopalians I met who lived near Newark's giant power stations faced intensified asthma risks. Rural Washington migrant workers connected their exposure to toxic pesticides to the headaches, school absenteeism, and cancer rates their communities experienced.

Pablo and Maria, who work with the migrants of rural Washington, talk about how teaching a course in licensed and unlicensed chemical spraying empowered them to defend themselves and encourage their friends and families to do likewise. The course was taught under the auspices of the Catholic National Rural Life Conference. After studying pesticide impacts and regulations, they knew the risks and knew their rights. Armed with this information, they could protest inappropriate pesticide exposure. As Maria said,

---

5. Natural Resources Defense Council, "The Environmental Justice Movement" (2013), http://www.nrdc.org (accessed July 8, 2013).

6. Environmental Protection Agency, "Addressing Uranium Contamination on the Navajo Nation" (2013), http://www.epa.gov (accessed July 8, 2013).

"I heard people who attended the meeting, who said they have not talked about pesticides before, that the pesticides are killing them. We taught them all, and then the people are more conscientious. They say that though they may be nervous, it is better for them to do it, to cut short the work."

People were nervous about confronting the overseer at the fields, and concerned about losing their jobs. Maria stated that "actually, too many people are scared. Scared to ask the farmer or say we can't work in there because you spray. The people stay there because they are scared to lose their job." Having a certificate from the course meant they could prove that they knew their rights. Pablo explained the power of this small certificate that trainees were issued.

> *Pablo: Well, actually when we give this course, we give a little card to these people that says that they took this course and if they go to the orchard they have this card and if they see something that is not labeled [an unlicensed chemical], they can tell the foreman. And say hey, I know these basics and you cannot fire me for this or for that.*

Having knowledge, and a card to prove it, provided a measure of courage when the power is visibly concentrated in the overseer.

Everyone experiences the impact of polluted air, water, climate change. But these impacts attack the most vulnerable most directly. As Pablo insisted, environmental action is self-defense in a situation where the attacker won't stop. As he said, "that's the main reason to educate these people, and nobody else is going to take care of them as their own. It's like me: if I'm walking through the street and I know a car is coming, I have to stop. If I want to be killed, I'll keep walking."

Scientific literacy can greatly empower those most threatened by environmental toxins. Knowledge is a motivator, a source of energy and power to protect the environment and all whose lives are threatened by the same practices that threaten the earth itself.

The harm comes from many sources. Migrant workers run risks of cancers. Urban residents feel the impact of concentrated industrial particulates, bus depots, garbage incinerators, and toxic-waste dumps. These toxic sites are concentrated in our nation's poorest neighborhoods, causing asthma, contributing to school absentee-ism, and learning delays. As shown by the "Toxic Wastes and Race" report, children in low-income neighborhoods are exposed to more toxins from the disproportionate number of toxic-waste sites in their neighborhoods. Sometimes the exposure that can cause learn-ing disabilities begins *in utero*. A study reported in *U.S. News and World Report* showed that mercury levels rose from 25 to 30 per-cent in American women between 1999 and 2006. Children may then be born already exposed to mercury. This is especially trou-bling because children are particularly susceptible to harm from environmental toxins, a point underscored by the American Asso-ciation of Pediatrics in a letter to Congress.

The situation has not improved. A follow-up report, "Toxic Wastes and Race at Twenty," finds that racial disparities in the dis-tribution of hazardous wastes are greater in 2007 than reported in the original study.[7] At the other end of the life span, summer urban heat waves take a rising death toll, especially on seniors. Also, the urban poor are additionally vulnerable to climate change because global warming heavily impacts rising food and energy prices.[8]

---

7. Recent data from the U.S. Centers for Disease Control and Prevention's National Health and Nutrition Examination Survey (NHANES) show that while inorganic mercury was detected in the blood of 2 percent of women aged 18 to 49 in the 1999–2000 NHANES survey, that level rose to 30 per-cent of women by 2005–2006." See "Blood Mercury Levels Rising among Us Women," *U.S. News and World Report*, August 24, 2009, http://health.usnews.com. Such rising levels pose intensified risks to child-bearing women. In a letter to Congress, the American Pediatric Association emphasized the particular vulnerability of children because of their smaller size. The letter states that "neurologic and endocrine systems have demonstrated particu-lar sensitivity to environmental toxicants at certain stages of growth, but all organ systems can be affected." This letter is available at http://greenfaith.org. The document reaffirming the correlation of race and the concentration of toxic-waste sites is Robert D. Bullard, Paul Mohai, Robin Saha, and Beverly Wright, *Toxic Wastes and Race at Twenty: 1987–2007: Grassroots Struggles to Dismantle Environmental Racism in the United States. A Report Prepared for the United Church of Christ Justice and Witness Ministries* (2007).

8. There are an estimated 1 billion-plus people living on less than 1 dollar a day, and the impact of climate change aggravates their living conditions.

Some of the people I interviewed feel bitterly that the information about the need for justice as a critical message of the church is being channeled to the wrong people—the poor people. Jorge questioned the strategy of placing brochures about Catholic social teaching in churches to encourage concern for workers. The brochures were written in Spanish but not in English. To him, the wrong audience was being targeted.

> *Jorge (Catholic): We were in Mass and we found this brochure. These are the principles of social justice, Catholic social justice, but this is in Spanish? Do we have it in English in every single church? We don't have it in English. See, in Spanish, the dignity and the right of the workers, it is talking about the dignity and the right of the workers, but this is in Spanish. But what is the message for the growers?*

Jorge pointedly asks if the right people are being challenged to live out the church's message. This is a crucial question: "What is the message for the growers?" It is important and necessary for the church to support the poor in their struggle, as the National Catholic Rural Life Conference did by sponsoring the pesticide education programs. But are wealthy growers in the churches also being invited to consider their obligations according to Catholic social justice teaching? Because they are not in the fields, the owners are isolated from the problems that drive the workers to ask for safer pesticide practices. The growers do not see the problems and experience the risks directly, and layers of supervisors and managers distance them from those who do. Jorge is right to want a brochure in English that makes plain the wealthy growers' responsibility to protect the dignity and rights of the workers. Ironically, on the other hand, being wealthy can support environmental action. Some have argued that environmentalism is a hobby of the rich whose basic needs are met.[9] The wealthy can afford to worry about polar

---

9. Maslow's hierarchy of needs is relevant here; see also the discussion of relative concerns addressed by Denton E. Morrison, "Some Notes toward

bears; those struggling with rent and grocery bills can't. There is some truth to that. As Charles Callaway, an urban organizer with a major Harlem advocacy group, WE ACT for Environmental Justice, said to me, "If their basic needs aren't met, there's no way—if you're hungry and your apartment is no good and everything, it's kind of hard for you to see beyond that."

Still, when basic needs such as breathing are affected by urban pollution, even environmental concerns gain significance. But this can only happen if people understand the links between bus depots, garbage incinerators, particulates, and asthma. Creating awareness of the sources of asthma was a driving motivator for the congregations in Elizabeth, New Jersey, for Gladys in Queens, New York, and Charles in Harlem. GreenFaith, an interfaith coalition, sponsors "toxic tours" through Newark's industrial areas near the dioxin factories that once supplied Agent Orange to Vietnam. The dioxin has since leaked into Newark Bay, endangering the locals who continue to fish for crabs from the bay. Such initiatives expand the themes of scientific literacy beyond climate change and species extinction to crises in human health. Toxins in the air, water, soil, and climate are borne by all in an interdependent world.

Awareness of Global Interdependence

The multiple interdependent dimensions of life were absolutely foremost in the minds of the research participants. After scientific literacy, awareness of interdependence was the second most compelling motivating factor for faith-based environmentalists.[10] Engaged religious environmentalists are strongly aware of how people affect one another through economic, social, ecological, and spiritual networks, through both institutional and personal choices. In other

---

Theory on Relative Deprivation, Social Movements, and Social Change," *American Behavioral Scientist* 14, no. 5 (1971), 675.

10. Awareness of spiritual interdependence was most frequent (75 references), with related subgroups: social (47), ecological (34), and economic interdependence (11). If taken as a single set, awareness of global interdependence is the largest set, with 167 total references. See Appendix C.2.

words, participants were clearly aware that the world is "flat," and sensed their links to life around the globe.[11]

As Madeleine put it, "The God that I believe in is with us here, and I'm connected to it. And that means the place that I'm in as well." Her own understanding of interdependence was itself expressed with interlinking religious symbols: Buddhist interdependence and a Christian view of God's presence on earth through the Incarnation of Jesus Christ. She went on, "I'm not Buddhist, but I think my connection to the environment is sort of Buddhist-like with the Incarnation added." Latha, a Hindu woman, also affirmed the importance of an interconnected view of the world as her favorite thing about Hinduism. "It's very insightful ... you're really connected, with not just the humans but also with the whole cosmos." Yet at the same time, she did not elevate this interconnected view as marking or isolating Hindus within a superior, more insightful faith. For her, all religions, languages, and social divisions faded away in the greater union of all life.

> *Latha: You're that little part of this whole scheme, this beautiful picture. So everything else vanishes—religions, languages, countries—I love that!*

Among the members of my focus groups, statements about global interdependence fell into four subcategories: social interdependence, economic interdependence, ecological interdependence, and spiritual interdependence. These categories applied to statements that acknowledged the globalized nature of society and ecology in the twenty-first century.

Social and economic interdependence. Charlie explained that he became involved in environmental work when a stream on his property was destroyed by a development without storm water controls. Earlier in his career, the impact of unregulated water flows—and the impact of toxins in the water—had not struck him as "an ethical situation."

---

11. Thomas L. Friedman, *The World Is Flat: A Brief History of the Twenty-First Century* (New York: Farrar, Straus, & Giroux, 2005).

> *Charlie: I worked at a polluting industry, a steel industry, for thirty years. We would do things at night that we wouldn't do during the day because at night nobody would see it. I never had thought about it as an ethical situation. . . . What I did in my property wasn't going to affect Mary at all. But what I'm finding out is that that's not the case, that what I do on my property affects the downstream person and unfortunately it affects those—what did Jesus say about the least? It affects the least. It affects the least.*

Recognizing the impact of pollution transformed the act of draining industrial chemicals into the river by night from one that merited no second thought to one that provoked a religious revelation of responsibility for the neighbor. Because of their strong sense of interconnection, religious environmentalists feel both related and responsible. Feeling a sense of responsibility gave Charlie a heightened sense of awareness about how his actions impacted others, and supported an attitude of sacrifice: being aware of how others were affected by his energy use, if the energy sources were power plants spewing out pollutants and greenhouse gases. Even in a small way, that awareness might lead him to turn on the lights less often.

> *Charlie: I come to this environmental effort because I appreciate, and based on what I've been told by people who I respect, scientists and things like that, that what I do impacts those that can't take care of themselves. Therefore, I feel that if I turn a light on. . . .*

Sarah, a young evangelical Christian, explained how her view of individual sin was influenced by her study of sustainability and social theory. For her, "almost any sin is both personal and social and having social repercussions." For her, sin meant not being in the right relationship with God or with one another. The social repercussions of injustice meant that "it might not be as simple as to point a finger at one individual person and say I think this is your sin." But despite the complexity of moral accountability in an interdependent world, it was clear to her that somewhere in the system, there was culpability. Her academic study of interdependent globalized systems helped her rethink the social repercussions of sin and how those repercussions threatened earth's sustainability. And that threat remained as a moral responsibility with which she had to wrestle. Thus, for Madeleine, Charlie, Latha, and Sarah, central doctrines such as Incarnation, sacrifice, and sin were being recontextualized by their perception of global moral interdependence.

Ecological interdependence. In sensing ecological interdependence as a real relationship, people are rethinking their relationship with ecosystems, plants and animals, and water and air. Some participants were just becoming aware of the interlinkages between chemical and physical systems; others had more sophisticated knowledge. Donna experienced a conceptual breakthrough: all the elements of the earth are the same throughout earth's history. There is no place to find a new clean earth if we pollute what we have. Her new mental model of the interconnection of earth's matter led to a new appreciation for preserving it.

> *Donna: Two or three years ago, it had never really occurred to me that the earth is here, the air is here, and somehow we breathe this air, and the Egyptians breathed it in the past, and the dust moves around. That this is what we have, and we use it well or we don't; this is what we're given.*

Judy, a Catholic woman from New Jersey, already recognized the chemical links of toxins that run into water systems and was angry about their impact. "It kills me when I see stuff people put on their lawns. Or when they dump stuff down the storm drains, thinking it's a sewer. But it's not. Eventually it's affecting all of us somehow."

I had a fascinating conversation with members of the Creation Care Task Force of Northland, A Church Distributed. Northland is a megachurch in Florida that identifies as a Christ-centered, evangelical church, that is "distributed" among locations and online worship communities, linking over 15,000 people. Several people shared a sophisticated knowledge of carbon chemistry and the signature of coal molecules.

Paul: The government is going to impose regulations on U.S. businesses so that a lot of them shifted offshore to countries that have less environmental controls. There was a recent study outside of San Francisco, and they can actually take air samples and coal actually has a signature to it, and air pollution developed from coal has a signature. They're collecting air pollution samples and 20 percent of the air pollution in that part of California comes from China. So here we are, we shipped it all to China, and it comes right back.

Q. And it all comes back! What does that tell us?

Ted: Is that why we live on the East coast?

Alison: Wait ten years; it will blow over. (Laughter)

I later checked out the details in Paul's description of traveling coal signatures with a climate scientist (Paul was right).

The group's humorous discussion of air pollution tracked how molecules moved around in a physical system, regulative legislation moved incentives around in an economic system, jobs moved around in the globalized industrial system—and the final health impacts moved: nowhere. The group clearly saw the irony of attempting to corral pollution within one country or another, ignoring the greater power of global wind currents. Furthermore, they perceived the foolishness of attempting to put moral boundaries around the creation of pollution. In the globalized marketplace of production and demand, of trade and outsourcing, we are all responsible. Chemical interdependence is closely linked to moral and spiritual interdependence. Paul's sophisticated knowledge of carbon chemistry undergirded a cynical, but accurate, recognition of pollution's permeability. Like original sin, it affects everyone, no matter where one might think it originated.

Spiritual interdependence. Participants sensed the moral rightness of respecting the order of the universe. Belonging to God's creation is an important part of their spirituality. Members of a regional Chesapeake-area Presbyterian council (PCUSA) were developing a conscious awareness of their spiritual relationship with the cosmos as part of their uniquely theological commitment to the environment. They explored a spiritual understanding of an identity linked with the cosmos, with God and creation, being not "apart *from* creation, but a part *of* creation." While acknowledging that these ideas were still being worked out, one member began to clarify the distinct nature of his faith-based environmentalism and what he called "earth spirituality."

> Tom: *Our understanding of the nature of God and the nature of the cosmos and how the cosmos came into being and earth as part of that and us as part of that ... that is what the church can speak about. We don't have any special exper-tise in energy generation or in water conservation or things like that but we do have a special way of speaking about the moral and spiritual issues.*

Another member of the discussion expressed that spiritual connec-tion through a concrete example of the personal bonds created by knowing a creature's name.

> Branch: *We were at a meeting in our church where some-body suggested that we ought to get to know the names of the plants in your woods and what their history is and what their individual characteristics [were]. And I was reminded of another meeting earlier where four homeless people were at that same room and they started by saying "My name is ... my name is. ... So we're not homeless. We have names." And then this justice stuff came into play for me again. That you treat plants that you know with care and justice, just like you do a person whose name you know.*

Complete silence followed Branch's comment as people digested what resonated as a profound and simple truth: plants are funda-mental to our ecologies and well-being. They must be protected to survive; they have needs, and indeed, have names. They are deeply valuable; they are family.

Mohamad emphasized that to name something is to make it real in your consciousness. A plant or animal you don't know the name of is relatively obscure to you; it's just some animal, some plant.

But when you know the name of it, everything you know about it becomes virtually present to you. "Oh, that's an *elder* tree; you can make preserves out of the berries, and its flowers are good for colds; they are used in cough drops."[12] And the same thing is even more true of another human being; when you learn a person's name, he or she becomes more real to you.

In the Unitarian-Universalist discussion, Roshan shared his developing sense of interdependence with the world, a sense of spiritual connection that was growing to encompass even the inanimate world of rocks and stones.

> *Roshan: I think when I was growing up I treated inanimate things differently from animate things. And I don't now. I think that that definition has enlarged for me. It isn't just that human beings don't have any special privilege on this earth, that was okay, that's how I grew up. But I don't now regard the inanimate piece as to be left out, that is part of the totality of my cosmology.*

Within such expanding religious visions, people, plants, and even rocks are kin. All earth's communities are part of divine concern. These are elements of an ecological identity: an embodied identity that goes beyond a scientific description of relationship between humanity and creation to focus on people's self-perception. The community model also has the ability to create an emotional or even spiritual basis for environmentally ethical behavior. Environmental educator Mitchell Thomashow sees the scientific understanding of human interconnectedness with the rest of the natural world as central to the creation of an "ecological identity." This ecological identity is defined as the state when "people perceive themselves in reference to nature, as living breathing beings connected to the rhythms of the earth, the biogeochemical cycles, the grand and complex diversity of ecological systems."[13]

---

12. See also Camille Adams Helminski, ed., *The Book of Nature* (Bristol, UK: Book Foundation, 2006).

13. Mitchell Thomashow, *Ecological Identity: Becoming a Reflective Environmentalist* (Cambridge, MA: MIT Press, 1996), xiii.

Interdependence expresses itself in a perception of unity for those who grasp it—the multiple levels of interdependence that participants recognize weave them into spiritual relationship with all of life. For some, this unity is shaped and experienced institutionally; their congregation is a source and expression of that unity. For Rafael, a pesticide educator working with immigrant apple pickers in rural Yakima County of eastern Washington, the Catholic Church is a source and expression of that unity.

> *Rafael: For me the most important thing about being Catholic is the unity that it inculcates in us, the Catholics, and we help, not only the Catholics, but we help everyone in general, and that Catholicism teaches that all are equals. No differences. And that it says we are united with every person and before all.*

For Rafael, the spiritual awareness of unity then issues a call for solidarity. He went on to say, "So we are like that in our house, with any person, because we have that teaching inside us. As it is in the church, it starts at home, and it will go on to change the world."

Commitment to Social Justice

Awareness of all these strands of interdependence wove a strong bond of commitment to social justice, which emerged as the third defining characteristic of green spirituality. For Gladys, Charlie, Jorge, and Rafael, understanding the impacts of toxins created a demand for justice. The demand for social justice, fueled by knowledge of the risks that people and living ecosystems endured, was again and again the spark that lit the fire of action. It got people moving—*to do* something. As Pat said,

> *Pat: I guess it's our moral responsibility to cause this to happen for all people like the woman that spoke yesterday. When she talked about global warming and she talked about our moral responsibility and she used an example of Bangladesh and how many people live there and they're, what, three*

*feet under sea level. And with this change in the weather pat-
tern and everything, we have a responsibility to those people.
"Who is our neighbor?"*

Commitment to social justice was widespread among the participants in my focus groups; comments about social justice emerged
in conversations almost as frequently as comments about scientific
literacy. While participants related environmental issues to many
doctrines— stewardship, mission, care for the poor, their political
voice, charity, prayer, honoring the glory of creation, and simplicity—the largest category of influential doctrines concerned social
justice.

Like Pat, many used the classic teaching known as Jesus's "great
command" to express their moral obligation as "loving the neighbor." This teaching, of course, was borrowed by Jesus from the
Torah (Leviticus 19:18; Deuteronomy 6:5). Wendy expressed environmental care as love of neighbor very clearly.

*Wendy (Reform Christian): There are a few things in the
Bible that talk about how to care for the earth but so little.
What we do have in the Bible is a whole bunch of times when
Jesus says love your neighbor as yourself. And here's where
I think the church can get on board. If we love our neighbor
as ourselves, and if we see our neighbor as that third world
community that doesn't have access to water, or the people
in our town who don't have enough food, then there's no end
to what we can do.*

Social justice, often expressed by Christians as "love of neighbor,"
remained absolutely central, but its compass widened. Now the
earth community belonged to a larger definition of the neighbor,
and social justice serves the entire earth community, seeing the
"earth as the new poor." Many persons expressed this in diverse
ways reflecting their faith traditions.

For Ellen, concern for social justice flowed naturally from an
awareness of spiritual interconnection, terms characteristic to her
Buddhist tradition.

Ellen (Buddhist): Compassion, certainly it's a huge word in Buddhist practice. But the word for me is reverence; I feel a real reverence in interconnectedness. The first image that came up for me is the people who are suffering and the people who will suffer. Towns disappearing in Alaska, there is tremendous suffering with this change in the environment. The more aware you are, the more I read or meditate, the ways I feed my consciousness, you know what comes around goes around, it's a cycle. What I take in is given out for sure, one way or another.

The centrality of social justice beliefs and the recurrent expression of the neighbor as the "global neighbor" suggest that theological adaptations that build on this common religious passion do increase the energy of green spirituality. Faith-based environmentalists seek to respect the earth for ethical reasons common to all environmentalists, as well as for additional faith reasons. Their combination in green spirituality adds fuel to the fire of both ethical inclinations and benefits from the social dynamics of congregational life.

David (Reformed Christian): The spiritual or religious aspect of it and the social responsibility, the action. To be Christian, to be spiritual, I won't even limit it to Christian, is to have respect for everything [including] the place that we've been given to live. So for me, it's a continuum. There's no front or back to it. It's just two twists of the same discussion.

Social justice commitments to the "global neighbor" are given an even deeper, planetary context when suffused by a reverent relationship to the earth community, which suggests that these core religious passions do increase the energy of green spirituality. The energy of green spirituality adds fuel to the fire of environmental concern. As Paul Gorman, a cofounder of the National Religious Partnership for the Environment, stated, the organization was not "the environmental movement at prayer." Their work was "not about providing more shock troops for the embattled American greens. We have to see the inescapable, thrilling, renewing religious dimension of this challenge."[14]

For faith-based environmentalists, a coherent worldview required environmental awareness. Thus, maintaining affiliation with their faith in a relevant and authentic way required the incorporation of green consciousness. But precisely because their traditions proposed the values of social justice, reverence for life, honoring creation, and spiritual unity, that faith itself was a powerful source of energy and motivation for the conceivably narrow problem of ecological degradation, if viewed purely as a pollution or wildlife or energy crisis. That is exactly why they engaged in congregational activity rather than seek an exclusive outlet for their environmental concern in a local chapter of the Sierra Club or another conservation society.

Many did belong to such organizations. Many showed strains of "dark green" religion.[15] More than one acknowledged an agnostic, even atheistic outlook, yet found meaning in the congregation's sustainability committee nonetheless. Certainly this ethnographic project confirms the vast diversity and complexity of spiritual beliefs, even while identifying recognizable categories of spiritual motivation.

But along with thousands, perhaps millions, of other faith-based environmentalists, the research participants also felt empowered and obligated to bring that green consciousness back to their faith traditions. As loyal pioneers, they developed ways to express the spirit of their tradition in an age of ecological crisis. To affirm the moral claim of environmental risks, they renegotiated the meaning of faith life in a morally globalized world and inhabited the religious paradox of loyalty as novelty.

Environmental Justice. This emphasis on social justice is not surprising because caring for the poor and working for social

---

14. Bill McKibben, "The Gospel of Green: Will Evangelicals Help Save the Earth?," *OnEarth* (Fall 2006), http://www.nrdc.org.

15. While I differ with many of his assumptions, Bron Taylor offers important analyses in *Dark Green Religion: Nature Spirituality and the Planetary Future* (Berkeley: University of California Press, 2010), 10.

justice are traditionally central concerns for virtually all faith traditions. Social justice is the natural link to environmental justice. As the faith-based environmentalists grew in their understanding of the ecological threats to the earth, aware that a degraded environment harms the poor, they interpreted traditional teachings about caring for the poor as a mandate for ecological responsibility.

The environmental justice movement's focus on the disproportionate burden of toxins and climate change on the poor is a critical contribution of religious environmentalists to the broader ecological movement because it punctures the reduction of environmentalism to a romanticized, nostalgic, and distant concern for lost, pure, wild nature. Environmental justice calls attention to the inequalities and injustices in human society that wreak damage on ecologies *and* persons. This call does not in any way underplay the crises of species extinction, deforestation, glacier retreat, or any other ecological problem. The very point is that these issues are inseparable for all in the community of life.

Unquestionably, the great wildernesses are treasures to preserve and reclaim. For many, the lonely, holy, and beautiful wilderness is their truest sanctuary. Generations of nature writers speak to this spirituality, and sacred scriptures also celebrate the presence and creativity of the divine therein. But two kinds of moral myopia are possible. On the one hand, wilderness preservation can seem like a luxurious, if not hypocritical, concern of privileged people who might overlook the damage (for example) to migrant workers who are sprayed while harvesting their beautiful food. On the other hand, many people are simply less interested in wilderness preservation, and to them conservation arguments are less pressing than their daily concerns. As Pablo said, "If I want to be killed, I'll keep walking." He knew his own survival was at stake. For Rafael, working for his own survival and dignity was integral to his community life and faith identity. It was not about himself alone; nor was he passively looking for help from others. Seeking unity and seeking social justice were central to his faith.

Reverence for Creation

Scientific literacy is one dimension of appreciating the earth that is complemented by a religious reverence. Religious reverence goes beyond love of nature itself because it includes a conviction that nature is God's creation, and that God's creation is certainly good. Love is also a powerful source of energy. It spurs active concern. Reverence and awe thus draw people into action more than simple understanding of the facts of climate science. In this bond of love, as Augustine wrote, we are what we love. Life on the planet is part of the self—and so the distinction of caring for "nature" outside of us disappears. The reverence owed to God invites respect for God's creation.

The combination of scientific sophistication and literacy together with religious reverence and love of nature produces a strong sense of being related and responsible. Faith-based environmentalists perceive an obligation to protect the earth as part of their responsibility to care for their neighbors. Indeed, the earth and its many living systems are increasingly sensed as neighbors in their own right, deserving protection as beautiful, good, as beloved creation. They are rethinking moral obligation within these expanding horizons of meaning—what it means to be creation, to be sacred, to be just, to care for the poor.

Finding God in nature. Many participants sensed God most closely in nature. Promoting experiences in nature is a key strategy for several faith-based environmental groups. *Renewal*, an important documentary film often used in religious environmental education programs, portrays a Jewish summer camp that celebrates God's gift of nature and encourages environmental awareness. Hiking expeditions are central to the environmental ministry of the Orthodox Fellowship of the Transfiguration. My participants emphasized how nature served as a meeting place with God and a space in which to experience their emotional connection to God.

Alison is an evangelical Christian and also a member of Florida's environmental protection agency. In a dramatic example of the fusion of faith and ecological activism, she arrived late to the focus group because she had just been out in a boat trying to find a manatee trapped by a fishing line twisted around its flipper. For her, "being in nature is one place where I'm closest to God, and it's a very strong connection."

The connection with nature does not have to be an encounter with Mt. Everest or Niagara Falls. Angelina, raised in a very different environment, would agree. She grew up in a New Jersey town facing the New York City skyline.

> *Angelina: I grew up on a busy street, above the store, but down the street was a fence with rambler roses, and I would just look at them and take in the scent and it was really amazing. I think you can only come to God through nature; it's realizing that these things come from something bigger than themselves.*

Their closeness to God through nature makes the pain of nature's degradation all the more poignant. It is not just a loss of some green space, but a spiritual diminishment. Reverence for nature and God unite—and combine into a profound sense of spiritual loss. Chris, an Episcopalian and a minister's wife, grew up on a beach in South Carolina and found a haven for her own soul and a place for self-discovery walking on it. "I grew up on the beach, and I worked my life out walking up and down the beach. And that was a spiritual place for me. And it's still a spiritual place for me, and it breaks my heart when I see the things that happen to the things that live there."

Like Chris, Bob, who was an evangelical Christian, saw the presence of God in nature's beauty and experienced the destruction of nature as a spiritual loss. Both expressed the loss in physical terms: a broken heart, a scar on one's inner faith. He was also a scuba diver and commented on the bleaching of coral reefs. "You know, I've been all around the world and seen how creation cries out invisible attributes of God, and I've seen it firsthand. And so to see that diminished in our society because of the environment is a scar on our faith."

To Shonto, a Navajo artist, reverence for nature precludes exploiting nature for its commercial value. Simply honoring a sacred mountain by letting it be, however, was not an easy religious practice to explain to the Forest Service.

> *Shonto: Right now, we're in this constant state of struggle with the Forest Service and a ski resort. How can we make them understand that we're not out to just close deals with them, but to block the use of sewer water to make artificial snow on the sacred mountain? That is sacred! I think they expect us to be up there holding some sort of powwow, holding some sort of a vigil, having some sort of a temple up there.*

As Shonto insisted, "We're not up there because the mountain itself is a temple. They say, 'Okay, you're not using it. Why don't you use this land?'" He characterized the utilitarian view of the Forest Service as implying that the tribe isn't adequately "resourceful with our resources, meaning that we don't suck the blood out of it." The tribe chose not to make money off of their mountain, but for everyone else, "that's the only thing they talk about."

In observing nature, reverent believers find more reasons to praise God. Dr. Joel Hunter, the charismatic leader of Northland Church, the megachurch in Florida, shared his own ecological spirituality.

> *Joel: I have found myself more and more just sitting around in my back yard and looking at the turtles. We have a little pond with little turtles. And I just love to sit for fifteen minutes and just say God this is so beautiful, how did you think of all this stuff? How did you do it? It has really given me permission, it has given me reminders to just sit and appreciate what God has done with creation.*

Interfaith Connections

Interfaith collaboration is very typical of practical actions and environmental advocacy at the congregational level. Different religious traditions experienced the impact of shared social issues such as consumerism, scientific illiteracy, or globalization in similar ways, and found natural partners among other value-based groups.

Within towns and counties, persons from different congregations worked together on clean-ups and local issues. During announcements at a service I attended, the Atonement Episcopal Church shared news of a ceremony at a local Hindu temple with whom the environmental committee had worked. As already mentioned, the Maryland Towson Presbyterian Church had been cleaning streams with a Muslim girls' club, and both the New Jersey Unitarian-Universalists and Catholics at St. Mary's Church mentioned their work with each other.

Organizations that support grass-roots congregations are growing as well. GreenFaith, a New Jersey based organization specifically dedicated to supporting faith-based environmentalism, promotes multiple collaborations, hosts interfaith spiritual and intellectual forums, conducts toxic tours, collaborates on important local legal advocacy, and provides leadership education to persons from multiple traditions. Interfaith Power and Light grew from a San Francisco advocacy group to a national organization with over 35 state chapters. The National Religious Partnership for the Environment organizes Christian and Jewish education and political action on the environment. The Alliance for Religion and Conservation has promoted long-term strategic sustainability planning by religions for their worldwide membership, among other initiatives. Other coalitions include Religious Witness for the Earth, Interfaith Moral Action for Climate Change, the Interfaith Environmental Programme of the United Nations . . . the list goes on.

At a deeper level, there are commonalities in worldview transformation. The Forum on Religion and Ecology at Yale sponsored multiple academic conferences, one on each major religious tradition, to examine how worldviews are responding to the new priority and needs of the earth. Through this ground-breaking scholarship, the unique resources of each tradition—its own history, symbols, texts, and traditions—have been better understood and their potential to inspire care for the earth developed.

Religious faiths offer different conceptions of God and of their place in the universe. As theologian Elizabeth Johnson has put it, "The incomprehensible mystery of the living God shines ever brighter as the God of Abraham and Sarah, the God of Jesus Christ, meets Allah, Brahman, Krishna, Kali, Sunyata, Kwan yin, the Buddha, the Tao."[16]

Despite different conceptions of God and of humanity's place in the universe, there is the same hope for ecological renewal and a common impulse to "green" their religions. Sacred laws teach obligation to the earth variously: by not cutting down fruit trees, by respecting sentient beings. Moral obligations are framed using the diverse concepts of karma, interbeing, submission, covenant, and blessing.[17] Christians often employed terms such as Incarnation, creation, sacrifice, and grace. All were unique forms of inspiration for their green missions. Participants stressed the importance of their unique identities, expressed through these different obligations, doctrines, and concepts. Many, like Satya, felt particular pride in their own traditions. Satya quoted a saying from a swami of his Hindu tradition that "no religion is wrong, but it's how far away that they are from the sun. And I think that we are the sun. And other religions are not, I'm not saying ... the other religions seem to get a part of it, but not to get to the whole of it. That's why I feel really great and proud of being a Hindu."

Many others found inspiration in stretching some of their traditional religious concepts by engaging the language of others. One rabbi who led his congregation in environmental advocacy alluded to the contemporary Buddhist teacher Thich Nhat Hanh in order to explore ways Jews might capture the deep sense of Eastern interconnection. In a sermon once posted on his temple's website, he writes, "We must move toward a Judaism of interconnectedness, a Torah of interbeing." A Jewish teacher from a more Orthodox

---

16. Elizabeth A. Johnson, *Quest for the Living God: Mapping Frontiers in the Theology of God* (New York: Continuum, 2008), 155.

17. For an excellent overview of how diverse faiths draw out the environmental implications of traditional symbols, texts, and themes, see the collected essays in *Daedalus: Religion and Ecology: Can the Climate Change?* (Cambridge: MIT Press, Fall 2001).

community drew comparisons between the Islamic and Jewish ablutions before prayer.[18]

Overall, a wide and generous theological appreciation for the gifts and insights of other traditions was common, beyond practical collaboration. Participants used insights from other traditions to clarify their own distinctive spiritualities. Madeleine did this by observing that her view of the world was both incarnational and perhaps Buddhist. Mohamad had a striking way of interpreting that borrowing, making interreligious borrowing legitimate on internal grounds. He said, "Wisdom is the lost riding beast of the Muslim, so that wherever he finds it he has the right to claim it." For Mohamad practical borrowing had a kind of urgency: we need all the useful ideas we can find. If there is a teaching from another tradition that brings clarity or inspiration, use it! The many faith-based environmentalists did feel free to engage and explore diverse spiritual gifts, and found this sharing to be a true gift of energy and renewal.

Expanding Religious Visions of God, Neighbor, and Self

Participants spoke of their expanding horizons, of finding a "bigger God": one who embraces the more-than-human cosmos. For Elaine, her sense that the immensity of the universe was directly linked with her identity and her spiritual responsibility came from a talk at her Unitarian congregation about the "Greatest Story." When a child told the lecturer that he was six years old, the speaker responded that "you are really thirteen billion and six," because thirteen billion years ago the same hydrogen was created that exists in each of us. As Elaine put it, "Just thinking about that in connection with the whole universe, that's a pretty big huge idea. But we

---

18. These comments were part of a sermon by Rabbi Gil Steinlauf posted on the website of Temple Israel, Ridgewood, NJ. See also Ora Sheinson, "The Halachos of Netilas Yadayim and Water Conservation," in *Compendium of Sources in Halacha and the Environment*, ed. Ora Sheinson and Shai Spetgang (New York: Canfei Nesharim, 2005), 45.

can be part of my little part of the universe, which is earth, and try to not harm it, try to cut down where I am harming it right now."

Personal ethical identity expands when moral relationships share a global stage through the indirect webs of globalization and planetary ecology. Neighbors in need include plants, animals, and even nonsentient parts of planetary systems.

Faith-based environmentalists reinterpreted doctrines not as simply the concerns of the individual soul but as beliefs with planetary implications. In short, many came to recognize a "bigger God" whose concerns included the earth. They saw a larger sphere for the action of the divine—which implied broader moral responsibility.

To give voice to the environmental concerns and sense of planetary citizenship that inspired them, many participants expressed classic concepts in new ways. No one said this more powerfully than Ted, an evangelical Christian minister, who found that his understanding of God's sphere of concern expanded. Always all-powerful and supreme, God's action expanded to include the land.

Ted: I mean your last question is how your view of God has changed. That was a fascinating question because I think my God has gotten bigger since I've embraced this effort. Even just thinking, in 2 Chronicles 14, "if my people will hear my voice and turn from their wicked ways, and call upon the Lord I will heal their land." What does that mean? You know, could that be an environmental answer that revival could bring about the cleansing of the land. It's land, it's not just people. So, you know, it's my view of God, I've read that verse for 30 years and I've never seen that verse that way. And so, it's my view of God getting much bigger since I've started thinking about the stewardship aspect of this environmental concern.

Q. I am assuming God was almighty before ... well, how much bigger can he get? What is bigger?

Ted: Well, he was almighty, he's pretty consistent, I'm the inconsistent factor. I think that's good theology? What do you think? (Laughter)

Ted simply realized that through his advocacy for creation, his "God has gotten bigger."

Erik's new view of redemption recast the central Christian concept of salvation into relational terms that suggest the interdependence of ecology, citing "wholeness" and "integration."

> *Erik (Baptist): I used to think in terms of redemption all the time, the act of being saved. And that was always in the context of confessing sin and being good enough and being worthy of Christ's sacrifice. Instead of thinking of being redeemed I think of being brought into the wholeness that God has for me. . . . God's interest is for me to be a whole integrated person. And I think that kind of directs my environmental perspective as well, that the earth was meant to be an integrated system of life and it's all a cycle.*

Participants are consciously aware of the adaptations they are forging. For Shonto, reinterpreting traditional symbols creates bridges back to the land of his people. New symbols were critical for the young people living both on and off the reservation, whose relationship to the land is as altered by modernity as is the landscape itself.

> *Shonto (Navajo): In some sense, we always have to be ready to rearm ourselves with the prayers and chants, and the stories, and the strength of the hero twins. So in this case, the young people today have the legacy of rearming themselves to fight the latter-day Ye'is, the monsters, in the form of draglines and things eating the earth.*

Independent Thinkers

I started every focus group with the question, "What is your favorite thing about your faith tradition?" This question yielded two dominant responses: the pleasure of being in a friendly community, and the satisfaction of sharing free inquiry. I was not surprised to hear that being part of a family-like community with shared values was one of the top two favorite characteristics. However, given the common assumption that religious affiliation translates into set ideas, I was fascinated to find that freedom of inquiry was equally cherished.[19] Almost half of all participants volunteered that free inquiry was their favorite thing about their community, equal to those who most appreciated finding a group that shared their values.

An emphasis on freedom is perhaps a uniquely American experience of religious faith. This phenomenon has been a staple of religious commentary since De Tocqueville. Freedom is a primary source of energy for the journey into a new and unfamiliar path of living sustainably.

> *John: I think for me it's the freedom of inquiry that will allow the fact that we're not given a dogma or set of beliefs, we're not told what to believe but invited to believe what we find to be true and try and work that out with other people who want to engage in that journey.*

Free inquiry, openness to wide-ranging discourse, affirmation of exploring new meanings and forms of expressing ancient meanings—these values were shared spontaneously and immediately by almost all. Cheryl valued "the sense of diversity in the sense of opinions, a willingness to consider various options." As she said, not being "a rigid denomination" was very important. In her view, there were certainly core beliefs, but also "room for a lot of discussion."

It is not surprising that a Unitarian-Universalist community would comment on the value of spiritual diversity. But this was a priority shared by members of all the groups I encountered. In fact, for Julie, the openness to considering various options created a spiritual responsibility, which she interpreted using the traditional term "priesthood of all believers."

---

19. Paul A. Djupe and Patrick Kieran Hunt, "Beyond the Lynn White Thesis: Congregational Effects on Environmental Concern," *Journal for the Scientific Study of Religion* 48, no. 4 (2009): 671; Douglas Lee and T. Jean Blocker Eckberg, "Varieties of Religious Involvement and Environmental Concerns: Testing the Lynn White Thesis," *Journal for the Scientific Study of Religion* 28, no. 4 (1989): 510.

> *Julie: Good and bad, you don't get straightforward answers
> … you don't get an answer. You're challenged and expected
> to do the work on your own. I think the concept of the priest-
> hood of all believers is absolutely vital for me. I have a hard
> time with groups that can't accept that I have a valid way to
> interpret and understand things in my experience.*

Furthermore, she added, getting straightforward answers wouldn't
be appreciated. "I don't like you telling me any answers. The group
laughed at this. Being engaged in this way, in a tension between
searching for answers and experiencing the challenge of creating
these new interpretations, was both frustrating and rewarding.
Being free to pursue the meaning of her faith within her community—and as an exercise of the traditionally recognized priesthood
of all believers—probably played a large part in her significant
leadership within her congregation and in her regional faith group
as a whole. Julie was the representative of the Maryland Presbytery
to the Maryland legislature: she was the presbytery's policy representative and brought to the legislature her community's views on
environmental advocacy and justice. As she said, "It's hard, too,
and it's frustrating, but it keeps the spice in your life."

The power of their congregations to affirm free thinking, spirituality, and service to the earth is not incidental. The energy of
freedom is the power to break the bond of inaction, to transcend
the action gap.

More traditionally conservative groups also talked about spiritual
freedom. When I asked the gathering of Catholic migrant workers
what was their favorite thing about being Catholic, one man said,
"Well, it's too many things for me, because we have different rules
and different things, and we are free to make every decision."

Clearly people choose to join like-minded groups. But joining a
like-minded group does not preclude thoughtful reflection in selecting the group. Participants valued the ability to continue to think
freely about their beliefs and principles. Because the trust within
a familiar community enabled free inquiry, committee members
were able to examine and develop their attitudes about spiritual-

ity and the environment. In a safe community, they were able to explore new ideas and new actions productively.

To conclude this exploration of the seven observed patterns in green spirituality, I review the seven patterns. They are a good sense of scientific literacy; awareness of global interdependence; commitment to social justice; reverence for creation; interfaith connections; expanding religious visions of God, neighbor, and self; and prizing freedom of inquiry within their communities. The atmosphere of shared values and free inquiry allowed members of environmental committees to rethink their attitudes and actions related to spirituality and the environment. Inspired by a sense of spiritual interdependence and driven by knowledge of scientific reality, they developed new doctrinal understandings and patterns of action. Now, the question is, what sparked the interest in the environment in the first place?

Igniting the Fire

Having observed certain patterns in green spirituality, we can wonder: How did they get there? How did that spirituality develop, and what sparked an environmental dimension to their preexisting faith?

For many of the people I interviewed, green spirituality blossomed through a process like a conversion, an experience of shifting values and priorities. In the process, they have drawn energy from a sense of freedom to express their religious convictions through ecological action, have a certain sense of social justice obligation and a clear awareness of global interdependence. In the words of African-American womanist theologian Dolores Williams, these pioneers have found "a way where there is no way." They have seen that a new road is needed, that the signs from their faith point to the need to care for the earth.

But awareness of a need is not sufficient to meet that need. In this next section, I will explore the challenging question of how hope and commitment emerge. Where did participants find the energy to take on new commitments? What gets them noticing the crises in the environment?

The Spark That Starts It: Noticing Something

Sometimes, a dramatic moment changed their attitudes to the environment. Tragedy struck, leaving Gladys fiercely dedicated to asthma awareness and fighting pollution after her daughter-in-law died in a hospital parking lot, an hour after an asthma attack began.

> Q: *What about you, Gladys, was there a moment or was it gradual or always in the back of your mind, the pollution and the environmental issues?*
>
> *Gladys: Well, I would have to say when our daughter-in-law died. I mean that woke me up completely because I never— we never even thought about somebody dying from asthma; it just wasn't heard of, we just never heard of it. But I mean the realization that somebody could die in that short a period of time was a real wake-up call. It just gave us the impetus to say let's hope that we can stop that from happening again to someone else. Because it's a devastating experience, you know, when somebody dies in less than an hour, it's a—it's— it's really a devastating experience.*

Gladys lives in a neighborhood with five garbage incinerators, whose particulate exhaust leads to high rates of asthma, learning disabilities, school absenteeism. Grief for her daughter-in-law drove Gladys to create citizen-science air quality monitoring programs, results of which she delivered regularly to her local politicians. She started a parish environmental committee and invited me to speak at an educational seminar the committee organized, which is how I first met her. She gave me a paper fan, a memento printed with the name of the foundation she established to honor her daughter-in-law. Perhaps this fan was meant inspire me to combat the New York City summer heat the old-fashioned way, without turning up the air-conditioning and creating more greenhouse gases and industrial particulates. It also included inspiration of the spiritual kind, being inscribed with a scripture text about the Breath of God. This homemade paper fan was one way she could spread awareness, and offer practical comfort and a cool breeze at the same time.

More often, awareness grew from small encounters that struck a chord and resounded with people. In the case of Pat and Sarah, remarks heard long ago were remembered, and their impacts were still felt. Both women were exposed to the scarcity of resources many Americans take for granted. Pat, a Presbyterian woman, recounted that during a visit to Jamaica, somebody tore up a piece of paper. Another woman gasped, "Don't throw that away! Paper is precious to us! We'll use this." For Pat, this was an "aha!" moment, a breakthrough in awareness that stuck with her for twenty years. Nancy, a Unitarian, had a similar awakening to the crises of water, something so easily taken for granted in the First World full of faucets. She attended a seminar at the United Nations that discussed water issues. But the impact came from the African teenagers she heard.

> *Nancy: They had some teenagers there that had come from some countries in Africa, and they talked about how far they had to walk every day to get water, and we're flushing our toilets with drinking water. So I guess for me it's sort of been a gradual process. At a lecture I went to one time they said our biggest export is used clothes, and I just think all of this over-consuming. But it hasn't been anything like a bolt of lightning out of the sky.*

In each of these cases the preciousness of resources ordinarily seen as so common and unremarkable took on a new quality—rare, essential, absolutely indispensable. For Pat and Nancy, the message hit home because of the emotional reaction directly expressed by a person shocked by waste.

Likewise, Mohamad's reaction to finding a great tree cut down on his college campus also shows how other people's emotional evaluations can powerfully shape others' perceptions. He had just left a class in which the professor said that cutting down a tree is a crime.

> *Mohamad: They had cut down a tree, and it was a tree that I just learned the name of, so it was like lying there, and I, I just kind of remember the words of the professor about cutting*

down a tree without reason is a crime—it's murder. And so I
just kind of looked at it and it hit me.

And like Branch, who learned the names of plants, the tree now
had a name. The crime became personal. At that time Mohamad
was trying to figure out what I was going to do, and he in fact
became an environmental engineer after graduating. He started a
blog called DC Muslims that brought together many young, professional, environmentally conscious Muslims and significantly
increased the visibility of Muslim environmental activism.

Bringing on the Heat: Influential Information

Books and films also played a role in influencing people's thoughts
about the environment. Joel Hunter remembered reading Tim Flan-
nery's *The Weather Makers*, which made him start to pay attention.
After reading that, he sought out other books, "just for a balanced
approach." Hunter read the writings of climate skeptics who were
portraying climate science as overhyped and politically motivated.
Fortunately, Hunter kept reading and found the research promul-
gated by the Intergovernmental Panel on Climate Change (IPCC) of
the United Nations. These reports surveyed peer-reviewed articles
from thousands of scientists across the globe and included summary reports assembled by high-profile scientists such as Sir John
Haughton, the chair of one report. "But I got to the IPCC stuff,
and I thought oh my goodness, just because of the number of scientists, and then I heard Sir John Haughton." Dr. Hunter was invited
to attend a meeting between evangelicals and scientists, where he
heard Haughton describe the science and the international consensus. Hearing Haughton's authoritative account of the changes
occurring on earth, Hunter recognized the incompleteness of the
climate denial and skeptic position. Hunter also realized how climate change would affect the poor, and this connected with his vital
sense of his own ministry as a vocation for social justice. "I was
brought to Christ during the Martin Luther King Jr. era. A matter
of fact, it was his assassination that was the occasion to my coming
to Christ."

Carol realized the impact of commercial investment in polluting practices from a film. "I think I've always really been very strongly in favor of protecting the natural world, but I didn't think I really understood the commercial side of it. How seriously industries and farms contribute most to pollution of the waterways and pollution of the air." For Carol, the films she saw also revealed concrete options for sustainable living of which she had not been aware. Madeleine likewise saw hope in the (at least temporary) groundswell of interest and attention brought to global warming by Al Gore's movie, *An Inconvenient Truth*. Other movies such as *Renewal*, *The Story of Stuff*, even *Erin Brockovich*, and most recently *Gasland*, all have caused surges in attention and concern.

Local experiences were powerful, and losses in people's local environment hit hard. As a Maryland environmental policy advocate said of her neighbors, "They want those crabs!" She could see how polluting the bay forced changes in people's recreational options. The frustration couldn't be explained away.

Julie: We have friends that have waterfront property that feeds into the Chesapeake Bay. The grandchildren were going to jump off the dock and swim. And I said, "Think about it because of the contamination of the water." And she said, "Julie, you just ruined our Sunday afternoon." Because you can't swim in those waters anymore, and that is what's getting to people. When they can see it and it changes their lifestyle and what they would like to be able to do. So there I just see passion.

Getting the picture in a way that ignited that passion—whether through films, the news, stories from friends, lectures—provided the essential spark. The passion could take the form of reengaging a fundamental sense of ministry, or just the aggravation and frustration of having one's Sunday afternoon ruined. Information floods our society, but when it catches onto an emotional foundation, it can ignite into action. Leadership is then needed to help people realize what can they do with this information, this irritation, this need to do something.

Stoking the Flame: Leadership

The power of leadership within communities is incredibly significant. One person's example, enthusiasm, and championship have
a critical, galvanizing power. Directly communicated passion is
catching, and a personal invitation to become involved has almost
unfailing success. Sometimes, leadership can be as simple as just
stating one's views clearly. A simple comment can lock into another
person's memory with unanticipated impact. Sarah, the evangelical Christian who studies sustainable development, remembered a
comment from a classmate in her Christian high school, at a time
when Sarah wasn't thinking about climate change. She remembers
widespread dismissal of any environmental concern. "Everyone in
the class was like, well, I don't believe it, who cares. But one girl in
the class was like, no, we are supposed to care about this. And that
stuck with me."

Trusted leadership. The sustainability committees were able
to connect the environment to local concerns, gave friendly and
persistent encouragement, and facilitated nonauthoritarian leadership. While clergy were often powerful leaders, in many cases, lay
leaders carried the torch. My research particularly focused on lay
leaders. Pragmatically, laity are more likely to have the time for
new initiatives. Let me be clear: clergy leadership provides critical authority, validation, and permission. Clergy are uniquely able
to galvanize people into action. Their authority and prominence
are essential to champion the cause. Without the permission from
local clergy to continue with environmental work, it won't start. At
the same time, lay leaders held great sway as both educators and
motivators, and it is the reasons for their success—precisely as non-
ordained leaders—that are tracked here.

Persistent and personal. Participants often stated that people
respond not primarily to data but to inspiration, enthusiasm, calls
for courage, and reminders of core-group priorities. Local leaders
effectively highlighted the moral and religious dimensions of ecological awareness: the loss of the beauty and sanctity of creation,
the justice implications of environmental degradation, and the
needs of the poor.

Other frequently cited qualities of a strong leader were persistence, setting an example, peer pressure, ability to be a pioneer, issuing personal invitations to friends, respectability, sharing goals, enthusiasm, and religious vision. Personal outreach was frequently cited as the reason people became involved. Persistent, passionate leadership kept a project going. Friendly, repeated contact with respected leaders in a congregation invited people to reconsider default behavior patterns.

Lay leaders could often leverage activity precisely because they were not ordained leaders. From a less public position, they could advocate for a new and unfamiliar cause, and take on some of the risk that could deter a pastor. Preaching on controversial topics with a political tinge was a real risk for pastors, whose job security is threatened by decamping members, especially in a small congregation. Dr. Joel Hunter, a national leader in the evangelical environmental movement, explained the dilemma in no uncertain terms: job security.

> *Joel (evangelical): Pastoring is the only job that we've been trained for. Pastors are very sincere people; they got in because they wanted to do good, they wanted to shepherd their people, but they're very insecure. And if they lose their job, they have to put on a hat and say, do you want fries with that?*

Clergy are in a sensitive position. One leader recalled hearing, "I don't want to be legislated from the pulpit. Don't tell me how to live." Lay leaders may be able to raise ideas and invite participation without seeming to overstep the boundaries of pulpit admonitions, restricted in the minds of some to "spiritual" matters.

The cherished freedom to express and act on their own values noted above empowered people to "demand" green leadership from their church, temple, synagogue, or mosque. Often, pastors and congregants are coming to this mission together. Monica, a Reform Christian, observed, "We're not the last word in green but I've been paying attention to that for so long I can't imagine not doing it." However, her earlier environmental activities affected her private choices about commuting, light bulbs, recycling. As her pastor rejoined, "Yet you never demanded it of your church before, did you?" His comment indicated a vacuum of leadership waiting to be filled and the willingness to take the first steps of leadership together.

Those smaller communities, in turn, are sometimes more responsive than the governance or regulatory bodies of a city, state, or nation. In sum, local leaders can light a spark that ignites action by reframing ecological concern spiritually—explaining, inspiring, and nudging.

Following Friends: Models Make it Possible

Sustainability committees modeled more sustainable ways to do common things. Among the group, participants could discuss concerns and share practices. The comic frustrations of car pooling, advice on green cleaners, the technicalities and practicalities of installing solar panels, ways to eat less meat, or avoid out-of-season produce took on a tone of humor and warmth among friends. Sharing models of new behaviors demonstrated that new practices are possible, permitted, and even preferred. These behaviors might be countercultural. But the groups' awareness of the seriousness of the environmental crisis helped them realize their importance.

Possible (and preferred) practices. New practices ranged from forgoing small conveniences to making radically austere decisions. By simply having the time to share ideas, people could learn about new practices and see that such practices might be preferable. Recycling more might be possible, cheaper, better for the earth, and morally significant to one's peer group. Elaine never thought a party was possible without bags of trash afterward. After discussions with her Catholic committee, Elaine hosted a party with pitchers of homemade iced tea, flatware, and cloth napkins. Recounting the story, she said, "When we were all finished, I have to say my husband came to me and he said, 'There's no garbage.' I just smiled."

Another woman, Madeleine, listened to her friend Ann talk about avoiding out-of-season produce that had been trucked or flown in from continents far away. Hearing about someone else's struggle with what had become a cultural norm—raspberries *any time you want them*— connected instantly with her own subdued guilt about endless asparagus purchases. Madeleine felt impatient with the constant barrage of unsustainable, foreign, and unseasonable produce. This barrage had dulled her conscience to the "what the hell" stage, but her friend's experience with raspberries helped her awaken the energy to care once more about these wasteful and fossil-fuel intensive indulgences. Just as important, she could focus once more on the specialness of fresh spring berries. She said,

> *Madeleine: I love that little story about the raspberries. We talked earlier about leadership. Now, I had been in that situation with the food thing as well. . . . I had lost the seasonal nature. I know now because somebody's told me, "These foods have been trucked in; this is not good for the environment." I get to the point where I think, "Oh what the hell. Throw it in the basket." I hate to keep saying what the hell. But now I've heard Ann's story, and I'm telling you, this is leadership because I am going to think, "Well if Ann can do it . . ."*

In other words, group dynamics show that participants can, and should, take on new practices. The group offered a place to share ideas; often, the congregation was the only place some people could find for environmental collaboration that fired their passions. Judy, a Catholic woman and teacher, remembers getting ecological training, but not finding an outlet for her activism and desire to teach about the environment.

> *Judy: In the '70s with the Clean Air Act, I remember there was an opportunity to go to Rutgers to a course to help teachers teach about ecology. For years and years and years I would always try to educate, but I've never found someone who I could share that same passion with.*

Lastly, groups exerted peer pressure to make these practices the new norm.

Q: You plan to enlist people further in moving this into their own lifestyles. What's your game plan for interrupting the busy people?

Bob (Unitarian-Universalist): I think it's peer pressure.

Nancy: Yeah, nobody would dare drive a Hummer in here.

Peer pressure works very effectively when it is applied upward—that is, from children to parents! Congregations often wisely employed this strategy and, as social organizations involving the whole family, were excellent venues for involving young people. St. Mary's Environmental Expo took off when it highlighted exhibits and hands-on projects for kids. When children gathered around the pets or explored light-bulb displays, it gave reluctant parents "permission" to check out the exhibits as well. Teenagers took the lead at the Episcopal Church of the Atonement by starting a church garden as a Scouts project. And at the highly active Reformed Church of Highland Park, all the environmental energy began when one college student insisted on getting rid of all the Styrofoam cups and washing all the coffee mugs himself, inspiring and educating his whole community in the process.

One family made radical adjustments to their winter thermostat settings, motivated by personal ideals as well as the price of heating fuel. Despite their discomfort, they were also sustained by a desire to live out the green spirituality visibly proclaimed by the new solar panels on their church's roof.

Marc (Reform Christian): The hardest thing we have done, it is green and it is economic, is turn our heat down to 40 at night. We wear more clothes and we use more blankets.

While living right where frugal and conservationist values intersect himself, Marc also emphasized the difference between "economically green" and "spiritually green" that he observed in Wendy.

Marc: Wendy said something that really summed up the difference between economics and spirituality. We're all pretty frugal people, but at the end of the day she takes what she saves and gives it away by supporting a family. That's the spiritual connection, that action turns it from economics, political, to spiritual. We all buy our clothes at the thrift shop and everything, and her actions speak for the spirituality, for Christianity, because you can be cheap and frugal and all of that, and if you squirrel it away until you are 90 you haven't fulfilled the Christian ethic. She gives that which she could have lavished on herself and her family; she gives away to a charity and being green and ethically green, politically green, she's turned it into spiritually green.

Marc captured the essential truth that must be sown to reap a just global society in which resources are shared. Even more significantly, excess resources must be identified as excess so they can be given to others. Marc observes in his friend the gift for renewing a sense of unity that enables caring for one's neighbor, a gift rooted in a spirituality that is open and eager to share with others.

Hope and Realism

Religious hope does have the potential to empower people with the courage and stamina to seek solutions and work for change. Marie was a founding leader of the creation committee in her Catholic parish. Her hope was rooted in belief in "a transforming God somehow connected with the Eucharist. I am always looking for transformation, not only for myself but for my family." Transformation was the key dynamic needed: a power that can transform the way things are, a sustaining presence that can impart this gift of transformation, and a ritual of hope and thanksgiving. She was not looking for magic, but for inspiration. She trusted that she was not alone: that with all of her tireless efforts, God was working toward transformation as well. "That's important to me, that I feel that there's somewhere I can go to express that, or to hope for that, or to thank for that, if transformation does take place."

Faith-based groups promote hope in a community, renewing and strengthening people's moral commitment to act. If spiritual inspiration enables some small sprig of hope to emerge, faith communities can be the brace to help that sprig grow. Religious conviction about human unity and equality inspired Rafael to hope for an ongoing transformation, personally, ecclesially, and globally. As previously cited, he said with conviction, "As it is in the church, it starts at home, and it will go on to change the world."

Interestingly, though, hope was not a universally driving factor. Many participants expressed a commitment to act virtuously regardless of whether they felt it would make a difference to the earth. Religious values motivated many to keep working despite a sense that "the system" and the tides of time were against them. Indeed, the felt sense of obligation to act regardless of hope was a topic that arose as many times as did the sense of hopefulness.

Recognizing that young people will inherit the earth, its problems, and the ultimate (if unfair) responsibility to address them, Shonto believed strongly that the biggest threat to the earth is that many youth are disengaged from these problems. He did not blame young people for this position but wondered how to give them inspiration, get them "jazzed up" to do something. However, blame does seem to figure in the nexus of apathy and resentment felt by some young people who are angry at the previous generation about being handed a degraded planet on a downward spiral. One young leader linked her own anger with apathy by stating, "I have a chip on my shoulder the size of a boulder." In effect, she was saying: your generation caused this problem, and now we have to fix it? I don't want to do anything. Their apathy may well cover anxiety and resentment, elements of a painful and ambiguous emotional experience that facing the environmental crisis honestly can bring about.

Erika, a college student who joined the University Baptist Church discussion in Seattle, also felt that apathy was epidemic among her peers, and she was alone in her environmental concern. "Most people don't really think the way I do. They just say, well people before me have come and gone, they did their thing and didn't care about the earth, so that's what I'm going to do now. I'm going to die before the earth is gone. They don't really care about future generations." She observed that some people wanted to help the community for the sake of the future, "and there's people that really care about now, their life, and then screw it, you know."

To her, creating any kind of change seemed overwhelming. Change would require challenging central American views of land as private property to use as one pleases, and driving cars as a sacrosanct freedom. To Erika, freedom required sacrifice—a familiar notion in the context of war, but one she applied to environmental health. "How much of our freedoms come because of our sacrifice? You can't just have a lot of freedom because if there's no sacrifice there's no real balance. I think a lot of Americans don't see that. As soon as you say, 'You're losing your freedom,' they just go, 'Oh my God! Oh my God!'" As she saw it, widespread apathy and defensiveness drained what little effectiveness truly concerned people might have. "Yeah, there are a lot of people that care; there's nothing really feels like it is happening. We're just sustaining this level of okay, we aren't going down as fast as we could be you know. Dumping water out of the boat but still sinking."

In a different discussion, Jim raised the same theme. He spoke to his pessimism from another generation of college advocacy.

> *Jim (Unitarian): I grew up in Students for a Democratic Society, and I believe that there is no revolution down the road; whatever life we are living is the revolution. This is the world, the way it's going to be forever. And so if you are going to take action, don't wait for the revolution. Now is the time to do it. And it doesn't matter to me whether I am optimistic or pessimistic. My values are robust enough so that it's important to keep working even though I'm actually very pessimistic about the overall situation in the next probably hundred years.*

> *Lynn: You mean we are the people we've been waiting for? Darn.*

Sarah also lacked confidence in the political system. Instead, she put her trust in God and in Christ—reaching for courageous spiritual language but seeming to express despair nonetheless by her repeated emphasis on the failure of creating change by the vote.

Sarah (evangelical): I would ... well, I mean I wouldn't have hope if it wasn't for Christ. I wouldn't have hope in the political system. I still will vote based on that but it's not where my hope is. So ... that's definitely what it comes down to. I mean, I take courage and I have hope but it's not in us figuring it all out; it's us partnering with God, and God figuring it all out.

Being overwhelmed is an extremely common feeling among environmental advocates. To many, it does look really hopeless much of the time. But for faith-based environmentalists, there seems to be a religious dimension to feeling overwhelmed. Charlie expressed a sadness that lies below the common feeling of being overwhelmed by the magnitude of climate change. When Charlie really grasped how his practices at home and at work affected others, he felt a sorrow for harming them that was magnified by his own recognition that no action is truly isolated. Coached by his faith to see those harmed as the "least ones" whom Jesus protects, this became a source of religious pain. He went on to say, "From my perspective, I'm suffering from mass depression sometimes, thinking that what I do is going to touch somebody negatively, and that upsets me." Charlie and others shared their moral grief for the almost unavoidable complicity they share in destructive systems simply by participating in society. His awareness of total connection and thus total responsibility in an interdependent worldview contributed to the "green blues," a religious dimension of grief for the environment that experienced the diminution of creation's beauty as a spiritual loss.

The critical question that confronts us is how to find the energy to walk the road when the outlook ahead for a healthy planet appears grim, and it is one that does not have easy answers. Roshan stated that he was "grateful for small victories but I am not too sanguine about where we are going." In Ralph's words, it's time to confront the lack of action.

Ralph: I just have to say that I don't think we've really pushed the issue. I think the real issue that you're referring to is that we are going to have to change our lifestyle. We in the West. . . . I don't think the church has said, "Look, we've got . . . I mean we'll recycle, we'll change our light bulbs, we'll drive a hybrid car." But that's not enough, that's not going to do it. It's going to take something much more radical. We've got to stop people from driving to work in the morning; we've got to take radical steps. . . . If we want to change it, we've got to take radical steps to change people's behavior, and I don't think that we have really confronted that issue.

Ralph would agree with Patriarch Bartholomew of the international Orthodox Christian Church. The Orthodox Church has had a special impact on faith-based environmentalism due to the highly visible, passionate, and bridge-building leadership of the Ecumenical Patriarch Bartholomew.[20] Bartholomew has personally hosted a series of symposia on the great waterways of the earth to bring scientists and theologians together to discuss the environmental crises. Despite his unusual sensitivity to scientific causes of the environmental crisis, he identifies the crux of the issue as spiritual. As Patriarch Bartholomew has said,

We are all painfully aware of the fundamental obstacle that confronts us in our work for the environment. It is precisely this: how are we to move from theory to action, from words to deeds? We do not lack technical scientific information about the nature of the present ecological crisis. We know, not simply what needs to be done, but also how to do it. Yet, despite all this information, unfortunately little is actually done. It is a long journey from the head to the heart, and an even longer journey from the heart to the hands.[21]

---

20. I especially wish to note this important work; despite outreach to several Orthodox churches, none was able to participate in this study during the research period.

21. Ecumenical Patriarch Bartholomew, "Sacrifice: The Missing Dimension," *Address at the Closing Ceremony of the Fourth International Environmental Symposium* (2001), http://www.ec-patr.org.

We know what to do, but little is actually done. As Erika said, "Yeah, some people care, but nothing really feels like it is happening." And the boat is still sinking. If not animated by hope, a sense of urgency and the conviction that imparts the strength to act make religious environmentalists willing to hold the flame—to keep working—even when realistic about the depth of the darkness.

The next chapter considers the contrasting faith experience of "the green blues," and how people find the energy to journey on from the head, to the heart, to the hands: to taking action.

CHAPTER TWO

Engaging Head, Heart, and Hands to Get Over the Gaps

At one statewide conference of religious environmentalists hosted by the New Jersey Catholic Coalition for Environmental Justice at Princeton University, a Catholic priest serving in Jersey City said, "I guess I have the environmental blues." That term grabbed my attention and hasn't let go. In my mind, I turned this phrase into the "green blues," and this simple statement became the nucleus for green blues theory, a *cri de coeur* from a struggling activist that called out for interpretation. With this lament, the first step of the hermeneutical circle of green blues theory is taken: apprehending ecocide as shockingly real, a reality that demands understanding and action.

The previous chapter highlighted the energy of spirituality and hope. In this chapter, the blues are heard: testimonies of struggle, explanations of delays, and tales of obstacles met and sometimes overcome. The blues give voice to frustration, discouragement, dismay—why aren't communities and individuals acting faster to clean up our earth?

That conference took place in 2003. At this writing, the bottom line is that after years of authoritative scientific reports and staggering weather experiences well outside historical norms such as Superstorm Sandy, which wrecked miles of shoreline communities in the Eastern United States, the climate situation is worsening and climate denial is not dead. Reports from the Intergovernmental Panel on Climate Change show that the impact of the crisis is accelerating.[1] Bill McKibben, the Methodist activist once called by *Time* magazine the most important environmentalist, calculates the "terrifying new math," which indicates the planet is headed toward the more extreme temperature scenarios outlined by scientists.[2] Other calculations come from economic studies such as *Prosperity without Growth?* a report of the British Sustainability Commission, which bluntly counts the costs of environmental destruction. The costs are high, from the sixty billion dollar price tag on rebuilding after Superstorm Sandy, and the yet uncountable cost of geopolitical instability fomented by climate refugees, estimated to reach fifty million people by 2050.[3]

These scenarios are so bad that any amount of action to prevent them seems reasonable—and yet, many are taking very little action at all. The *motivation* of American society to act against climate change doesn't seem to have changed, let alone accelerated. Given these frightening scenarios, why aren't we doing the things we know *can* be done? Scientists have argued since 2004 that the necessary technologies exist to address climate change if they are implemented at scale.[4] But the reality is that becoming really green takes more than know-how. Simply having technical solutions is not enough. Jeffrey Sachs, the Columbia University economist, United Nations advisor, and author of *The End of Poverty*, says as much, acknowledging that "scientific, engineering, and organizational solutions are not enough. Societies must be motivated and empowered to adopt the needed changes."[5]

---

1. Working Group I Contribution to the Fifth Assessment Report, *Climate Change 2013: The Physical Science Basis* (Intergovernmental Panel on Climate Change, 2013).

2. Bill McKibben, "Global Warming's Terrifying New Math," *Rolling Stone*, July 19, 2012, http://rollingstone.com.

3. United Nations High Commissioner for Refugees, "UN Refugee Agency Chief Warns of Security, Displacement Threats from Climate Change" (New York, 2011); http://www.unhcr.org.

4. Robert H. Socolow and Stephen Pacala, "Stabilization Wedges: Solving the Climate Problem for the Next 50 Years with Current Technologies," *Science* 305, no. 5686 (2004): 968.

5. Center for Research on Environmental Decisions (CRED), *The Psy-

To build positive social engagement with climate change, it is essential to understand what factors motivate actions and what blocks motivation. In other words, what enables just shrugging it all off and staying stuck with the blues?

The Christian Orthodox Patriarch Bartholomew of Constantinople sees the problem of motivation as a profoundly spiritual challenge that calls people to fully own their values and integrate them into their conscious priorities. In his contemplative way, Bartholomew sees that the struggle to renew our relationship with the earth requires engaging the head, the heart, and the hands. This is no simple task, however, as legions of frustrated environmental advocates know. Too often, it seems that the head is confused, the heart is overwhelmed, and the hands are busy. Bartholomew writes,

> We are all painfully aware of the fundamental obstacle that confronts us in our work for the environment. It is precisely this: how are we to move from theory to action, from words to deeds? We do not lack technical scientific information about the nature of the present ecological crisis. We know, not simply what needs to be done, but also how to do it. Yet, despite all this information, unfortunately little is actually done. It is a long journey from the head to the heart, and an even longer journey from the heart to the hands. How shall we bridge this tragic gap between theory and practice, between ideas and actuality?[6]

---

chology of Climate Change Communication: A Guide for Scientists, Journalists, Educators, Political Aides, and the Interested Public (New York, 2009), 48; http://guide.cred.columbia.edu.

6. Ecumenical Patriarch Bartholomew, the honorary head of the Eastern Orthodox Communion, has been one of the world's most dedicated religious leaders calling for environmental action. He has hosted scientific journeys on many of the world's waterways to bring scientists and religious leaders together to share their common concern for the earth and rally support for action. Ecumenical Patriarch Bartholomew, "Sacrifice: The Missing Dimension," *Address at the Closing Ceremony of the Fourth International Environmental Symposium* (2001), http://www.ec.patr.org.

How can the confusing and overwhelming experience of climate change be better understood to inspire action as well as wistful ideals? What is really the source of the green blues? What are the patterns in people's resistance to seriously addressing climate change?

Ari, a member of the Jain group, offers a way to understand the lack of action by baldly stating the difference between ideals and practice. Like Charlie, and Patriarch Bartholomew, he described this impasse between ideally green and really green as a "gap." Ari didn't expect a large gap between environmental ideals and practice in his community. He naturally assumed his Jain community would embody high standards for sustainable living. Jainism is an Indian religion devoted to nonviolence, and Jains are known for their uniquely dedicated nonviolence toward animals, simple vegetarian living, and recognition of the interconnection of all life (which they share with many Eastern religions). Given these Jain values, Ari was predisposed to expect more from Jains, but he found that even in his community, the gap between ideals and practice persisted.

> *Ari: In real life, whether you are Jain or non-Jain, people are using vehicles a lot more, walking less. All those things impact. So even though the ideals are there, they're not in practice. You can look at people, a hundred of them are Jain, and nine hundred are not, and take the average consumption, and there's no difference.*

> *Q: Why is that?*

> *Ari: That's because the Jains have not kept up with the ideals. There's a gap between ideal and practice. We have been talking more about the ideals. And unfortunately in practice— whether you go to a Jain house or a non-Jain house, you see the same thing.*

Ari recognizes the gap between ideals and practice, and this recognition sparks the suspicion that ideals aren't enough. He is not alone in noting that widespread social engagement is painfully absent. In fact, a group of British clerics launched an anti-apathy campaign deliberately targeting what they called the "shrug culture."[7] Ari spoke for his Jain community, but the charge of apathy despite ideals fits Christians in the United States as well. Researchers who compared data from the 1993 and 2010 editions of the General Social Survey, an ongoing, large-scale measure of societal trends, found that Christians continue to report lower levels of environmental concern than non-Christians and nonreligious individuals even after twenty years of official religious teaching on the need to care for the environment.[8]

Thus, the second step of the hermeneutical circle is taken: the suspicions that religious statements about the environment *are not enough to drive action*. Some conflict blocks the realization of ideals, and a new interpretation of that inner conflict is needed. In all fairness, it's not easy being green and navigating this gap. Like any trailblazer, environmentalists who walk the walk are charting an uphill path, with difficult footing and unclear directions. There are inspiring vistas of a healthy and beautiful restored earth that keeps them on the path. But keeping on the path requires certainty, concern, and energy—and good company to keep them inspired through the difficult terrain. Despite the dedication and creativity of many volunteers, and the official endorsement of environmental justice as a faith concern by all major religious groups, many feel pessimistic about how much "greening" is actually getting done. Despite the best intentions of many people, a gap persists between green ideals and actual practice, causing the blues.

---

7. Religious leaders in the United Kingdom have used Ash Wednesday as a call to all Christians to repent for the "shrug culture" existing in many parts of the world toward climate change. See Brian Roewe, "Ash Wednesday Declaration: Repent for 'Shrug-Culture' on Climate Change," *National Catholic Reporter*, February 22, 2012.

8. "Self-identified Christians identified with lower levels of environmental concern than did non-Christians and nonreligious individuals." The comparison of data from the 1993 and 2010 editions of the General Social Survey found "no statistically significant change in this divide [between Christians and non-Christians] about two decades after the first wave of mobilization to greet U.S. Christianity." See Tom Jacobs, "The 'Greening' of Christianity Is Not Actually Happening," *Pacific Standard*, July 8, 2014.

To interpret this cry from the heart, I employ the green blues theory described in the Methods section of this book: a grounded liberation theology that arises from the particular and committed questions of faith-based environmentalists. This method of analysis moves in a hermeneutical circle by interpreting the content source of ethnographic data with environmental decision theory, in this chapter and the next. In chapter 4 the ethnographic data will be interpreted with Ricoeur's philosophy of conflict, and in chapter 5, insight from world religions will be used.

In this chapter, analyzing participant remarks about climate action *and* inaction alongside the insights of environmental decision theory generate the central concepts of the knowledge, caring, and action gaps. The gap is a concept that spontaneously emerges from participant comments and proves capable of robust conceptual depth under analysis. The analysis proceeds *with the suspicion that the conflict itself is revelatory* and that searching for clarity about the gaps will be liberating. By identifying the gaps, they may be bridged, and a clearer basis for ethical and ecological self-interpretation may be established.

Identifying the Gaps

First, the *knowledge gap* is a black hole extinguishing the first feeble sparks of concern. Without knowledge about the causes and impacts of climate change, concern is nonexistent, motivation is impossible, and behavioral change is unreasonable. It's reasonable to expect that people would react to painful realities and want change once they understand what is at stake and what kinds of actions create the problem. But often the impacts of climate change aren't directly experienced by North Americans. Or, perhaps more accurately, "weird weather" isn't attributed to climate change.[9] Too often, the privileged world is insulated from the suffering that swamps billions of indigent people.[10] Or the opposite occurs, and the media issue a

---

9. Thomas L. Friedman, "Global Weirding Is Here," *New York Times*, February 17, 2010.

10. Cynthia Moe-Lobeda, *Resisting Structural Evil: Love as Ecological-Economic Vocation* (Minneapolis: Fortress Press, 2013).

torrent of disaster images that only lead to "compassion fatigue." Can people reasonably be expected to protest and resist when the crisis is not even perceived? Cultivating concern and action without the conviction of knowledge seems virtually impossible.

Second, a *caring gap* weakens the link between knowledge and action. Knowing what needs to be done makes no difference if one doesn't care—enough. And the inconvenient truth is that personal concerns do affect what one is willing to know. Values can be affected by disinterest, denial, politics, or preoccupation. When knowledge about the problem isn't sharp, neither is motivation; we don't care enough.

Third, and most significant, there is the *action gap*. Even those who understand *and* care don't always commit to action. And furthermore, commitment is still not yet action. A decision to act is not the same as action. Good intentions can be quickly dissipated by the continually competing concerns of daily life, concerns that may be legitimate or trivial. Getter over all the gaps is a formidable challenge, and one that needs the kind of social support and encouragement that is hard to find in the "shrug culture," or the cultures of denial and willed ignorance. No wonder the green blues keep returning.

Maybe you have felt the environmental blues. Seeing the earth's beauty diminished is unquestionably sad. Facing increased risks of asthma or cancer because of toxins is enraging. With weather becoming more unpredictable, planning a summer wedding or travel in hurricane season is unsettling. These are all dimensions of ecological pain, the "green blues." Seeking to avoid the blues, people understandably suppress their awareness of climate change, because as awareness grows, the blues set in. The very painfulness of environmental awareness creates a greater need to suppress it, and willed ignorance dampens the potential sparks of action even more.

The Knowledge Gap: Climate Change—Really?

Scientific literacy galvanizes environmental action, as discussed in chapter 1. But, as illustrated by Charles's account of the fear and anguish of someone with firsthand knowledge of climate change, it can be devastating to really experience and understand what is happening to the earth. Charles is a doctor who regularly gathers with a group of largely Southern U.S. Christians for a conference on medicine and ministry. Charles told our group about a patient of his, a geochemist who studies the Arctic and Antarctic.

Charles (Episcopalian): My patient cries, talking about what's going on. He actually has a fear of going to the Arctic anymore, and falling through the ice, having just watched square-mile chunks of ice disappear. So I get that kind of feedback from somebody who's in the sciences and with the [political] reality of the last eight years; it's scary.

The powerful connection between anxiety and awareness was evident in Charles's account of how he came to understand the environmental crisis through his patient's eye-witness accounts of Arctic ice loss. His account tells not only of ice loss but of a literal and existential loss of stability, the unease and sorrow of the green blues.

The blues set in after one becomes aware of the environmental crisis. But becoming aware in the first place, in a way that claims our moral attention, is difficult because of three overlapping filters within the knowledge gap. First, there is widespread scientific illiteracy: straightforward facts can have a hard time filtering into minds unused to complicated science. Second, beyond this basic scientific illiteracy, cognitive limitations filter the ways people process and retain information. Third, and this is the most ambiguous aspect of the knowledge gap, there is a moral filter that affects how people accept knowledge—a filter composed of bias, ideology, and willed ignorance.

Distinguishing between these filters is important because identifying the properly factual issues of environmental literacy lifts some of the moral weight off this highly charged issue. People often feel blamed or ridiculed for lack of sympathy to environmental causes. Some may feel guilty for their seemingly unavoidable participation in systemic structures that accelerate climate change. In fact, a lack of action doesn't point immediately to callous indifference. Views on the environment may simply reflect the difficulty of obtaining or processing information—the challenge of scientific literacy and natural human cognitive limits in absorbing new information. Those aspects of the knowledge gap reflect cognitive limits that are morally neutral.

But other aspects of the knowledge gap have moral significance, in the eyes of the participants, if the ignorance is deliberate and inaction harms others. Because willed ignorance was often discussed by the participants, it points to conflicts that persist in blocking motivation and so merits deeper exploration. Distinguishing between basic scientific literacy, built-in cognitive limits, and moral use of knowledge is essential to diagnose the gaps that block motivation and action, and thus identify appropriate ways to bridge them.

Literacy Limitations

First, in the United States, the knowledge gap is deep and wide. The environmental crisis is a morass of multiple problems: deforestation, loss of habitat and biodiversity, air and water pollution, and the overarching specter of climate change above all. This specter of climate change is by itself a deeply complex problem. Climate is a chaotic process under any circumstances. Ordinary weather predictions often are unreliable. Broader climate patterns can't be put in a test tube in order to experiment with the conditions that affect weather, so statements about climate must be based on predictions and models that may seem abstract. It is natural that most people are confused about this admittedly extremely complex issue, and our brains conveniently supply mechanisms to suppress the complexity.

For example, learning new information is complicated by a common phenomenon called the "confirmation bias." Mental models are preconceptions that shape the reception of experience—but such models can also filter information. People are more able to incorporate and remember information that correlates with prior expectations. Furthermore, "people seek out less situational information if they hold strong preconceptions about a given relationship."[11] The

---

11. Elke Weber, "Perception and Expectation of Climate Change: Precondition for Economic and Technological Adaptation," in *Psychological*

confirmation bias means that people more readily accept information that matches their current models and filter out novel or discomforting information by selective inattention or dismissal. For example, many people have a mental model for climate change that confuses it with the ozone hole (and then they propose letting the excess greenhouse gas out the hole).[12] No matter what the original mental model, new information requires revising it, which is difficult work.

Energy is a similarly complex issue that confuses many people. Beth's confusion about light illustrates this. Recall how Charlie answered the question asked by a group of Muslim girls on a river clean-up: how do we get light? He answered, "It comes from a man shoveling coal into a furnace." Hearing this, a light went on for Beth, a very well-meaning and highly active member of the Towson Presbyterian Church. She certainly understood the reality of electric light. But she had not consciously made the connection between energy sources, mines, pollution, worker hazards, electric grids, and her concrete choices regarding plugging in appliances and flipping off switches.

> Beth: I would just say, Charlie, you just simplified for me how we get light. I never really thought about it. Okay, it's somebody shoveling coal into a furnace. . . . I know about the coal dust and all the people getting killed in the mines and all of that. . . . So if you depress a few people, you probably enlightened a lot more.

Charlie's discussion of how "we get light" enlightened Beth on several levels. Before the focus group, she did not have a clear under-

---

Perspectives to Environmental and Ethical Issues in Management, ed. D. Messick, M. Bazerman, A. Tenbrunsel, and K. Wade-Benzoni (San Francisco: Jossey-Bass, 1997), 317. Weber cites numerous studies that establish the various ways people "focus on observations that conform to their beliefs." Expectations cause people to underestimate or overestimate relationships in data. Expectations cause people to seek out less situational information. Finally, people encode and retrieve correlated information much more effectively when their prior expectations explain those correlations.

12. CRED, *Psychology of Climate Change Communication,* 5.

standing of how light came into her living-room lamp through electricity that went over wires that came from a grid and a generator that was powered by ... something. Ultimately, she came to understand that "something" was a human being digging coal in a mine that might collapse on his head. Before Charlie spelled it out, she "never really thought about it," and as a consequence was unable to see the social consequences of electrical sources and energy systems. When the systems behind the flow of electricity were made more clear, she quickly saw how people were affected by ordinary choices to turn on lights. But, Beth's response that "you depress a few people ... [and] enlighten a lot more" illustrates the low levels of scientific literacy that are a huge part of the knowledge gap. Beth is not alone by any means. The National Environmental Education Foundation found that only 12 percent of American adults could answer seven out of ten questions about energy correctly in a 2001 study.[13]

However, confusion about climate science, or energy, or other environmental topics has been deepened by a false debate about the authority of science and the nature of scientific knowledge. Debate in the United States about climate change has introduced an insidious resistance to accepting the authority of science that obstructs a straightforward progress toward learning. Though difficult to understand, climate scientists offer us a clear consensus about climate change. That consensus has been frequently subject to political spin, allowing pundits to rattle the clear and distinct foundations of scientific method. Media misrepresentation, in the form of giving equal weight to positions that are not equally informed, undermines the effort of scientists and activists to educate citizens about what is actually happening to the earth.

Statements like "do you believe in global warming?" make it seem as though science lacks the authority of science to assert its own findings as evidence-based conclusions. Like the still-raging battle over evolution and creationism ("do you believe in evolution?"), the question "do you believe in global warming" falsely presents the process of establishing data through investigation and validating

---

13. "America's Low 'Energy IQ,'" http://www.energyliteracy.com.

conclusions through scientific review as equal to positions based on anecdotal evidence or personal experience. In fact, the scientific consensus on climate change is not an equal debate between fairly based sides.[14] Science does not propose an object of belief at the rhetorical level of personal opinion, like belief in Santa or the Easter Bunny. The problem with perpetuating a false appearance of "debate" about climate is that scientific arguments are reduced to unsubstantiated opinion and allowed to persist uncritically.

Even when people move beyond the antiscientific bias that surfaces in climate-change debates, understanding the science of climate change or complexities of many environmental issues faces challenges. Scientific literacy is a product of both an individual's education and a natural interest in science. However, some challenges to understanding are better described not as scientific illiteracy—a lack of information about a scientific topic—but as cognitive barriers. "Cognitive barriers" are the partially unconscious filters on the cognitive acceptance of data. That is, there are mental pathways and patterns of perception that affect the ways people prioritize or process information. These mental pathways and patterns of perception rooted in built-in cognitive structures can keep people from understanding and processing scientific information as well as from taking action; these are discussed below as the next filter in the knowledge gap.

Built-in Cognitive Limitations

Our learning styles, motivations, and choices are shaped by unconscious psychological processes, including built-in cognitive limitations that filter the perception and retention of new information. These filters may restrict one's receptivity to unfamiliar, analytical, or alarming information about the environment. Other psychological processes enhance the ability to learn, to remember, and,

---

14. See Mary-Elena Carr and Madeleine Rubenstein, "Challenges to Authority: Understanding Critiques of the Intergovernmental Panel on Climate Change," *Union Theological Seminary Quarterly Review* 63, nos. 1-2 (2011): 45; Paul Bloom and Deena Skolnick Weisberg, "Childhood Origins of Adult Resistance to Science," *Science* 316 (2007): 996.

critically, to act. Marketing has long excelled at using information about how people learn and act to influence their behavior, whether it be shopping, choosing a movie, or voting on policies. By contrast, one reason climate science has failed to influence policy is due to the complicated layers of psychological reactions to climate change. Researchers Sabine Marx and Debika Shome argue that social science offers important insights that help individuals and groups process information about climate uncertainty and environmental risk.[15] But they represent an emerging field within social science that illuminates the complexity of our human interaction with knowledge, and also suggests strategies that help people get past their cognitive limitations. This emerging field of research, which I am calling environmental decision theory, analyzes the psychological reactions and cognitive limitations at work when people process information about climate. The research-based strategies make it easier to embrace new knowledge, and get into action: in other words, to get across the gaps.

The Center for Research on Environmental Decisions (CRED) at Columbia University is a leading center for research on the limits of cognition and perception. The center's founder, David Krantz, is a psychologist and statistician who has fostered investigations into multiple subfields of behavioral, cognitive, and social psychology, sociological and economic analysis of behavior, as well as decision theory. All these investigations clarify the way that unconscious, psychological, and emotional mechanisms may influence behavior as much as, if not more than, straightforward rational analysis.

To presume that decisions are made on a strictly rational basis, for the greatest economic or practical utility, overlooks the complexity of human behavior, which is both rational and emotional.[16] Decisions are not always made in a calculated or wholly reasonable fashion as might be assumed by rational-economic models of choice. Furthermore, behavior is influenced by unconscious processes as well as by conscious knowledge. The center's codirector,

---

15. CRED, *Psychology of Climate Change Communication*, 24.

16. Daniel Kahneman, "A Psychological Perspective on Economics," *American Economic Review* 93, no. 2 (2003): 162.

Elke Weber, describes behavior as "determined by unconscious and conscious inference and decision processes, which are elicited by conditions in the external environment in combination with internal factors that include prior experience, expectations, and goals."[17] Thus, rational thinking doesn't determine decisions as much as common assumptions or economic models might suggest.

Like Weber, social psychologist Anthony Leiserowitz challenges the dominance of the cognitive paradigm. The cognitive paradigm in past behavioral research has created models focused on rational, analytical choices, thus overlooking the role of affect and emotion. As he writes, "Affect (a person's good or bad, positive or negative feelings about specific objects, ideas or images) and emotions (e.g., anger, fear) are typically ignored in these models or viewed as mere epiphenomena of the decision making process. Thus, most theorists assume that decision making about risk is essentially a *cognitive* activity." As a result, the significant role of emotion and affect within human judgment and decision making has been overlooked.[18]

Emotional and affective reactions have particular influence because such reactions happen fast, even before cognitive processing. Affective reactions spring up initially, automatically, and influentially. Emotions and feelings are often evoked before cognitive processing and direct the path of rational information processing. Feelings are not by-products of thinking about something, but can play a critical role in what is thought.[19] Emotions and mental mod-

---

17. Elke Weber, "Doing the Right Thing Willingly: Behavioral Decision Theory and Environmental Policy," in *The Behavioral Foundations of Policy*, ed. E. Shafir (Princeton: Princeton University Press, 2007), 3.

18. Anthony Leiserowitz, "Climate Change Risk Perception and Policy Preferences: The Role of Affect, Imagery, and Values," *Climatic Change* 77 (2006): 47. As Paul Slovic affirms, "Perhaps befitting its rationalistic origins, the main focus of descriptive research has been cognitive rather than affective"; see "The Affect Heuristic," in *Heuristics and Biases: The Psychology of Intuitive Judgment*, ed. Thomas Gilovich, Dale W. Griffin, and Daniel Kahneman (New York: Cambridge University Press, 2002), 397.

19. Robert Zajonc, "Feeling and Thinking: Preferences Need No Inferences," *American Psychologist* 35 (1980): 151.

els thus have a formative, if submerged, power to shape the information that people accept and recall.

Many reaction patterns reflect evolved constraints. The evolving human brain developed cognitive and emotional response patterns that were suited to very different interactions among small clans. As Weber writes, some response patterns that evolved early in human history "have not yet had time to adapt to the current high-density, high-complexity, resource-constrained world."[20] What used to be an evolutionary advantage—the ability to focus totally on immediate threats and respond to a charging tiger—becomes the evolved handicap of short-term focus. The tendency to respond to dramatic, immediate danger does not easily recognize the slow advance of climate change. The handicap of short-term focus now prevents people from rapidly responding to changes in climate as they would to a charging tiger.

Let us now consider some of those unconscious processes, including (a) short-term thinking; (b) concern for local issues; (c) attention limits; (d) the different impacts of experiential versus analytical processing; (e) susceptibility to framing; and (f) a "finite pool of worry" and risk perception. That is a long list of cognitive limitations: no wonder the knowledge gap is so deep.

Short-term Thinking: Is It a Crisis NOW? A consequence of the evolved tendency to react to immediate threats is that people think and act in the short term unless there is real impetus for them to think long term. Crises that haven't happened yet just don't seize our attention. This short-term focus indicates humanity's evolved hard-wiring, not necessarily indifference or laziness. Social science research suggests at least three ways people demonstrate a preference for short-term thinking and acting. First, unless there is a visible, concrete reason to adopt a long-term time frame—like an immediate threat—people tend to resist long-term thinking.

The second short-term habit is the tendency to undervalue future risks. Because people generally react more urgently to immediate threats than to future risks, people tend to undervalue future risks. Future losses are "discounted," that is, people see problems in the

---

20. Weber, "Doing the Right Thing Willingly," 4.

future as less and less important for every year into the future they are expected.

And third, when people make decisions and judgments based on their experiences—which are inevitably limited in various ways— their judgments tend to give priority to their most recent experiences. Interestingly, this contrasts to judgments based on descriptions, or formal teaching, when people are more likely to take the full range of described events into account. As a result, people tend to take more seriously the events that happened most recently. Social scientists call this the "recency effect."[21] Decisions thus privilege the most recent experience out of a range of events, and underweight rare events. By the sheer reduced odds of occurring, rare events are more likely *not* to be recent. So by definition, future events (like the risk that Greenland will melt) cannot have been recent, so their probability and credibility are also underweighted.

In summary, people tend to resist long-term thinking, discount future threats, and privilege recently experienced events, thus underweighting risks that are not recently experienced (or experienced yet at all).

Given the strong tendencies to short-term thinking, religious long-term thinking is a positive resource. The ability to imagine the long duration of a greater time scale counters the tendency toward temporal discounting. Ralph and Eric from the University Baptist Church of Seattle discussed how thinking in the short or long term affected their decisions, and how they see that perception in the actions of others. They felt that their own religious perspective encouraged the long-term thinking that favored environmental action.

Ralph: The difference between recycling or not recycling or whether you drive or take the bus is what your analytical time frame is. If you're worried about right now there are a lot of things that have rewards now but the costs are in the future. If you're going to analyze your actions in the context of five

---

21. Ralph Hertwig, Greg Barron, Elke U. Weber, and Ido Erev, "Decisions from Experience and the Effect of Rare Events in Risky Choice," *Psychological Science* 15, no. 8 (2004): 538.

minutes, not recycling is the sane thing to do. A lot of things like riding your bike when it's rainy benefit you a few years out.

Eric: And the theological corollary of that is, if you think the end of the world is going to come any minute, then why recycle.

Ralph: So faith can be an excuse for short-sightedness, if the world is going to end. I also understand that part of why I show up each Sunday is that Tim reminds me that the world is longer than this weekend. That's his job.

When thinking in the short term, it made no sense to be inconvenienced by a slow, uphill bike ride in the Seattle rain for the sake of some distant ecological benefit to the earth. But Ralph believed that his pastor, Tim, helped him remember the long view. Furthermore, as a geologist, Ralph more easily adopted the long view. As Ralph observed, "A mortgage is a thirty-year time frame; the next election is a two-year time frame or less. I'm a geologist, and my analytical time frame is 10 or 15 million years. That's an act of faith on my part." That long view of faith focuses beyond the short term, on the consequences of actions that unfold in the longer time scale.

Religious vision celebrates this long view in the time scale of the Jewish week, Sabbath to Sabbath, or the shared Jewish and Christian view of the reign of God slowly growing in human society, a better time not yet realized but already on the way. The preference for short-term thinking is today intensified by the digital time of text messages and video games and on-demand movie downloads that click on at speeds so fast as to leave no record. Geological time and holy time—*kairos*—both require patience and imagination to become attuned to the slower pace of changes in ecosystems.

Tim: Time takes on a different character; it isn't that I have to rush off to the next thing because there's only so much time. God knows I need to be there for the world to change. You begin to say no, the religion of my life is that stewardship is important and it will take a certain amount of time, it will take a certain amount of planning.

Taking time for stewardship is one of the sacrifices that Bartholomew called for, a sacrifice of time and a conscious resistance to the short-term focus that is both evolved, habitual, and culturally reinforced in our instant, digital age.

Concern with local Issues: is it a crisis HERE? Furthermore, to be influential, the experience of climate change must be local and personal. One evangelical Christian was a scuba diver. He was deeply troubled by seeing the bleaching of beautiful reefs he had explored years before. The loss of that beauty motivated him to join his church's environmental committee: it was concrete evidence of environmental harm he could see here and now. Emphasizing the problems that exist here and now helps overcome the tendency to discount events that seem too far distant in time and space and motivate action. In Weber's words, "the concretization of future events and moving them closer in time and space seem to hold promise as interventions that will raise visceral concern."[22]

At the same time, local experiences must be interpreted and framed in a way that people can accept. After Superstorm Sandy, one might expect that disaster would fuel widespread responses. Certainly protective measures were taken. Flood plains were re-analyzed, insurance policies updated, and home generators flew off the shelves at Home Depot. But rebuilding of vulnerable shoreline houses raced on. There is a paradoxical response to disaster—the strangely recalcitrant resistance to accepting that we need to live in new ways with the climate we are affecting. George Marshall, a climate communication analyst, observes that survivors can be particularly reluctant to accept some level of responsibility for the suffering they've experienced: "Disasters encourage powerful and compelling survival narratives (that can overwhelm weaker and more complex climate change narratives.)"[23] The paradox of being

---

22. Elke Weber, "Experience-Based and Description-Based Perceptions of Long-Term Risk: Why Global Warming Does Not Scare Us (Yet)," *Climatic Change* 77 (2006): 116.

23. Andrew Revkin, "Why Climate Change Disasters Might Not Boost Public Engagement on Climate Change," *New York Times*, November 12, 2012; http://dotearth.blogs.nytimes.com.

victims makes some survivors less willing to adopt the painful narrative of climate change *when it implies responsibility for causing
harm to themselves.* A more positive and reassuring response to
disasters is to concentrate on how neighbors helped one another,
or how Americans used their ingenuity and resourcefulness. So
while intense storms or wildfires or droughts may provoke some to
action, they may shore up the denial of others.

Attention limits. People also have built-in limits to their attention spans, memory, and processing of information.[24] So, when
searching for information, people tend to limit their search
attempts. Short-term-memory capacity may control this limitation
(sometimes associated with seven attempts). With limited attempts
to search for information, there is less chance they will encounter
evidence of a risky phenomenon (such as an adverse climate event).[25]
Similarly, reliance on small samples of experience means not all
outcomes are experienced. As a result, one perceives that there is
a smaller range of actual possible outcomes. By not paying attention to more than a few events, it is easy to conclude that the other
events don't happen, and don't exist. In short, people simplify their
judgment and decision tasks to manageable levels of complexity.
This understandable need to simplify nonetheless affects people's
ability to respond appropriately to risks in the future and restricts
the information they can process. When making judgments based
on self-limited experience, people differ little from bumblebees—
unable to process vast amounts of information, acting on limited
samples— literally bumbling along, going in circles.[26]

Seeing is believing: analytical vs. experiential processing. The
reality of climate change can be assessed in two ways. The first way,
experiential processing, recalls one's own experience. The second
way, analytic thinking, is analysis that appeals to described information.[27] Both kinds of learning are bounded by different limits.

---

24. These limitations are also expressed as "bounded rationality." See
Weber, "Doing the Right Thing Willingly," 3.
25. Hertwig et al., "Decisions from Experience," 537.
26. Ibid., 539.
27. Sabine Marx, Elke U. Weber, Benjamin S. Orlove, David H. Krantz,

Decision-science researchers have observed that decisions made on the basis of experience and decisions made on the basis of description can lead to dramatically different choices.[28]

Experiential processing compares a situation to one's own memories, engages emotions and instincts that summon survival responses. This experiential imagination may identify an "average" or typical situation but does not easily handle abstract concepts like sample size and probability. If people do not feel they are experiencing global warming, all the data in the world in brief news clips or confusing scientific articles will not be effective. Assessing risk from experience in this way causes people to underweight risks, to discount possible dangers, and ignore warnings.[29] Experience overcomes more reliable statistical information because of the competition between experiential and analytical processing systems. Factual probabilities have little impact if contradicted by one's own more visceral experience. "Yeah, right—I shoveled two feet of global warming off my porch today." Experiential information is persuasive, but not because of its greater scientific reliability. Sabine Marx observed that Bernard Russell expressed this in another way: "Popular induction depends on the emotional interest of the instances, not upon their number."[30]

In contrast, *analytic thinking* relates a situation to processed sets of data and theoretically collated past experience. Such statisti-

---

Anthony Leiserowitz, Carla Roncoli, and Jennifer Phillips, "Communication and Mental Processes: Experiential and Analytic Processing of Uncertain Climate Information," *Global Environmental Change* 17 (2007): 48.

28. Hertwig et al., "Decisions from Experience," 534. In the case of decisions from description, people make choices as if they overweight the probability of rare events. In the case of decisions from experience, on the other hand, people make choices as if they underweight the probability of rare events, and we explored the impact of two possible causes of this underweighting—reliance on relatively small samples of information and overweighting of recently sampled information. Thus, if people consult their experience of extreme weather events, they will consider them less likely to occur than is probable, because they focus on their own limited and recent experience.

29. Hertwig et al., "Decisions from Experience," 538.

30. Marx et al., "Communication and Mental Processes," 48-49.

cal information may be more complete, but it is hard to process and understand. Graphs do not convey urgency and concern to lay people the way they might to a scientist trained to interpret their implications instantly.[31] Grasping the implications of the "hockey-stick" graph requires interest, familiarity with graphic presentations, and some expertise with the technical vocabulary. Thus, simply filling an information deficit with more information doesn't mean people will act. People need a different type of information, information that has a greater affective or emotional tone, and not too much or else they will experience "input overload." Pictures before and after glacial retreat, stories from elders, the effects on children—these have impact, whereas graphs of temperatures do not.

Scientific jargon frustrates communication unintentionally as well. A "positive feedback loop" sounds like a good thing—but its true meaning of "cycle of intensifying effects" is closer to "a vicious circle." Because the planet's atmosphere can't be duplicated in a lab for testing and the future cannot be absolutely predicted, there is a certain amount of uncertainty inherent in climate science. The Intergovernmental Panel on Climate Change (IPCC) has assigned different future projects different levels of uncertainty to help assess the difference between risks scientists agree are inevitable and scenarios that are less likely. But even scientifically graded levels of uncertainty can be uncomfortable for people who prefer predictability. And, those scientifically graded levels of uncertainty are certainly open to misunderstanding. Terms used to label the levels of uncertainty such as "very likely" have precise statistical meanings in the IPCC report. But just as "several" or "few" can mean different things to different people, nonspecialists can easily interpret a term like "very likely" to mean possible, but not certain, when in fact, climate change is certainly underway.

The power of "framing." Short-term focus can be overcome by communication strategies that grab our attention. As comments by the unusually scientifically literate green blues participants show, closing the knowledge gap is highly effective when appropriately

---

31. CRED, *Psychology of Climate Change Communication,* 15.

communicated. To communicate appropriately, the message must be placed within a context that matters to the audience. Framing is the process of creating that context, appealing to perspectives that shift people's responses and choices.[32]

One of the key findings of environmental decision theory is that "frames," or personalized messages, matter. Effective communication strategies choose meaningful frames for educational messages, adapting messages to our cognitive limits. Communicating scientific issues effectively despite cognitive limitations is like opening a fireplace door to let light and heat emerge.

Framing resituates the message within a preexisting understanding, an evaluation people already have about a given issues. For example, in policy terms, a "carbon tax" is more acceptable to some voters when described as a "carbon offset." This preexisting understanding forms part of a mental model, or a representation of how something works. The model may include images, facts (and perhaps misinformation), past experience, and intuitions. However, if the message doesn't correlate with the model, often the model takes precedence.

Scientific jargon, statistical reports, and temperature graphs rarely help people grasp the complexities of climate change in a way that commands attention and action. The "hockey-stick" graph, a representation of global temperatures over time published in 1998, soon became an icon within the global warming debate. However, this is not because it was clearly understood. On the contrary, this graph, which showed a dramatic upswing in temperatures (the upswing resembling the blade end of a hockey stick) after centuries of more regular variation, remains unfamiliar to many unengaged in climate debates. Among those debating climate change, it became the "most controversial chart in science."[33]

---

32. Daniel Kahneman and Amos Tversky, "Choices, Values, and Frames," *American Psychologist* 397 (1984): 343.

33. Climate deniers focused their attention on the graph, though the data behind the graph was confirmed in 2006 by the National Academy of Sciences and employed by the Intergovernmental Panel on Climate Change in its Third Assessment Report. See Chris Mooney, "The Hockey Stick: The Most Controversial Chart in Science, Explained," *The Atlantic*, May 10, 2013.

Instead of graphs and other technical data, research from CRED shows that in order for climate-science information to be heard and understood, several things should happen. The information must "be actively communicated with appropriate language, metaphor, and analogy; combined with narrative storytelling; made vivid through visual imagery and experiential scenarios; balanced with scientific information; and delivered by trusted messengers in group settings."[34]

These qualities match characteristics of communication within religious communities, whose traditions are carried by narrative storytelling and deeply resonant images. Emotional responses, imagery, and values are the currency of religion. Anthony Leiserowitz shows why they can have an intriguingly profound impact. Imagery is deeply influential. Imagery refers to all forms of mental representation or cognitive content. Images include both "perceptual representations (pictures, sounds, smells) and symbolic representations (words, numbers, symbols)."[35] In fact, in his study, "affect, imagery and values were better predictors of support for global warming policies than all socio-demographic variables, including political identification and ideology."[36] This is a strong claim given the overwhelming association of environmental views with political views, and it validates further study. It also validates the effectiveness of faith-based environmentalists.

Religiously infused celebrations that emphasize care of the environment therefore provide the kind of vivid experiences that are emotionally easier to accept than complex conceptual information, especially when facilitated by trusted leaders within a community.

Tailored messages were not simply memorable catchphrases but ways to summon deep religious motivations, such as the commitment, behavioral scrutiny, and personal renewal of traditional

---

34. CRED, *Psychology of Climate Change Communication*, 2.

35. Americans' risk perception and subsequent policy support were found to be strongly linked to experiential factors, such as affect, imagery, and values. See Anthony Leiserowitz, "Climate Change Risk Perception," 48.

36. Ibid., 59.

Lenten practices. For example, various Christian groups have developed their own creative frame for energy conservation patterned on their Lenten disciplines, calling it the "Carbon Fast."[37]

For Susan, an Episcopalian from North Carolina, central religious symbols expressed physical survival but also conveyed spiritual meaning. Such symbols demonstrated the moral necessity of caring for air and water. These frames were so powerful they almost demanded that envrionmental issues be taken seriously.

> *Susan (Episcopalian): The metaphors of our lives, the basic truth of our being, is immersed in these things we call environmental. Water is the central metaphor for us. How can it be negotiated? Not to mention our air. No, it's not a choice, it's not a choice for the church.*

For religious congregations, there are multiple frames that resonate deeply with their members and also relate to climate change: the loss of the beauty and sanctity of creation, the justice implications, and the needs of the poor. These and many other values are powerful religious motivators—once you get past the complicated message with an effective frame.

Constrained by a "finite pool of worry." "Sufficient unto the day is the evil thereof." This biblical truth has a parallel in cognitive science. There is only so much worry that people can maintain. In other words, people have a "finite pool of worry." This vivid image conveys that there is only so much emotional space into which we can cram worry. The amount of anxiety people can carry at any one time is limited. As a result, if one source of worry increases, another must diminish. If the economy becomes a more urgent concern, climate change drops on people's lists of priorities. Emotional appeals for concern work in the short term but need to be bolstered by additional reasons for concern in the long run. After too much expo-

---

37. I first noted this practice of the United Church of Christ in 2012. In 2013 several Catholic dioceses observed a Lenten Carbon Fast. In 2014, it was both a national and a global Catholic observance, sponsored by the Catholic Climate Covenant and the Global Catholic Climate Movement.

sure to worrying ideas, people grow numb to repeated warnings.[38] Growing numb is adaptive and protective; its helps keep the total level of anxiety within the capacities of our finite pools of worry.

Risk perception. How one handles worry is a subjective, personal response. Personality and disposition do affect one's readiness to receive information with certain kinds of political or scientific content. Positively, this is part of the diversity of human intelligence and particularity that gives rise to creativity and new perspectives. Negatively, aversions from certain kinds of information can become blinders. Aspects of personal inclination that can positively or negatively influence the way people receive information include their risk-assessment style. As Paul Hawken warns, we are "playing dice with the planet."[39] Humanity seems willing to gamble with disaster. But there are different types of gamblers. People with different risk-taking personalities assess circumstances in various ways, and then tend to favor different responses or policies. A branch of social psychology called cultural theory argues that hierarchists, individualists, egalitarians, and fatalists each focus on the different risks that threaten their own preferred way of life. Each different risk-taking personality thus represents a different set of presuppositions about the ideal nature of society, which leads each group to perceive different risks and prefer different policy responses.

Research on risk perception shows that people's perceptions of dangers such as climate threats are influenced not only by scientific and technical descriptions "but also by a variety of psychological and social factors, including personal experience, affect and emotion, imagery, trust, values and worldviews—dimensions of risk perception that are rarely examined by opinion."[40]

---

38. CRED, *Psychology of Climate Change Communication*, 21.

39. See Leiserowitz, "Climate Change Risk Perception and Policy Preferences," 48, and Paul Hawken, *Blessed Unrest: How the Largest Movement in the World Came into Being and Why No One Saw It Coming* (New York: Viking Press, 2007), 174.

40. Ibid., 46. "Hierarchists" most fear social deviance, which threatens the structure of status quo. They call for the active management of risk by "experts," in whom they place great trust. "Individualists" most fear restrictions on their autonomy, such as government regulation. They promote

We started this survey by studying the limited ways people perceive information and prioritize their responses to that information. These ways are not few, as we have seen: short-term thinking, concern for local issues, attention limits, the different impacts of experiential versus analytical processing, susceptibility to framing, the "finite pool of worry," and risk perception. By recognizing these limits and unconscious mental preferences, we can choose to change or adapt them to transcend the knowledge gap that is so critical for our move toward climate action. Climate communicators and educators can strive for more nuanced, targeted, and thus more effective outreach strategies. Environmental decision theory offers us clues, tools, and resources for how to overcome these limits in ourselves and in our communication with others. For better or for worse, these cognitive limitations only describe the built-in limitations of how our brains and behavioral patterns evolved. We now turn toward what social psychology has to teach about how our personal inclinations shape our ability to receive and respond to important information, such as climate knowledge, where our response has major consequences for society. Here, the use of knowledge takes on moral meaning, because the use of knowledge enters the realm of choice.

Social science thus complements ethical reflections about the distinctions between the cognitive and moral limits at play when people resist new behaviors. Built-in, evolutionarily driven structures of cognition and behavior affect people's ease and willingness

---

market-based strategies that maintain their autonomy and provide opportunities for personal gain, believing that the "invisible hand"—of self-interested actors seeking to maximize their own personal gain—leads to optimal social results. Both hierarchists and individualists tend to embrace technology, which is viewed instrumentally as providing either more social control (if sanctioned by the "experts") or more individual efficacy, respectively. "Egalitarians," however, are most concerned about injustice in the distribution of risk costs and benefits, tolerate or celebrate social deviance and diversity, and view technology with suspicion. They often promote participatory, democratic, and consensus-based decision making that includes all affected parties as equals. Interestingly, most of the religious environmentalists appear to share the characteristics of prototypical egalitarians, themes that resonate with the awareness of social interdependence they discussed.

to learn and their tendency to choose or resist new behaviors. While such structures influence people to act in ways that deserve moral attention, the actions may not reflect conscious moral choices as much as built-in cognitive structures that require thoughtful and caring effort to overcome.

These distinctions are extremely fine but worth exploring precisely through the use of both social scientific and theological disciplines in order to better understand how some manage to get really green and what keeps others from doing so. Social science addresses human limitations descriptively, while religion focuses more deeply on how individual choice influences and amplifies the moral meaning of those limitations.

Moral Limitations

This subtle but critical dimension of the knowledge gap might be called the "unwilling-to-know gap." Here the line between legitimate cognitive challenge and moral choice begins to blur.

As discussed above, scientific literacy often depends on morally neutral factors beyond one's control: education, scientific inclination, and access to information. Moral struggle follows mental understanding. It is only possible to speak of a moral problem once someone understands the severity of a problem and one's contribution to it. Gaining climate literacy in particular is particularly challenging, and the knowledge gap is legitimately wide. Grasping the complexities that baffle scientists is even harder for "ordinary" people (i.e., nonscientists).

Willful ignorance. Some factors affecting one's openness to knowledge do have moral weight. Ralph's comment on the willful ignorance of the Hummer driver, cited in chapter 1, is worth repeating. He stated, "I'd say we have a great ability to be willfully blind in the consequence of our actions to externalize costs and now see that we are affecting ourselves. I think the ability to change that is one of our great hopes." In his anger at the destruction of the common goods of the earth by individual greed, Ralph put his finger on the slippery reality of willful ignorance—and the potential of a revised perspective.

Through willful ignorance or deliberate inattention people are able to ignore important issues that lay claim to their moral attention. Holocaust studies identified the protective defenses of deliberate inattention. People afraid for their families under repressive regimes can claim to know less than they do. By maintaining their ignorance, they exaggerate their powerlessness and wait for someone else to do something first. This is called the "passive bystander effect."[41] Adopting the stance of a passive bystander won't make climate change go away, but it offers the superficial bliss of ignorance.

Thus moral meaning is not just relevant to external action alone, but permeates one's *willingness to know*. While in theory knowing is morally neutral, there are moral dimensions embedded even in the process of understanding. Even the etymology of "error," rooted in the term "to wander," reveals this connection between being mistaken and being at fault. At some point, failing to see is not nearsightedness but willful blindness. Tim felt he could see this willful ignorance in the jeering dismissal of global warming by his father.

> *Tim: I think there's ignorance and then there's ignorance and then there's willful ignorance. I think the price of gas is going to destroy some of that willful ignorance. The reality is that there are forces out there who want to take advantage of people's naiveté, let's say, maybe not ignorance exactly. My own dad's a Baptist minister, now retired, and every time it's really cold and snowy he'll say, "That's global warming for you!"*

His father was willing to observe weather events only long enough to dismiss them. Tim went on to say that his father had "absolutely no concept of what the bigger picture is." More to the point, his father was satisfied with dismissal, not acknowledging that a serious societal issue might be at stake, that more com-

---

41. George Marshall, "Why We Find It So Hard to Act against Climate Change," *YES Magazine* (Winter 2010): 44.

plex scientific understanding might be needed, and that he might be called on as a moral leader to investigate the bigger picture of weather.

Like Tim's father, societies also find ways to marginalize inconvenient problems. Distancing oneself from climate change is an extremely effective insulation against action. The problem is "in the future," "unclear even to scientists," "only for tree-hugging environmentalists," "a distraction from jobs and security," etc. Furthermore, climate change appears inconsistent with our felt experience of a cold winter, which emphasizes the point about how powerfully focus on local experience determines one's assessment of a global phenomenon.

Misinformation. If willful ignorance is the "demand side" of the morally charged knowledge gap about environmental crises, misinformation is the "supply side." Misinformation is a serious contributor to the knowledge gap. Industry can misinform through the subtleties of "greenwashed" advertising—for example, too many ads for gas-guzzling SUVs disguised as exploring the great outdoors. Industry also misinforms by a policy of silence or nondisclosure, as Charlie confessed: "I worked at a polluting industry, a steel industry, for thirty-six years. We would do things at night that we wouldn't do during the day because at night nobody would see it." Government suppression of information also exists. A scientist employed at the National Oceanic and Atmospheric Administration (NOAA) related to me that he was personally pressured by his superiors in Washington not to hold press releases about climate-change findings. Industry misinformation colludes with government suppression when industry donations buy the independence of congressional leaders.[42]

---

42. As Richard Miller documents, the climate threat has been recognized for decades but has been unaddressed because of "the failure of central institutions of democracy: namely, our media, politicians, and preeminently a vast disinformation campaign by corporations making short-term profits off of the burning of fossil fuels. He cites the history of the climate problem from the U.S. Senate testimony of historian of science Naomi Oreskes, available at http://www.gpo.gov (Richard W. Miller, "Discussion of 'Reflections on the

The research participants saw misinformation, industry power, and political lobbying as among the greatest obstacles to action and progress. This topic was one of the most frequently discussed, and anger about lobbies loomed extremely large in participants.

> *Rich: I think lobbies from industry are a big part of it. I think I blame both lobbies and the lack of any government push to make it known to us.*

> *Pablo: I remember in Michoacán, there was a river where we could get fish and shrimp and all that. Right now you can go and you can find nothing there. So I can see the change of the environment, and it's coming rapidly. And why is that? I think it's because the people, they don't have any conscience. All they want is power, power, power, in the industries and all that. They don't care about the people. All they care about is themselves. Make money, money, money and that's it. They're forgetting that we just have only one world and what we're leaving behind for the kids I don't know. Deserts.*

The Buddhist group felt political power was blocking the advancement of environmentally sustainable technology. Dick began commenting on the political shaping of technology and energy policy, which not only dictated social options but restricted individual choices to use less energy.

> *Dick (Buddhist): Well I think it's political because a lot that happens is based on governmental policy. In terms of individual versus collective, you've got a governmental policy in one direction, it's very, very hard for an individual to do something counter to that instead of going along with it. And energy, and energy use, and who's on different energy committees. Whether we're looking for alternative energy*

Energy Crisis': A Statement by the Committee on Social Development and World Peace, United States Catholic Conference, April 2, 1981," conference paper for the Catholic Theological Society of America Interest Group on Discipleship and Sustainability, 2014), http://ctsa-online.org.

seriously or whether we're just pushing oil, it's very much a political issue.

Jason provided a concrete example that is close to home for most Americans: fuel efficiency. He couldn't understand the lack of progress in fuel economies otherwise. "The last thing Dick said is something I've been thinking a lot about lately. I work in the technology field. The technological advances over the last 20 or 30 years are outstanding, but the average car still only gets 25 miles per gallon? Why is that? It has to be politically oriented. There's just no way of explaining why they can't make cars that are more fuel efficient."

Ellen at least tried to avoid demonizing political powers that seemed to oppress environmental progress, as a way of expressing her Buddhist spirituality of interconnection—but in the end, couldn't. "I think one thing is the issue that ... one way that practice can help people that are involved in political activism is not to get into the intense dichotomy of the good guys, the bad guys. But really to try in an effective way to do the most you can without demonizing the others. Which I certainly can't do at the moment."

Part of what made misinformers the "bad guys" is the perception of manipulation that compromised others' freedom to get accurate information, to educate others, and to make fair choices. Bob from the Unitarian group viewed this as deeply unsettling, saying, "I believe they skewed things, they actually changed scientific write-ups to suit their own needs, and you know, that's very, very discouraging." Participants like Bob felt misinformation made the challenge of getting past the knowledge gap of illiteracy that much harder. Thus, combating scientific illiteracy must move past formidable efforts to misinform funded by very powerful, very rich, and highly invested corporations. Information suppression points to the negative impact of someone else's dishonesty on my moral choices. Theologians describe this condition of human existence as social sin. The concept of social sin acknowledges that the wrongful actions of others affect our decisions without our consent, before we even consciously act. If lobbyists, industry misinformation campaigns, and government suppression of scientific findings control the information available to the public, citizens' moral choices have been limited without their consent.

While identifying the moral dimension of inattention is very hard to clearly capture, it is useful to pursue this fine distinction because identifying moral problems allows for moral solutions. Moral problems respond not just to information but to leadership, inspiration, enthusiasm, calls for courage, and reminders of what we love.

Since knowledge is influenced by attention, then to some degree it is also shaped by the things people value and to what they attend. Attention is inescapably fundamental, no matter one's perspective. Scientific observation, contemplative awareness, religious wonder, psychological analysis—all begin with attending to the phenomenon at stake.[43] Participants spoke frequently about how attention was sucked away by consumerism, the need for convenience, a bias toward "progress," constant busyness, and the force of habit. Social patterns, economic structures, and consumerism reinforce and influence attitudes. The circumstances of daily and social life in what is for most of us a technologically accelerated, Type-A lifestyle prevent noticing the nature and impact of one's regular activities, and much less reflectively attending to, researching their impact, or changing them—or creating sustainable alternatives where none exist. This leads to the next section, the observed aspects of the caring gap.

The Caring Gap: I'd Love to but . . .

The knowledge gap comprised scientific illiteracy and the built-in cognitive, emotional, and personal filters that limit understanding.

---

43. Many religious philosophers emphasize mindfulness and attentiveness, and Bernard Lonergan, S.J., is one notable example. Lonergan's epistemology explores how we know truth and act well through four imperatives. The imperatives are be attentive, be intelligent, be reasonable, and be responsible. Together with his accounts of conversion (intellectual, moral, and religious), Lonergan's epistemology aligns with my analyses of the knowledge gap, the caring gap, and the action gap. I am indebted to Julia Brumbaugh for emphasizing this connection.

The caring gap deals with what is already understood. This discussion among Ari, Naresh, and Vinay teased out this distinction clearly.

> *Ari: It's more than just awareness. In this country I would say most of the people are aware. Like I am aware. But I'm not doing much about it. So it's not simply that they are not aware. Even after they are aware they are doing little about it.*
>
> *Q: Can I push you a little, Ari, why aren't you doing more? You keep bringing this up; I want to keep asking you.*
>
> *Naresh: Who's holding your hand to keep you from acting? I can understand that in someone who doesn't want to talk about the environment.*
>
> *Ari: One thing to be aware of something, and the other to put it to practice, and do it. There is a big gap there. If you are not even aware you can't do anything. So that's the first step. But I think you are kind of implying if people are aware the problems are solved. It's not that simple.*
>
> *Vinay: You are just making the point more real. First you must be aware, and then you have to get out and get something done about it.*

The caring gap sounds like someone saying, "The environment may be in trouble but . . . I have so many other things to deal with first." Multiple distractions, competing responsibilities, and social pressures make it easy to put the environmental low on the list of priorities.

Erika, a college student from Seattle, felt that a lot of people really don't care *enough* to make the environment "high on their list," something worth doing first.

> *Erika (Baptist): They may care on a certain level, but it's not high enough on their list. When I talk to a lot of people at college, they're like, whatever, they know it's a problem, but they've got their classes, and it's just not a priority in any way*

and it's not going to be. I don't know if that's what you're calling willful ignorance, but it's just not a priority.

Another young professional, a Muslim woman in Washington, DC, also worried about people whose lack of caring went beyond the simple distraction that might simply push caring inclinations aside. Sarah feared actual apathy, which to her meant not sensing a moral imperative to learn about the climate and to act. She links the knowledge, caring, and action gaps in her discussion of apathy.

Q. *What do you think is the worst thing we have to fear?*

Sarah (Muslim): I think apathy, just lack of knowledge on what the issues are, and then just not caring, not feeling like you have this moral imperative to find out what's going on, and change the way that you live your lifestyle and the decisions that you make that are negatively impacting the environment. So just that feeling of not caring, you know—and that's really scary.

As Sarah understands in a way that frightens her, apathy has an insidious power to undermine moral engagement with climate change. Sarah deepens the critique of willed ignorance by linking apathy and lack of knowledge to a disengaged moral imperative. If one doesn't care, it's hard to feel morally implicated and accept the moral imperative to act. Sarah expresses this insidious failure to feel responsible as apathy, listlessness, and disengagement.

Moral failure can be so well disguised as listlessness, acedia, sloth—just not doing it. This failure hides under the appearance of banality, not vice, but the experience of the participants, as well as classic religious moralism, tell us otherwise. For Christianity, sloth has long been listed as one of the seven deadly sins.

In the view of one Catholic parishioner from New Jersey, caring doesn't always drive action anyway. Steve felt people seem willing to accept some level of damnation. Steve's frustration with the failure of education to create an impact led him to conclude there is an "ah hell" stage of self-conscious, apathetic velleity.

Steve: You think the education is going to do it, but we've been educating. It's been all over the place. For a while there, we were kind of a voice in the wind kind of thing. Everything that's been in the paper and magazines for the last couple years, it's hard not to be a little bit educated. Now I think we're in the next step, which is, "Ah Hell, I don't want to do this."

Steve points to knowing what is right, but not having the force of will or the courage to act: a failure of nerve that must pave the road to hell as surely as ineffective good intentions.

Furthermore, deciding to care doesn't make action any easier, especially given the vast distance between my presence at the gas pump and the greenhouse gases in the atmosphere. Even for those who care, it is very easy to wonder if action will make a difference. This question leads to the absolutely critical moment: when caring and deciding peers over the brink of actual ... action. The great leap in getting from ideally green to really green is summoned by the question, "Will I act, if I decide I should?"

In what follows, I will trace the forces that drag people down into a caring gap, according to the research participants. These forces are an onslaught of consumerism, the defeat of environmental values by "background values," the perception that some environmental actions reverse "progress," and simple disinterest.

Consumerism

Consumerism is a temptation, a seductress, an encroaching army! Participants used these vivid images to describe the battle against "stuff." Participants were keenly aware of the pressures of consumerism, and often stated that social values about consumerism and progress significantly affect what people care about and obstruct personal and communal action. Consumerism was felt to be supported by ideals of progress, buttressed by social values and class, and integrated into a worldview dominated by capitalism.

As Latha, a Hindu woman in New Jersey, put it, consumerism is an unstoppable power. "It's not about being sensitive; it's just being able to fight this consumerism. It's not that they don't know [consumerism is bad] or they don't want to do something about it. But this onslaught, I don't know how..." Instead of an onslaught, Lynn described the power of consumerism as a more subtle tyranny, a "seductive" power.

> *Lynn (Unitarian-Universalist): It's so seductive. I used to be a counselor in a school in not a real rich town, and all the kids had TVs in their rooms and they had Gameboys and they had all of these gadgets and that's just their life. I mean, how do you break out of that?*

Lynn lamented the all-powerful social reinforcement of consumption among the students she knew. Social scientists attribute part of the tenacity of consumerism to a phenomenon called the "endowment effect," by which people value things more because they already have them. The momentum of consumerism keeps rolling simply because the "things" are there. Clearly, ideas about consumerism reflect social values for both young people and adults in any community.

Defeated by "Hidden" Values

The value of simplicity can easily become lost and ineffective—a good example of what environmental ethicist Anna Peterson means by a religious ideal defeated by class values. Petersen observes that religious groups may teach the importance of honoring the environment, but those teachings do not automatically transform the members' behavior. People may value the earth, but they do not always act on their values. More to the point, people act on the social values *that have the most traction.* Taking the example of simplicity, the consumerist actions that contradict the environmental value and religious value of simplicity are reflecting *other* values, particularly class values.

Katrina lamented how her ideal of natural playthings was somehow torpedoed without her consent by "the feeling about consumption that we need so much . . . that we seem take it for granted."

Katrina: We have so much stuff and it's considered normal to have so much stuff. When my kids were born I said I was only going to buy wood toys, and that's all I had, wood toys. And now I look in the basement and it's full of plastic, and I don't even know how it got there. I'm surprised with myself with how much stuff we have accumulated throughout the years. Part of it is the region where we live—there is this idea that we need so much stuff. Sometimes I get a glimpse of how much more basic things could be. How much less we really need.

Parents may want to provide only naturally made, chemical- and plastic-free toys for their young children, but those values are often overridden by baby showers and a culture where love is shown by increasingly extravagant gifts. Peterson identifies these driving values as "background values" shaped by class interests and social setting. This disjuncture between (some) values and actions is a source of potentially tragic self-contradiction.[44] This disjuncture was clearly evident in the consumerism that participants identified as a major barrier to choosing sustainable behaviors.

Habits of simplicity are defeated not only by progress and social values but by the complexity of defining what is excessive in a super-developed lifestyle. Traditional religions have always exhorted care for the poor and denounced luxury that took goods from the poor. But even with religious inspiration, drawing the line between well-being and greed is not easy. A World Council of Churches news release asked, "When does the pursuit of economical well-being turn into greed?" A gathering of churches in Africa attempted to reduce the gap between the rich and the poor which held destructive consequences for peace and for the environment. They met to define a "greed line" as "practical guidance to Christians regarding sources of growth—such as speculation or expropriation—and the

---

44. Anna L. Peterson, "Talking the Walk: A Practice-Based Environmental Ethic as Grounds for Hope," in *Ecospirit: Religions and Philosophies for the Earth*, ed. Laurel Kearns and Catherine Keller (New York: Fordham University Press, 2007), 47.

level or ratio of wealth accumulation that are unethical."[45] In the United States, a similar discourse exploded onto the public stage with the Occupy Wall Street movements and the clamor of many against the unequal ratios of wealth that favor the "1 percent." Michael Northcott, a climate ethicist, has drawn a line between livelihood and luxury emissions to define the difference between need and excess in terms of greenhouse gas consumption. These new definitions are part of the challenge of navigating ethical consumption in the face of climate change.[46]

Against the power of consumerism and social pressures, religious traditions offer countercultural ideals and support but fight the same onslaught of consumer pressure. Religious ideals, raised in a familiar community setting, offer alternate visions to consumerism as legitimate social norms. Religious leaders and peers keep alive the ideals of simplicity—ideals fundamental to both spirituality and long-term sustainability. Traditional simplicity turned environmental virtue is an example of retrieving and reinterpreting traditions: an example of "loyalty as novelty" that is transforming many traditions. Simplicity is an ancient, traditional religious value, not a new green invention. As Tim, the pastor of a small, progressive Baptist church in Seattle, said,

> *Tim (Baptist): The seeds of anticapitalism are to sell all your possessions and goods, give them to your neighbor. That's resident in the tradition and those things may come back to focus people's spiritual lives in a way that they haven't in the current time.*

> *Margaret: That resident may be in solitary confinement!*

> *Tim: Maybe safely locked away. It's there nonetheless.*

Margaret's witty comment that simplicity, once "resident" in religious traditions, is now a resident of solitary confinement, shows

---

45. "Report on the African Ecumenical Consultation on Linking Poverty, Wealth and Ecology, 2007," Dar es Salaam, Tanzania, http://www.oikoumene.org.

46. Michael S. Northcott, *A Moral Climate: The Ethics of Global Warming* (Maryknoll, NY: Orbis Books, 2007), 56.

how countercultural practices based on simplicity have become. Such values may be "safely locked away," defeated by social pressure.

Progress

Consumption is partially reinforced by ideas about what "progress" means. Elaine attempted to educate her mother-in-law about disposable paper towels, which represented progress after a lifetime of using rags. Green habits, like returning to a rag bag, require reversing the "progress" of a disposable product that sold on the power of easy, quick cleanup. As David from the Reformed Church of Highland Park in New Jersey said, "our society is built upon it, hell, forces it. We are marketers. This society, this country in particular, is built, designed, engineered, to be consumers; it has been legislated to be consumers." It's then easy to see why reversing progress seems like blasphemy: consumption is an article of faith.

Faith in the market began in the 1980s, according to Harvard philosopher Michael J. Sandel, when the Reagan/Thatcher era began to consolidate the faith that markets are the primary means for achieving the public good. Sandel raises the question of what happens when the reach of markets, and of market values, extends "into spheres of life traditionally governed by nonmarket norms."[47]

The market as religion. According to theologian Elizabeth Johnson, one consequence of this extension of the market into greater and greater sectors of life is that religions' ability to preach simplicity and moderation is countered by the globally dominant religion of unfettered capitalism. Ideological capitalism functions as a religion by propounding a worldview and a particular ethic. It is simply not recognized as a religion because its ideology is secular, though no less totalizing. Yet the gospel of profit and satisfaction through consumption competes effectively with religions and displaces their influence.

One could argue that the Market is the first truly world religion, binding all corners of the globe into a worldview and

---

47. Michael J. Sandel, "What Isn't for Sale?," *The Atlantic*, April 2012, http://www.theatlantic.com.

set of values whose religious role we overlook only because we insist on seeing them as "secular." This worldview has competed with the insights of traditional religions, and so far bested them in the public realm.[48]

Theologian Jay McDaniel similarly argues that consumerism is a barrier to spirituality. It is a "cultural atmosphere that empha-sized speed and busyness, productivity and progress, at the expense of being obedient to God's calling in each present moment."[49] As a worldwide religion, consumerism promotes overconsumption and urges the attitudes and behaviors that support constant orienta-tion toward producing, achieving, maintaining, and improving our image and social appearances and seeking greater affluence. Haste, anxiety, preoccupation with things, selfishness, and greed become compulsive, enslaving habits.[50]

Johnson does not deride responsible market practice but distin-guishes between responsible market practice and "unfettered capi-talism" that enables luxury for the few. Such distinctions are also made by economists. Jeffrey Sachs, an international advisor to indi-vidual nations and the United Nations on market crises, recognizes that there are places where markets cannot function. His recogni-tion reflects a profound commitment to economic justice, rooted in the discovery of places of extreme poverty where markets do not exist and people are, in his words, too poor to live. Sachs's power-ful book *The End of Poverty* argues that the countries able to live luxuriously must offer the material and technical support that will eventually allow the desperately poor to participate in markets.

---

48. Elizabeth A. Johnson, "'And God Saw That It Was Good': Why Reli-gion's Resources for Ecological Ethics Are Not More Effective," unpublished paper for the conference "Moral Heat: Ethical Dimensions of Environmental Regulation and Economics in the 21st Century" (Fordham University, Lin-coln Center, New York City, 2010).

49. Jay B. McDaniel, *Living from the Center: Spirituality in an Age of Consumerism* (St. Louis: Chalice Press, 2000), 13.

50. Ibid., 16. See also John Francis Kavanaugh, *Following Christ in a Consumer Society: The Spirituality of Cultural Resistance* (Maryknoll, NY: Orbis Books, 1981).

Stories about consumption among the Reformed congregation sparked strong questions about sacrifice, and what sacrifice truly entailed. They grappled with the relative costs of sacrifice, as well as the socially contextualized view of sacrifice. Would living within a sustainable footprint really be possible in American suburbia? How much are they called to reduce consumption in light of the varying social mores between New Jersey and Zambia? A well-timed "hmmm" from the pastor spurred more probing reflection. Should they take on radical simplicity or is it necessary to accommodate to American society? One woman asked pointedly if daily showers are socially necessary. Another asked, must one grow one's own food? This question seems outlandish, but in another context I in fact encountered a Quaker woman who grew all her own food—and froze and canned it for the winter—in a New Jersey suburban yard. Her choice, totally impossible and undesirable for most people, illustrates the quandary of living "normally" while conscious of global inequalities and vast differences in consumption.

Disinterest

Simple disinterest and distraction was remarked upon by many participants.

> *Pete (Baptist): I have to harp back to the idea that people stop caring. If you could measure how many people are really interested in the natural world versus being at the mall and television, there'd be this great big gathering of people and a very small group of people on the other end.*

Pete's point was underscored by a campaign by British ministers in the spring of 2012 that pointedly criticized the "shrug culture." Their advocacy efforts, Project Noah, attempted to round up flagging support.

Migrant workers who advocated for pesticide awareness and limits put disinterest at the top of the list, along with other reasons.

> *Pablo: I think the hardest thing right now is to make people attend to the meetings about pesticides and health that we*

are conducting, where we invite the people to have a meeting. Not everybody is interested.

Q. Why is that?

Pablo: Even though it's their health, they don't care.

Rafael: Too much time in the orchard. They want to spend time with their families. That's 50 percent and probably another 50 percent they no like the meeting.

But for Pablo, that wasn't a good enough answer. He blamed TV for absorbing people's time. "Way too much TV; that's what I've been seeing. People aren't willing to go to these meetings even though it's for their health, for their own safety and all that." For Pablo, this was just like walking into traffic—waiting to be hit by a car. Pablo expected a focus on personal survival to motivate concern; it didn't. Erika found a focus on personal survival actually to enable disregard for the earth. Both positions are illogical, but nonetheless dominate attitudes and behavior.

Recall what Erika said about apathy among her college peers born of complete personal disconnection from the earth beyond hosting their lives, until they are dead. "Well, people before me have come and gone; they did their thing and didn't care about the earth, so that's what I'm going to do now. I'm going to die before the earth is gone."

Even those most uninterested in the problem, such as Beth, agree that her faith teaches that God wants us to be stewards. She could understand and accept that, especially as within the context of worship she is reminded of that duty. It is simply not that important to her. As she said, "You know I couldn't be an Earth Corps person. Not because I'm not at all interested in it, but because I'm not interested enough in it."

The Action Gap: Just—Do It!
The Armchair Environmentalist

All those I interviewed were unusually active idealists. For them, values drove their life decisions. They cherished being in a community that supported and nurtured their values. But by their own account, even the most dedicated environmentalists are pulled by undercurrents of resistance despite themselves. Several participants even described this resistance directly as laziness—a sense that they could do more. This is the action gap: *I know the environmental crisis is happening but I am not taking action* . . . for any number of reasons.

Chapter 1 identified an environmental spirituality characterized by scientific literacy, sense of interdependence, and commitment to social justice that motivated the participants' action. Having observed their own self-critical reflections on their action and attempting to be very charitable, I now ask: Why is such action not more intense? How do participants themselves describe this occasional lack of intensity? What failures and impasses do they acknowledge? What insights can psychological theory provide? This analysis builds on participants' frequent references to the barriers to implementing values, including being busy, comfortable, used to their ways, and overwhelmed.

Being Busy

It doesn't take a rocket scientist to notice that people are busy, distracted, inconvenienced by change, and put off by complex issues. As Charlie said, "I think one of the most important things that we're confronted with in the Earth Corps is that 'I don't have time for that.'" Charlie was able to appreciate the many legitimate demands for people's time. He went on to say, "I fully appreciate that. That is not a negative statement to me, because I know the people in this church have a lot of good causes." Being too busy himself to help with one of the church's missions, a food pantry, he understood the challenges of making time for causes—and also understood the successful appeal by friends for a shared cause that needs help. "They finally have got me to go ... I'm going to go because they say, 'Hey, we don't have anybody to come.' And I know if I go, I'll love to go but it just means it's one more thing." Busyness is not in itself a bad thing. Having multiple commitments is a reality of life, and Charlie didn't judge it. However, busyness can become a way to protect oneself from questioning one's current priorities and making space for a response to real concerns. The Unitarian-Universalist committee strategized ways to work through busyness with the insight that busyness can be "an insulating layer between ourselves and concerns and actions."

Distraction. Being busy is just one of the layers of insulation that stand between caring and acting, and are easily justified precisely because they are so common. Another common reason for not making environmental changes is closely linked to busyness—the unrelenting distraction that busy lives and digital devices provide. The constant media barrages and alerts from hand-held digital devices entice people's attention away from pondering big decisions about what isn't immediately pressing. As Pete from the Baptist group said, "How are you going to get these people to care about trees instead of iPods? It's going to be pretty hard." If one can attend to the problem, deciding what to do is a challenge in itself.

Convenience is key. Because we are busy, convenience trumps extra effort. Riley E. Dunlap and Rik Scarce, environmental sociologists, observe that while priorities shift from protecting the economy to protecting the environment, personal convenience still trumps ecological concern. Their research shows an increase in the public's expressed willingness to pay higher prices for goods and services (including grocery items), "to the point that willingness to absorb the cost of environmental protection has clearly become the majority position." Nonetheless, they emphasize that the most popular behaviors are those that require minimal effort and personal cost. So, while an expressed willingness to absorb the cost of environmental protection is a majority position, "only a fifth of the public 'strongly agree' that they would be willing to give up convenience products to help preserve natural resources." Convenience has the highest trump.[51]

Likewise, James Cornwell has found that environmental policies gain more support when the phrasing of the policy suggests the guidelines are for "(other) people," not "you." People expect oth-

---

51. Riley E. Dunlap and Rik Scarce, "Poll Trends: Environmental Problems and Protection," *The Public Opinion Quarterly* 55, no. 4 (1991): 657.

ers to take the harder step (driving less), but they want to help the environment doing the easier things. In other words, environmental restrictions are fine "for thee, but not for me."[52] Convenience is key—especially for "me."

Decision avoidance. Busyness—as well as the complexity of making changes—can also make it hard simply to think about what to do, and then commit to doing something that one has thought up. Psychologists call this decision avoidance. The complexity of climate change can lead people to avoid all cognitive and behavioral activities involved with decision process. Climate change science is confusing; solutions seem impossible, and it is depressing to think about. Decision avoidance is itself rooted in an aversion to loss and ambiguity. Uncertainty is unpleasant, and even thinking about disasters is uncomfortable. But from a moral standpoint, in the end, not making a decision is still a decision.

Decisions can also be avoided through a prolonged justification of options. People become unable or unwilling to commit to available options (for example, they start to think about energy options but never actually choose solar or wind and stay with coal). When both choices seem similar, decisions are especially difficult. People can justify either option and never take action for the simple reason of being unable to decide *what to do*.[53]

Engaging the decision process can be helped by recognizing that people may be more influenced to act positively to obtain a good rather than avoid a negative. These are termed *approach motivators*, which initiate something positive, or *avoidance motivations*, which avoid something negative. For example, the Northland Church committee preferred to approach creation care as a positive task. Rather than attract the "negative avoidance" of threats expressed by science, such threats were not acknowledged as the primary motivation. Scientific warnings, as discussed in chapter 1, were deprioritized as authoritative in comparison to scriptural teachings to care for creation.

---

52. James Cornwell, Presentation at CRED Annual Meeting, May 2014.

53. Center for Research on Environmental Decisions, Decision Theory Seminar, September 30, 2008.

I changed my light bulbs: I'm done! Ironically, even taking action can backfire if people feel too much satisfaction from too little action. Another phenomenon noted by psychologists is the "single-action bias," which shows how doing one thing removes a sense of urgency to act further. People may take one action—for example, change a light bulb—then feel better about the planet and their own stewardship. Taking some response to a perceived risk includes a sense of relief after taking one action. But it is clear that people need to continue to take other actions. Educational programs offered by faith traditions offered positive encouragement for sustained action.

The detailed checklists provided by the Unitarian-Universalist Green Sanctuary program did just that. Multiple steps were needed to earn the designation. This functioned like the Leadership in Energy and Environmental Design (LEED) program, an extensive green building guideline with multiple checklists. In fact, Howard, whose congregation became the first house of worship in the United States to earn a Platinum LEED designation, compared the process to the detailed moral codes of Leviticus! "The LEED process is one that really holds your feet to the fire. Someone compared LEED to Leviticus, that Leviticus has all of these very arcane and specific [codes]. But by doing that it forced us to oversee the whole project to—to get where we were going." With their feet "held to the fire" by the LEED code or the UU Green Sanctuary code there was less of a chance of resting with a single action.

Being Comfortable

Consumption is comfortable, so it is natural to resist any change.

Samantha (evangelical): It's so much easier to go along with … I like material goods, I don't like to have to worry about how much I drive, you know, I don't want to have to worry about my gas mileage. I'd much rather make a lot of money and not have to worry about it, you know, it's just a lot more to think about and my experience is that it's a good thing. I mean it's good for me as a human being to think about them.

*I'm glad that God put that word in Pastor Joel and that I got
to hear that. I think it's better. This life is better, but initially
... it poses a lot of hard work you know.*

Marc ruefully admitted that he used a car more than he really,
really wanted to or intended to.

*Marc (Reformed Christian): We tried to leave one car there
and walk between, so if we need a vehicle, there's one in each
place. And we can, and morally, we should. We can do it. But
we don't always. Whether that's due to real creature com-
forts or habits or convenience or I don't know.*

Monica said something very similar about her three-block com-
mute. She identified her reasons for driving as "excuses," admitting
to a personal sense of doing something not really acceptable. "My
excuse is I have a lot of stuff to carry, and I need to bring a lot of
stuff back and forth. But really it's more I feel I don't have time to
walk, or it's creature comfort, it's too cold to walk, it's too rainy. I
shouldn't be using those excuses but I continue to use them." Monica
spoke very honestly, acknowledging a feeling that she was indulging
in a convenient practice. Her feeling, born of an acute green conscience, targeted a fairly mild practice of driving a few blocks. An
acute green conscience took Marc's family in a direction few would
call mild. Marc's family, as mentioned in chapter 1, turned down
the heat at night to 40 degrees, motivated by personal ideals as well
by as the price of heating fuel. Despite their discomfort, they were
also sustained by a desire to live out the green spirituality visibly
proclaimed by the new solar panels on their church's roof. They
were quite conscious that this practice was a sacrifice. Having taken
such an uncomfortable step, Marc could take a more critical view of
what our comfortable society considers to be a sacrifice.

*Marc (Reformed Christian): Is ONLY having one car? Is that
a sacrifice? Is it a sacrifice that gets 40 miles to the gallon
but won't do zero to sixty in nine seconds? Really? What's
a sacrifice? Putting your house down to 40 at night—that's
a sacrifice!*

Interestingly, other groups also discussed discomfort and sacrifice in relation to cultural expectations. A Unitarian congregation had voted to embark on a formal program of greening their sanctuary. Along with solar installations and efficient windows, they lowered the sanctuary temperature to 65 degrees in the winter—and provided a stack of shawls in the back. Their democratic process included discussions, surveys, and votes—all of which raised and reaffirmed the widely pro-environmental views of the congregation. As one leader said, "Whenever they have to go into that earth room and it's only sixty degrees in there and they have to wear their coat, hopefully they remember we voted for this."

I raise this example to underscore the previous findings on free inquiry. Freedom, in this case, was expressed in the act of voting and processing values within the context of a supportive community. The example is not meant to glorify a modern religious ascetic or validate "shivering in the dark," which was Ronald Reagan's dismissive caricature of environmentalists or those who choose to live simply. This famous scoff at environmentalists reflects his career as an advertiser for General Electric, during which he invited Americans to "live better electrically," and lead "a richer, fuller, more satisfying life."[54] The better electric life poses multiple moral challenges today, which the Unitarian congregation addressed on all fronts. They conserved energy for heating (using the shawls), installed state-of-the-art windows, sought renewable electricity through their own solar panels, and placed the earth at the center of their spiritual community—literally—with a stained-glass Earth window above the sanctuary.

Pleasure and comfort are necessary supports of human flourishing. But they can override other needs. This point was made particularly by the Native American participants. Tony and Gabe recalled working before dawn in freezing weather to herd sheep, alongside elderly grandparents, and none even gave the discomfort a thought. For them this was an unremarked part of life.

---

54. William L. Bird, Jr., "General Electric Theater," in *Encyclopedia of Television*, ed. Horace Newcomb (New York: Routledge, 2013), 970.

Others emphasized the great challenge of asking Americans to consider sacrifice. Mohamad recalled past conversations about the very word "sacrifice," saying "that's not a useful word in an American context. If you use it for Americans they have this reaction to it, we have this reaction to it."

Mohamad is right. Sacrifice is not at all easy. Mindy (Reformed Christian) stated baldly the challenge that keeping a smaller footprint would have.

> *What should I be doing about that? And I really don't know. Turn off the air conditioner? Pull out the air conditioner and sort of swelter in the summer? Go vegetarian? Find a job where I can walk to work? I don't know what it would take, but it would definitely be sacrifice to bring my lifestyle into conformance with a global sustainable life, and there's no way.*

But at the same time, their spirituality suggested that the true meaning of choosing to be green as a loving recognition of the needs of the neighbor and themselves meant that sacrifice had to be reconsidered.

Pragmatism carried the day for Paul, an evangelical, who felt that "I don't know if lifestyle change should be considered a sacrifice. To me it's just smart." Sarah agreed that practical changes, while difficult, offered an exciting, transformative possibility.

> *I wouldn't characterize it as a sacrifice. It can seem harder like initially but change always feels hard, you know to human beings. It's exciting for me to see how it can make life so really different, like some choices that are sustainable for my life, and I think will be better for me. I think will actually make me happier, you know, almost. So, yeah, I don't see it as a sacrifice at all.*

Nonetheless, the ambiguous "almost" reveals the persistent challenge of giving up material goods, which for her was made possible by her faith.

One or two participants candidly acknowledged the real resistance to doing hard things by using the loaded term "lazy." Some implicitly and even explicitly admitted that people could do more. Beth candidly acknowledged that "a lot of what you all say I intellectually believe. I'm just too lazy to do it. I don't have time to do it. It's not important enough to me at this point to do it." After Carmen noted that some workers were scared to complain about pesticide exposure, she added that laziness was also a factor. "The people stay there because they are scared to lose their job. Also, I think that it is laziness." When asked to explore all the factors that insulated people from acting on their concerns, people readily identified multiple factors: busyness, distraction, convenience, comfort, even laziness. There is little wonder more is not done, especially when the habitual nature of unsustainable lifestyles is taken into account.

Being Habituated

The powers of the will are codified or restricted in habits. Habits are the learned behaviors, attitudes, and even expectations that become consistent patterns of action, and as such limit the full range of possible action. This may be the foundation for great virtue, in which one no longer can even think of committing some vice. On the other hand, habits can close one off from new ways of acting.

Dan, an evangelical Christian, explained the no-holds-barred dedication of his daughter in testing the possibility of new habits.

Dan: So there are a number of habits, you know how long do you take a shower? My daughter was experimenting with rotating cold showers in her schedule.

Q: Out of concern for the earth she wanted to start taking cold showers?

Dan: Yeah, so the habit says what? You just go take the shower, you know, so you know. I think those are some of the main barriers from my point of view.

This young woman is a striking model of integrating values and actions. For her fourteenth birthday, she asked for a garden space so she could grow her own vegetables and eat more local produce. Instead of presents, she asked for donations to causes that helped move women out of prostitution. She had an amazing energy for experimenting with good habits, an energy the rest of the group couldn't quite match. As someone said, "She can have the cold showers; I'll eat the vegetables!"

Building good habits are an effective way to counter the risks of the "single-action bias." Habits are the confirmation of multiple choices, a recurrent tide of actions forming new outlines in character. Bad habits are just as persistent, unfortunately. Habits include both the trivial and significant obstacles to change that fulfill one's values. Choices and habits interact in several ways that the participants discussed, having to do with one's range of options and one's freedom to engage those options.

Where to start? First, choices are limited by a lack of models and options. Some are trivial and socially determined, such as the presence or absence of a five-cent tax on plastic bags. A more socially entrenched and challenging limitation is whether or not busses are available on one's corner. Or, whether one must buy an SUV as the family grows.

> *Seth (Reformed Christian): The thing that is a struggle for us right now, we're about to have our third kid and I'm convinced that the makers of vehicles are in cahoots with the makers of car seats and the fact that you can't get three butts this big in the back of a Civic makes me berserk.*

Old habits die hard. Second, choices are prejudiced by habits. The personal habits that have been internalized and accepted do indicate some responsibility for the actions caught in the form of habit. The Jain group discussed habits with the assumption that people are fundamentally free to change their habits but are held back by ignorance of this freedom. Satya illustrated this with a story about a cow restrained every day with a rope.

Satya: After so many years, you don't do this, you don't actually put the rope on the thing, you just act it, the cow will never move. The point is, we are free, but somehow, something in us is binding us, but we are always free, we are always with the God. What they call maya, *the concept of* maya, *is that illusion that we are not free.*

Q: So the analogy is that the soul is free like the cow that is not tied but perhaps senses its connection to divinity.

Satya: That's the ignorance, that is the thing.

This group interpreted habit as ignorance.[55] That model enabled a sense of freedom to release oneself from habits, by removing ignorance. Habits could be released by better knowing or thinking, by choices in the cognitive dimension of experience.

Piyush (Hindu): Well, okay, I'll explain, initially try to come to the sin. Hinduism we don't have this concept of things that you are born with sin. We don't have that concept. You have the full capability of maintaining and progressing your own life. So you are fully responsible for that, and based on how you act, what act you're going to do, though your previous karmic reactions will build as a scar, or impressions in your brain, mind, whatever are you going to classify, that's going to impact. But still you have the full opportunity to make progress. The whole universe is one family, so if she's suffering or he's suffering I feel some responsibility, some day, whatever I can help, I'm going to help that. So compassionate nature is also built into, despite the karma theories.

Among the Reconstructionist Jews, there was a fascinating similar conversation about the freedom to make choices. Carol offered a deeply thoughtful interpretation of the biblical idea that humanity

---

55. By contrast, Christian interpretations of habit often emphasize the weakening of the will, so that it loses its freedom. But the complexity of comparing the illusion of *maya* to the Christian view of depravity is not the point here.

is created in the image of God. She saw in this idea a way to imagine connecting to all the possibilities of being human, and transcending the habits that limited her own perceptions and choices.

> *Carol: I have to say that I think being the image of God means that if I were to look at a reflection in a mirror of some kind and see back my own reflection, could I see it in a way that didn't have the biases of the lenses that I wear? And my judgments or habits or thoughts, would that be all that I saw reflected back to me, or perhaps could I see the potential of humanity moving through the world?*

For Carol, Judaism meant "that we are partnered with God in God's creation. And if what reflects back to me is knowing that God is within me, it's going to be that attitude that I then bring back out through my hands and my speech and my deeds." Being God's partner, reflecting all the possibilities of humanity as the image of God: this profound self-image gave her a sense of great freedom to change habits. Another member of that group, Sybil, expressed a similar sense of conscious freedom to make choices: "It's living your life in a certain way, making judgments in that way and always being conscious of it—knowing you have choices."

Breaking a habit means sharply confronting priorities. The values that Anna Peterson described must be pulled up from their tightly lodged place in our motivational mechanisms.

> *Punam (Jain): Priorities could be different for different people. It could be job for one person, for one person money, for another they want to have children. Priorities are different. To set priorities, you break the habit. You know you have awareness but you don't practice because you don't want to break the habit of doing this way. Break the habit!*

Is it addiction? Third, choices may be dictated by deeper levels of habit that approach the dynamics of addiction. Such dynamics are studied by addiction psychology. When does a habit become an addiction, an action that seems to have lost the element of choice? As addiction theorists attempt to explain the irrational reality of self-destructive behavior, some emphasize a biochemical, disease model of addiction; others explore the relationship of neurological reward circuits to emotion and memory.[56] One fascinating insight relates to the normalization of self-destructive behavior. Hardcastle shows how destructive behavior that evokes strong emotions and memories—emotions that relate to the ways we imagine our identities and values—is ironically easiest to normalize because the emotions and memories are key to our identities.

> We and we alone are the sorts of creatures who become spontaneously addicted to things. What sets us apart? The connection between our motivational system and emotionally tainted memories holds the key, because it is these memories and feelings we use to create ourselves. Something turns off the normal horror reactions to self-destructive behaviour if you are caught in a cycle of addiction.[57]

The destructive behavior is retained because it evokes memories and emotions that are key to one's sense of self. And the bitter neurological underpinning of this is that the circuits that are dominated by drug abuse are directly connected to the circuits that underwrite memory.[58]

---

56. Jon Elster, *Strong Feelings: Emotion, Addiction, and Human Behavior* (Cambridge, MA: MIT Press, 1999); Dennis Wholey, *The Courage to Change: Hope and Help for Alcoholics and Their Families* (Boston: Houghton Mifflin Company, 1984). Some researchers discuss how people adapt to their current situation in terms of a "hedonistic reappraisal." The situation isn't any better, but people get used to it, and their comfort level increases. This psychological dynamic influences habituation. Similarly, people tend to validate the status quo. This is related to the "endowment effect," a process by which people overvalue their present goods simply because they have them (James Cornwell, personal communication).

57. Valerie Gray Hardcastle, "Life at the Borders: Habits, Addictions and Self-Control," *Journal of Experimental Theoretical Artifical Intelligence* 15 (2003): 249.

58. "More importantly for our purposes, the NAc-VTA circuit is directly tied to the circuits that underwrite our memories. Hence, drugs of abuse indirectly commandeer the circuits that create and maintain our emotionally-laden thoughts (Koob 1996). As is now commonly known, memories of

If habits, lifestyles, and consequences become familiar and normalized, even the destructive impacts of alcoholism—or, for our purposes, changing weather patterns—no longer evoke "normal horror reactions." Deserts may grow and houses are rebuilt on higher ground, yet this is accepted as normal. Buying new gadgets and enjoying "Bacardi breezers" help the problem go away. The poet Emily Hinshelwood associates the normalization of destructive habits—"gadgets to plug in the wall that need more electric that burns more coal"—with drinking and pleasure, the reassuring habits of relaxation enjoyed while denying that anything is amiss. This poem is in fact a compilation of comments solicited by the author, who walked across Wales two years ago asking everyone she met a single question: "What images come to mind when you think of climate change?" Her poem "A Moment of Your Time—A Verbatim Poem" reads in part:

> and everyone everywhere with their heads in the sand
> me
> me on a deckchair—with my head in the sand.
> Me—with a bacardi breezer,
> suntanned—with my head in the sand
> while the desert expands.
>
> we know what we're doing—we can't seem to stop
> Society says—Don't think—JUST SHOP!
> So we buy more gadgets to plug in the wall
> that need more electric that burns more coal
> till the last lump of ice falls off the North Pole
> and there's more freak weather
> and London's drowned
> and we knock up more houses on much higher ground.[59]

---

especially salient events are likely to be more vivid, more emotional, and more easily triggered. When addicts return to the sights and sounds of where they typically used, the memory of what they did can literally flood their brains" (Hardcastle, "Life at the Borders," 247).

59. http://emily-hinshelwood.co.uk, shared by George Marshall via the Garrison Institute Climate Mind and Behavior mailing list.

Her poem offers a brief artistic creation that is its own form of unique social research, a testimony to the power of denial, comfort, and our ability to normalize the absurd facilitation of destruction. Somehow, those are choices that make people more comfortable on the level of action.

Carol spoke powerfully to the spiritual freedom that makes true choice possible. For her, that freedom was rooted in a spiritual awareness of living in the present moment, a spirituality she took from the Jewish Torah as well as other spiritual practices such as yoga and meditation.

> *Carol: You have to wake up to this moment. And then we're all enslaved and we have to see who we are as slaves or not slaves and what enslaves us and what it means to be free versus being a slave. And the last question the Torah leaves you with is, "What do you want, what do you choose?" I mean that you have a choice, what do you choose? And when you live that philosophy you are living an engaged spiritual life.*

Congregations support the transformation of conscious values into habits. Religious practices can shape feeling into conscious environmental value when these values are affirmed by oneself or one's community (a process that is discussed further in chapter 3).

Being Overwhelmed

Being overwhelmed. Data overload. Compassion fatigue. Pessimism. Participants knew all of these ideas. Some offered the advice: keep it simple, recognizing that even small changes are not easy. The Unitarian-Universalist group had already achieved so much, and aimed even higher, through small steps. They hoped to encourage all the members to become carbon neutral in their own homes, not just in the sanctuary. How would they do this? Bob noted, "We will, I think, start out with small groups, a couple sizes and gradually expand. Start small, do well and don't try to do too big and fall flat on your face."

Across traditions, participants felt their religious teachings offered insights that helped them overcome pessimism and create new lifestyles. Reforming doctrines was not their concern. Finding moral strength and energy, given the tar baby of pessimism and fatigue, was the real problem. As Carol said, "I think the teachings are adequate. So the inadequacies are not with the teaching; it would be only in our inability to feel empowered enough to act on them." Howard agreed and extended this recognition to social policies that affect the environment as well.

> *Howard: I think the teachings are adequate, just like—I mean there are so many things that we can think of in terms of laws and policies, et cetera, that are adequate. But the real question is how do we in fact carry them out and how do we convince people to carry them out; how do we make things fairly easy to do and with a return that people can see and feel that's important?*

The Hindu participants felt strongly that making the effort to change is up to the individual. Satya explained the difference between karma and effort, "as my teacher says clearly."

> *Satya: Karma only explains the past. Effort explains the future and what the future will be. So, the karma concept is the way things are, is based on the past, which we have no control over. So you reap whatever has happened, an accumulation of previous life, a life before this current life or whatever. But that doesn't say that you cannot put effort; in fact it says that you have to put effort to change that. So that's not an excuse, but that's how it's interpreted. Karma is not an excuse to say you will continue to be the way you're going to be.*

Furthermore, for Satya, this teaching empowered the freedom to make change. "It's very nice though, rather than waste your energies worrying why you are the way you are, put your energy to the way you want to be."

Ultimately, deciding or acting involves more than scientific or ethical literacy. Behavior is neither always rational nor ethical. Among the multiple conflicting currents of the heart's priorities, how did environmental concern gain enough power to drive action?

How did religious environmentalists understand the dynamics of empowerment in their congregations?

The next chapter explores the sustaining power of groups who share environmental values and can inspire their members to choose new behaviors, as well as the ways that groups can reinforce unsustainable social habits as well.

CHAPTER THREE

Finding Strength in Numbers

The Power of Group Energy

The power of group energy coexists with the dangers of group influence—the silent reality of congregational complicity in society's general disengagement with climate change. But let's look at the good news first: part of the secret of the success of faith-based environmentalism is the congregation itself. Jack, an Episcopal priest, was part of a group of Southern Christian leaders, mostly pastors and physicians, who met annually for a faith-centered conference on the health of mind and body. During the focus group I conducted there, Jack cited 1 Corinthians to remind the group that inspiration itself has a communal aim and purpose.

> *Jack (Episcopalian): You know in the United States, we've become such individualists we forget about the community. And the church's blessing of the Holy Spirit was sent upon the community, not the individual.*

The congregation supports the individual who is developing new worldviews and reflecting on spiritual experiences in nature. The congregation also reinforces shared values and leverages individual action through group cooperation that brings ideas and values to life. The congregation is a source of group energy.

Group energy engages the American love of independence in a fascinating synergy of social bonds and independent thinking. I began every focus group with same question: what is your favorite thing about your faith tradition? This question yielded two main responses: the pleasure of being in a friendly community, and the satisfaction of sharing free inquiry. Almost half of all participants volunteered that free inquiry was their favorite thing about their community, equal to those who most appreciated finding a group that shared their values.

While I was not surprised to hear that being part of a family-like community with shared values was a favorite characteristic, I was fascinated to find that free inquiry was equally cherished. There is a common assumption that religious affiliation translates into set ideas.[1] Yet paradoxically, free inquiry in part emerges from community. Understanding begins with questioning, and questioning begins with the freedom to ask. Because the trust in the community enabled free inquiry, committee members were able to examine and develop their attitudes about spirituality and the environment, exploring challenging new ideas productively.[2]

The synergy of freedom and community means that freedom is not sheer individualism. Persons are not defined merely by their separateness as individuals, but by choosing their relationships and communities.

Nor does joining a group mean static conformity to standard beliefs. Groups reinforce shared goals up to a point; people can and do leave groups they do not agree with. In the United States, changing faith communities is one of the most common experiences among those who have belonged to one. As many as half of American adults change religious affiliation once in their lives. As

---

1. Paul A. Djupe and Patrick Kieran Hunt, "Beyond the Lynn White Thesis: Congregational Effects on Environmental Concern," *Journal for the Scientific Study of Religion* 48, no. 4 (2009): 672; Douglas Lee and T. Jean Blocker Eckberg, "Varieties of Religious Involvement and Environmental Concerns: Testing the Lynn White Thesis," *Journal for the Scientific Study of Religion* 28, no. 4 (1989): 510.

2. Group membership does not mean static conformity to standard beliefs. People can and do leave groups they do not agree with. In the United States, as many as half of American adults change religious affiliation once in their lives. See Pew Forum, "Faith in Flux: Changes in Religious Affiliation in the United States," http://www.pewforum.org.

their individual views change, the groups with which they identify may change. Clearly, people choose to join like-minded groups. But joining a like-minded group does not preclude thoughtful reflection in selecting the group. Participants valued the ability to continue to think freely about their beliefs and principles.

How do these communities and persons mutually develop their faith identities? This chapter examines five key effects of group dynamics. First, I show how discussion engages the minds and hearts of members of faith communities by (1) renegotiating worldviews through the creation of new doctrinal syntheses, and (2) integrating experiences in nature with spirituality. Then, building on minds and hearts attuned to climate change, discussion within faith communities further deepens and expands values by (3) reinforcing shared commitments to social justice, and (4) expanding the definition of social justice to embrace creation care. Finally, faith-based environmentalists are further empowered by (5) the unifying power of worship and celebration, and the ability of communal action to leverage the leadership of pioneers.[3]

Renegotiating Worldviews: Creating New Doctrinal Syntheses

The synergy of social bonds and free inquiry enables a renegotiation of religious worldviews toward new doctrinal syntheses that link core faith values and new environmental concerns. Through discussion, unfamiliar scientific ideas can be incorporated into existing worldviews, making space for understanding climate change and inspiring a faith-based moral response.

Social engagement is critical for the evolution of environmental awareness for religious environmentalists who identify with a community, listen to clergy, engage in congregational ministry, or otherwise acknowledge a social integration of their faith. For them, social engagement with the congregation is important in a way that

---

3. Sections of this chapter were previously published as "Come with Me into the Fields: Inspiring Creation Ministry among Faith Communities," *New Theology Review* 26, no. 2 (March 2013): 33-42.

might not be true for those who are "spiritual but not religious." The "spiritual but not religious" person may define her spiritual identity rather more flexibly. While there are certainly diversities of spiritual experience among the members of the same community, members of a faith community share at least some common ideas and values. When new environmental ideas and values clamor for attention, they then work out the evolving significance of those values *within* the group.

Group discussion provided the support to struggle and helped create new syntheses of familiar traditions and new green attitudes. Whether at the coffee hour among congregants generally unaware of new environmental ideas, or at sustainability committee meetings, open conversations introduced new ideas about the earth and incorporated new environmental perspectives into belief systems.

New ideas often disrupted stable worldviews. Just as the radical nature of climate change itself upset basic assumptions about the stability of earth's core systems, so too the disruptions of climate change provoked religious questions about earth's permanence, divine providence, the extent of human responsibility, and the global impact of one's actions. But within safe, supportive groups, members could process these destabilizing new realities in relation to the shared values that brought members together, and work toward new syntheses.

Because committee members treasured the same long-standing values, revising them was not simple. Communally accepted beliefs were influential, whether they reflected religious, political, or family values. Worldviews can be deeply rooted, multilayered, and full of contradictory messages. A simple exhortation to "be green" and heed new doctrines will not adequately address this complexity. Committee members wrestled with the moral implications of the connections they had drawn, and extricated old, anti-environmental beliefs from the emerging matrix of spiritual values and environmental concerns.

One woman commented that a scripture study group galvanized her to reappropriate traditional teachings and uncover pro-environment messages in scripture. In her early life, exploiting the earth had been an implicitly justified reading of scripture. Discussion teased out the environmental reverence in ancient messages.

Pat (Presbyterian): I was raised thinking, okay, it's my earth; you can do whatever you want. I can remember, I'm ashamed to say it, just throwing trash out on the street. I just did it; it was bad, and I learned from it.

Q. Did you feel that was overtly taught to you? You have dominion over the earth and that came as a church message or was it more oblique?

Pat: It was more oblique. But it was there. And so I think rethinking scripture has been enormously helpful to me. We are in progress with this, and I truly mean that because I think a lot of us are looking at the creation and creativity differently.

Pat went on to say, "It's hard. I'm trying desperately to get a little more of a handle on it." But this group process was an important part of critiquing her views. Being part of the group "made [her] go back and look at this," and ultimately revise the dominion ideas she perceived to be obliquely present in her mainstream Christian heritage. Responding that it was more oblique, but there nevertheless, she stated that the process then of examining those oblique but powerful foundations by rethinking scripture was enormously helpful.

Speaking for her group, she also believed it was a process in progress and a journey in which the group was looking at creation and even divine creativity differently. Howard, from the Jewish Reconstructionist Synagogue, also referred to the process of integrating faith and environmental spirituality, noting that "in terms of the relationship that's expressed between people and nature, between people and the environment, so that's an additional piece that I'm aware of in the whole value system that's expressed in Torah and in Judaism. I'm not exactly sure how it's going to wind up translating eventually, but it happens little by little." In this way, committee members wrestled with the moral implications of the connections they had drawn.

Thus for the faith-based environmentalists who felt a coherent worldview required environmental awareness, developing that environmentally conscious faith life entailed the social renegotiation of traditional identity. To maintain a sincere affiliation with their congregation, and affirm the intensely felt moral claim of the environmental crisis, they renegotiated the definition of a green faith identity together. That is the particular passion of the pioneers with whom I spoke. They did not simply carry on with private environmentalism. They were convinced that caring for creation is a necessary mission for their community to engage.

Integrating Experiences in Nature with Spirituality

The power of discussion. Discussion helps to synthesize not only faith and new green attitudes but draws on deep experiential convictions about the value and beauty of nature. New ideas and the power of experiences in nature are sources of green "conversion." Katrina, a member of the Buddhist community, reflected on how the power of nature affected her in a way that couldn't be precisely defined.

> *Katrina (Buddhist): I grew up in Puerto Rico. I spent a lot of time in nature, particularly in the ocean. Since I was a kid I remember saying I felt very at peace there. That definitely had a big impact on my thinking, I don't know how. I just felt it had an impact on me; I can't define exactly which way.*

For many, experiences in nature mediate the sacred and invite communion with God. As Howard, a member of the Jewish Reconstructionist Synagogue, said, "I've always been more in awe of things when I'm out of doors, whether I'm in the desert or whether I'm in the mountains or whether I'm just standing around on a clear night in Grant Park." But often these experiences are not explicitly reinforced in worship or catechesis, whether oriented to the environment or not. The considerable power of spiritual experiences in nature may not be integrated into people's conscious religious identities, connected with their consumption habits, or otherwise invoked to alter behaviors, unless processed by discussion. Reverend Fletcher Harper, executive director of GreenFaith, observes that shared discussion is essential to link the profound spiritual bond with nature to consumption habits or other behaviors.[4] Prayerful reflection allows the religious depths of environmental motivation to unfold, precisely as a spiritual renewal, not as a way to join the secular environmental movement.

Faith-based sustainability committees provided a rare context for sharing spiritual experiences in nature, unfolding the powerful religious depths of motivation latent in their environmental concern. Within her group, Katrina could begin to define the meaning of nature's peacefulness for her. Rima also recognized that her relationship with nature was intuitively spiritual, but she had not been raised to connect her love of nature with religious life.

> *Rima (Muslim): That's where I sought spirituality [in nature], maybe subconsciously, and there is the importance of connecting that to faith and our religion. That connection needs to be there, and I think that's what was lacking when I was growing up.*

Steve, a Catholic outdoorsman, described how his love of nature became not only explicitly connected to his faith but environmentally activist through group engagement. His faith and green spirituality connected through group engagement at his church. He agreed to participate in his church's sustainability committee at the urging of his wife, who was already a member. Before joining the group, his commitment to his faith community remained sealed off from his love of nature. Steve was influenced by his wife to connect his own love of nature with his faith but also credited his active involvement to committee participation.

---

4. Fletcher Harper, "Religion and the Earth on the Ground: The Experience of Greenfaith in New Jersey," in *Ecospirit: Religions and Philosophies for the Earth*, ed. Laurel and Catherine Keller Kearns (New York: Fordham University Press, 2007), 507.

Steve (Catholic): I guess for me it's because of [my wife's] love and interest. She said she wanted to get involved with this committee, and was I interested? I said, "No, I don't think so. I'm not too interested." She said, "Well maybe come and I will come up to meetings and whatever." I would say it's because of this committee and working with the Unitarians. We had a joint meeting and I saw what they were doing. I think that's where my education started. I had read periodically this stuff. I didn't see it as part of being a Catholic, nor did I hear pastors and priests and people all over the place saying it was. I respect you for looking at it that way, because I didn't look at it that way.

For Steve, these two potent sources of motivation and energy were linked through active discussion at the environmental committee meetings he attended. For others, making a connection between the environment and faith allowed a richer version of their faith to emerge. Garret was raised as a Reform Jew but incorporated many Hopi and Navajo elements in his adult spirituality as an Arizona resident and activist. He observed that environmental concerns "liberated me to find a form of Judaism with which I could resonate. It is a Judaism that recognizes the importance of land, "the whole earth is full of His glory" kind of thinking." In his view, that rich view was indeed traditional to the Hebrew scriptures but "not fundamental to the ethical Judaism in which I grew up."

Finally, in the case of the Native Americans with whom I spoke, that connection between environment and faith was clearly integral to their worldview from ancient times. The trouble was hanging on to the implications of it when their land use is contested. Shonto explained the frustration of being in a constant state of struggle with the Forest Service about a ski resort. "How can we make them understand that we're not out to just close deals with them but want to block making artificial snow [from waste water] on the sacred mountain? I think they expect us to be up there holding some sort of powwow, holding some sort of a vigil, having some sort of a temple up there. We're not up there because the mountain itself is a temple."

Religious reverence vs. a "secular" love of nature? Is there a distinctly religious origin or dimension to these experiences in nature? Most environmentalists, secular and faith-based, affirm the power and beauty of nature, often in language full of sacred and numinous imagery.

Green spirituality could also be viewed as a secondary justification of preexisting environmental concern. Faith-based environmentalists love the earth; they come to worship. Is the process like a recipe: start with faith, add nature and stir? In that case, religious beliefs would be a superstructure, a doctrinal gloss that is functionally irrelevant in terms of motivation. The focus group evidence is not decisive on this point. Participants spoke to the fundamental influence of both their experiences in nature and religious teachings about nature. Recall that Rima expressed her unconscious resonance with nature that was intuitively spiritual but not explicitly connected to religious terms. On the other hand, Sarah clearly attributed her religious attitude toward creation to teachings in the Christian scriptures.

> *Sarah (evangelical Christian): My identity as a Christian is so connected with creation care and helping the poor but I don't know if I would be that way if I wasn't Christian. As an individual I've always been so much more rational, logical, and pragmatic and not necessarily that caring. If I wasn't a Christian I'd probably just say, we're just human beings, we're just animals, we just need to make the best of it while we're here. And it was really searching through scripture that led me to the care that I have for creation.*

Experiences in nature were thus not acknowledged to be decisive for Sarah. But another young evangelical woman did speak strongly to meeting God in nature, in a way that blended with her evangelical desire to share her faith. "I work with natural resources and being in nature is one place where I'm closest to God and it's a very strong connection, so if I can work with others who care deeply about saving our resources I can also share my faith with them."

Again, the dual authority of scripture and science for evangelicals discussed in chapter 1 complicates a simplistic attribution of environmental concern to either source. Indeed, for any person, spiritual self-interpretation is often inseparable from experience itself. A given interpretive frame for receiving impressions (such as viewing nature as "creation") may be logically but not existentially split from the core awareness of self in the world. Love of nature, reverence for creation, green spirituality: these do not come from a recipe that can be analyzed but are the fusion of a lifetime of experiences.

Beyond fellowship . . . Whatever the first spark of environmental spirituality may be, it is true that religious members of secular environmental groups (like the Sierra Club) are more likely to consider environmental issues important than their coreligionists who are not Sierra Club members. However, congregational discussion adds to motivation beyond the effect of previous environmental affiliation. Sociologists have found that "church effects are found amid strong personal predispositions and secular sources of information . . . the effects due to the congregational context are real and not proxies for preexisting attitudes and affiliations."[5] That is, raising environmental concerns in a community has an additional impact on its members who are already active in environmental groups.

Clearly, group support, sharing ideas, and leadership help any group flourish. Congregations are not distinct in this regard.[6] Carl Pope, the longtime president of the Sierra Club, agreed that community support and community wisdom are essential. In a talk lauded by some Sierra Club members and excoriated by others, Pope apologized for the "profound error" of environmentalists who

---

5. Djupe and Hunt, "Beyond the Lynn White Thesis," 680. See also Dana R. Fisher and Marije Boekkooi, "Mobilizing Friends and Strangers: Understanding the Role of the Internet in Days of Action," *Information, Communication & Society* 13, no. 2 (2010): 200, for more analysis on the social reinforcement of activism.

6. I acknowledge the limitation in this study which does not explicitly compare faith-based and secular environmentalists, and my indebtedness to David Krantz for urging this comparison, which is indeed significant. Future studies may address this lacuna.

cut off engagement with faith institutions.[7] He felt they uncritically accepted White's diagnosis of thoroughgoing religious anthropocentrism and misunderstood "the mission of religion and the churches in preserving the Creation." He argued further that faith groups benefit from the power of social support.

> But the Sierra Club, while not a church, must be church-like, because only such a community can provide individuals with the *fellowship* they need to go out into the world and battle with hubris and mammon, and commit their souls and their lives to a cause whose realization is indefinite and uncertain at best (*emphasis added*).

Pope thus described fellowship as necessary to sustain "morally driven" organizations like the Sierra Club.

The significance of "fellowship" and other social dynamics raises again the question of whether religious environmentalists are just environmentalists with faith. Both religious activists and social scientists say no. Religious concern for the earth contains a distinct, transcendental element. Paul Gorman, a cofounder of the National Religious Partnership for the Environment, stated that the organization was not "the environmental movement at prayer." Nor was their work "about providing more shock troops for the embattled American greens. We have to see the inescapable, thrilling, renewing religious dimension of this challenge."[8]

In other words, fellowship is not the only thing faith communities provide. According to the participants, religious concern for the earth expresses characteristic moral insights and contains a distinct, transcendental element.

Moral insights. A group of young Muslim urban designers, environmental lawyers, and sustainability policy advocates perhaps articulated the transcendental element beyond fellowship and

---

7. Carl Pope, Address to the Sierra Club, November 10, 1997; http://www.christianecology.org.

8. Bill McKibben, "The Gospel of Green: Will Evangelicals Help Save the Earth?," *OnEarth* 3 (Fall 2006): 36.

group support best. They did seek to differentiate their religious views from the approach taken in conference rooms during the workday. In other words, they felt it important to articulate the difference between Carl Pope's call to be "morally driven" and Paul Gorman's reference to the "thrilling, renewing religious dimension of this challenge." Like the Baltimore Presbytery committee, they struggled with finding the right ways to articulate their spiritual commitments to the environment. They recognized that words like "religious," and "sacrifice" limited productive conversation with secular environmental professionals. Yet there was a strong desire to affirm the inescapably spiritual dimension of their advocacy. In fact, for Mohamad, "You can not NOT have that at the table. Policy needs to happen, community organizing is happening, but I think you can add one more piece—this is in part a values issue, a moral issue."

For Mohamad and Rima, that spiritual dimension meant profound moral insights. Mohamad pointed to the insights about happiness, poverty, and consumption found in traditional teaching, wisdom that was ancient but very relevant.

> *Mohamad (Muslim): Another part of our tradition is a hadith from the Prophet on this: beware of greed because it's instant poverty. And anytime you start talking about happiness and this internal state, for me I wanted environmentalists and economists and policymakers in the room to understand that religion has spoken about this for people since time immemorial.*

Such teachings offered greater insight into the psychological depth of greed and lack, need and fulfillment, that play into satisfaction as much as simple quantities of "stuff."[9]

Identifying this distinct element of religious motivation does not imply in any way a lesser ethical commitment among secular environmentalists. Rather, the difference is the larger religious frame,

---

9. Tim Jackson, *Prosperity without Growth?* (London: Sustainable Development Commission, 2009).

the worldview of the participants. Their moral insights about consumerism were held in a larger religious frame linking consumerism and social justice, linking concern for the environment to reverence for creation, and linking social justice to religious views on human dignity. Thus care for creation, once awakened by discussion and synthesized into new worldviews, drew on multiple motivations and inspirations: the "transcendental" energy of groups. For his community, this is what Jack would call the gift of the Spirit: a home for new environmental ideas nested in faith.

Reinforcing Shared Values

If social engagement helps birth new green worldviews and values, that same engagement can also reinforce the new values in ways that leverage cooperation and action. The social affiliations and group identity fostered by the congregation reinforce the nest of interwoven ideas about the world, responsibility, God, nature, others, pollution, etc.

First, social engagement reinforces shared values by linking personal motivations to relationships with other members. Given that people naturally tend to join groups based on their values, social relationships make it easier for people to identify with values about the earth that have surfaced during discussion, to commit to advocacy, and even undertake sacrificial actions. In other words, group dynamics naturally intensified people's commitment to the explicitly shared values of the group.

These group dynamics can be understood through the concept of a "social goal." David Krantz, a leading researcher on environmental decisions at the Center for Research on Environmental Decisions at Columbia University, defines a social goal as either "a goal to affiliate with a group or a goal that is a consequence of an affiliation."[10] Affiliations may exist with groups of any size, from a

---

10. Social goals theory explains why congregations are effective incubators for community transformation. See David H. Krantz, Nicole Peterson, Pooman Arora, Kerry Milch, and Ben Orlove, "Individual Values and Social Goals in Environmental Decision Making," in *Decision Modeling*

relationship with one other person to an abstract identity as "good citizen." When acting within a group context, individuals are more aware of shared social goals and group support for shared values. Group identity thus tends to reinforce group decision making that reflects those goals.

Second, social goals make cooperation more valuable to the individual. People report feeling good about cooperating with others. Their shared values and social goals are common assets that motivate cooperation. Group norms take on a greater importance to individuals, and individuals feel greater rewards when group goals are met.[11] Working as a group also promotes a willingness to choose delayed benefits and enables sacrificial decision making.

Cooperation is likely to be particularly high among faith-based environmentalists who meet as a group, rather than those who read the latest article about ecospirituality at home by themselves, because past collaborations and shared experiences build trust and cooperation.[12] In fact, the very process of sharing ideas inspires others to try to make changes themselves. Engaging in discussion increases the energy for seeking solutions. Their shared values and group identity sustain cooperation against our culture of multitasking and distraction.[13] This process counteracts the "single-action bias." Affirming shared social goals makes it easier to act on one's

---

and Behavior in Uncertain and Complex Environments, ed. T. Kugler, J. C. Smith, T. Connolly, and Y.-S. Son (New York: Springer, 2008): 167.

11. Center for Research on Environmental Decisions (CRED), *The Psychology of Climate Change Communication: A Guide for Scientists, Journalists, Educators, Political Aides, and the Interested Public* (New York, 2009), 31; http://guide.cred.columbia.edu.

12. Groups with some prior assumptions are more likely to cooperate and make decisions reflecting group values than individuals or groups put together without social cohesion. See Krantz et al, "Individual Values and Social Goals," 186.

13. Group meetings increase affiliation, and "affiliation made social goals (e.g. the concern for others) a greater priority; and the added benefit of cooperation more than made up for the sacrifice." See Ganna Pogrebna, David Krantz, Christian Schade, and Claudia Keser, "Pre-Game Communication in Social Dilemma Situations," *Social Science Research Network* (2008): 31; http://ssrn.com.

values, and fight the drag of the action gap: decision avoidance, distraction, and busyness.

Furthermore, because smaller groups create stronger affiliations, they also create greater cooperation. For example, the bonds within a congregation where people are well known tend to be stronger than those in nationwide political parties. Smaller bonds matter: studies show that people's tendency to cooperate with group goals may relate more to a stronger sense of group affiliation than to an altruistic personality.

People also cooperate in challenging ways—for example, agree to willingly restrain their consumption—because group membership reminds them of aims beyond economic concerns. [14] In a congregation, for example, people seek worship, friendship, meaning, a place to share values and sustain ideals, and express their concern for others through service. People look for opportunities to make a mark on their community. Given the multiple relationships that people form within different groups, and the roles and aspirations they have within the group, relationships within the group result in multiple rewards of belonging and contributing to a larger cause.

This relates precisely to the ability of groups to promote sacrificial actions and to think of others. Social relationships have the essential ability to cut through the "tragedy of the commons." Goals become communal, and relationships within a group lift individualistic decisions out of a self-serving economy into a communal exchange with multiple rewards.

---

14. "Recognizing a variety of context-dependent goals leads naturally to consideration of decision rules other than utility maximization, both in descriptive and in prescriptive analysis. Although these considerations about social goals and decision rules apply in most decision-making domains, they are particularly important for environmental decision making, because environmental problems typically involve many players, each with multiple economic, environmental, and social goals, and because examples abound where the players fail to attain the widespread cooperation that would benefit everyone (compared to widespread non-cooperation)" (Krantz et al., "Individual Values and Social Goals," 165-66). These multiple goals serve to overcome the tragedy of the commons, as the "commons dilemma" transforms from a simple self-serving economy.

There is a third dynamic related to reinforcing and enlarging shared values: how being part of a network of larger groups can expand the group's horizons.

Leadership at the local level provided necessary validation as well, confirming that the group was expressing authentic values of the congregation. Madeleine's church's leadership ended up agreeing that they supported the principles of the sustainability committee. "That's all we were doing: supporting those principles. But that's really important." At the national level, organizational support (such as provided by the Unitarian-Universalist Green Sanctuary program or the nonprofit organization GreenFaith) supported cooperation and stretched a group's aims. As Nancy said, having a model made them "think a little harder ... what could you do now?" Structures from the national level also provided validity.

Lynn: And it really helps to have that leadership with the national level for validity; I think it, they have the resources, we know that we're not alone. You can feel kind of lonely sometimes, if you're trying to make a difference all by yourself.

Lynn spoke to the benefit that in a community, individual actions can multiply and engage others, spread and catalyze changes in other aspects of congregation mission. The community creates a multiplier effect that transfers ideas and leverages leadership.

I've noted before that faith-based environmentalists tend to work in interfaith coalitions. Their familiarity with multiple worldviews, a sense of ontological and spiritual interdependence, practical interfaith collaboration, shared wisdoms and teachings all underscore the planetary links. Connecting to multiple identities makes it possible to empathize with those suffering from the ravages of environmental destruction.[15]

The possibility for group affiliations are wide indeed, going beyond congregational, denominational, and national links. The ultimate group may in fact be cosmic. Ved, a member of the Jain group, spoke with feeling about how the birth of a new baby

---

15. CRED, *The Psychology of Climate Change Communication*, 31.

reminded his community that they are part of the cosmos, relating to the position of the stars. "'Dharma' itself means a way of life, a tradition, or belief system, that is to live a life in consonance, in harmony with nature and the universe. The universe! When a child is born, we say, which stars are where in the universe?" This view may be characteristically Eastern, but most religious communities tend to emphasize concern for the other, identify their core identity in common origin from a creator, and recognize cosmic relationships that transcend more narrow groups.

Social Norms Give Values Traction

Congregations explicitly encourage ethical reflection and moral action as one of their main functions. Through the process sociologists call "normative diffusion," members observe others' behavioral cues while developing their own opinions.[16] Values spread in congregations, given the members' social affiliations and similar outlooks. As a result, sustainable ideals within worldviews take on new importance and meaning. The example of consumerism will illustrate how values are redefined through social channels, and more significantly, take on the traction to lead to real action.

Choices about behaviors and actions related to the environment, like many other choices, are made either by groups or by individuals within and influenced by a group. In the United States, consumer society has enormous power to define the goals of the individual and the aims that translate into social acceptance and approval.

Naresh (Jain): It is the value society places to that thing. Having a bigger or better car is, O man, you are doing good! So once saving the environment also gets into the value system, probably then we will do it.

Like Naresh, Ralph recognized that social consensus has the power to shape values, whether or not the value was a "truth" or not. Ralph observed that "we do create our values collectively and we can mold them. The way out, our salvation if you will, is to

---

16. Djupe and Hunt, "Beyond the Lynn White Thesis," 672.

mold them in ways that are useful. I don't have any faith that the truth is going to do anything." For Ralph, this meant that collectively held values were determinative *because* of their social influence, not necessarily because of their instrinsic merit.

The positive side of this possibly cynical view is that prosocial nudges are possible. An entire literature on "choice architecture" recognizes this. As Sabine Marx of CRED commented, referring to the popular book about structuring choices to encourage preferred behaviors, nudges work![17] In a small setting, being part of a group makes it very hard to backtrack on one's commitments.

Social goals that go beyond economic self-interest support nonconsumerist values and social justice values. These are precisely the values that are needed from faith communities to offset the dominant power of consumerism in the larger culture.

New religious norms helped counteract the "background values" of consumption, convenience, and endless distraction, all challenges strongly identified by research participants as barriers to making sustainable choices. Tim was the pastor of a church that had run a reduced-driving campaign. Then, he bought an SUV because his car couldn't handle certain hauling trips. The irony and presupposed hypocrisy of buying an SUV created more cognitive dissonance than *he* could handle. He had had a Jesus fish symbol on his previous car, but as he couldn't stomach putting it on the SUV; the Jesus fish ended up on his bicycle.

Worship and Celebration

Worship and other celebrations of the beauty and abundance of God's creation help transcend the sometimes contentious aspects of environmental conversation. Because group experiences of worship and celebration inscribed care for creation within ancient traditions, worship smoothed the way to accepting new ideas. The

---

17. Appealing to social goals can promote cooperation, as do appropriate "nudges"; see Richard H. Thaler and Cass Sunstein, *Nudge: Improving Decisions about Health, Wealth, and Happiness* (New Haven: Yale University Press, 2008).

creation-centered themes within familiar texts, hymns, and rituals are traditional resources that easily bring forth new environmental resonances. Worship was also a site of creative and inclusive celebration of the interfaith collaboration so central to faith-based environmentalism. At one Episcopal service I attended, an upcoming festival at a local Hindu temple was announced so that persons collaborating with them in environmental projects could attend. These interfaith collaborations reinforce the globally shared commitments to religious concern for the earth.

Worship has a unifying and communal authority that transcends the divisive taint of politics or wary mistrust of that global-warming science. As one woman put it, "On Creation Sunday we're reading something that's familiar to them that they know is not something we made up—the scriptures."

Tom, a member of the Baltimore Presbyterian leadership team, emphasized that things are most successful when they contain an element of celebration.

> *Tom: I think when it doesn't work so well is when it's done out of a sense of duty or obligation or "got to change those light bulbs." But when we have Earth Day celebration in our church, that's when we are going best because we have a service that's full of celebration, and interest, and excitement, and then we have some sort of project after that where we go out and get our hands dirty. In that sort of setting it seems to flow.*

The power of worship to ground environmental concern in traditional symbols is essential. Faith leaders can make creation care a moral issue, one that is permissible for churches to pursue. When framed as a moral issue, environmental concerns gain power despite the predisposing influence of political worldviews.

The Silent Side of Groups: Congregational Complicity in Society

Religious congregations—at their best—are experiments in increasing caring and action. There is much reason to place hope in our religious institutions—their numbers, their energy, and their traditional moral influence. But, the faith community's capacity for widespread impact has been questioned. Robert Booth Fowler tallies the critiques:

> Those who affirm the church as a significant agent for change . . . insist that small changes add up and that each act helps transform people's consciousness . . . [and] can make a difference . . . in ecological transformation. . . . Yet there are reasons to doubt these expectations. Such beliefs assume that churches have (or can have) much impact on their members' consciousness; they assume that Protestant churches can really mobilize on environmental issues and form a united front on what to do about them; about all, they assume that Protestantism at the end of this century in the United States still has a powerful enough vision to transform the culture in a serious way. Each assumption is debatable today, and each requires the kind of supporting argument that is only rarely offered.[18]

One may accurately substitute religions in general for Protestantism above. The moral influence of congregations cannot be assumed, even in areas of traditional ethical teachings. The moral status of ecological action is even less obvious to both congregants and clergy.

For clergy, the environment is not standard seminary fare. The problem of clergy preparedness has solutions, because excellent initiatives for professional development in environmental ministry exist.[19] Still, environmental issues are new to most clergy, and the complex grounding of environmental ethics in global socioeconomic

---

18. Robert Booth Fowler, *The Greening of Protestant Thought* (Chapel Hill: University of North Carolina Press, 1995), 164.

19. The work of the GreenFaith Fellowship Program and The Green Seminary Initiative are prime examples. See GreenFaith: Interfaith Partners for the Environment, "The GreenFaith Fellowship Program," http://green faith. org; and The Green Seminary Initiative, "Education and Syllabus Project," http://www.greenseminaries.org.

interactions go beyond the personal, sexual, and community ethics of traditional morality. And as Susan points out, traditional morality is often aligned with the status quo of a "bigger is better" country.

Susan: At least in this country, at least until fairly recently, the church has been immersed in some really complex ways with this culture. This was considered a Christian country. And there's a real domino effect because the church and its members have also bought into the culture. And the bottom line is, independence, and bigger is better, and entrepreneurism, have been identified with this country.

Thus, despite the hope that religious groups will be strong moral leaders for environmental advocacy, in reality, congregations are often as complicit with power structures that distort their missions as is any other organization in society. And because congregations explicitly claim to be centers of moral teaching, their failures to confront denial and be open to examining issues that might have moral relevance are more hypocritical than the greenhouse gas denial of an avowedly profit-oriented corporation.

Furthermore, congregations have their own reasons for complicity with society's environmental inertia, including both institutional and theological reasons. Four major issues converge in the perfect storm of congregational and societal inertia: (1) the framing and reduction of environmental questions to the level of politics; (2) the divisiveness of environmental politics; (3) the ability of political issues to trump doctrine; and (4) pastoral priorities that take precedence over new and unfamiliar environmental questions.

The Risk of Political Framing

Reducing environmental concerns to political issues is extremely risky. If environmental concerns were framed as a political issue, an ugly political taint could block congregational advocacy. This was not only because politically framed issues are divisive, but because political issues seem intrinsically less credible. Despite the influential nature of political worldviews, political issues lacked credibility by taint of association with politicians who, in the words of one woman, "play both sides of the table." Carol revealed her view of the problem with politicians by contrasting them to Jesus. She stated, "I don't think Jesus operated like a politician. They play both sides of the table." Likewise, scriptures are common authority while environmental issues might be "made up." Creation Sunday was effective because "we're reading something that's familiar to them that they know is not something we made up: the scriptures."

Joel Hunter also affirmed the corrosive power of conflicts based on the political culture wars between left and right. He noted that "we have had people in this church, many of them have left now, that linked the environmental cause not with the care of creation but with some sort of leftist agenda that was devising some great hoax so that they could gain power and take over our lives. Very conspiratorial." Similarly, Tim, a progressive Baptist pastor, related the attitude of his father, a retired Baptist minister, who viewed environmental concerns as part of a politically driven agenda, a piece of liberal propaganda intended to create fear (and presumably support for liberal policies). As Tim saw it, his father interpreted environmental concern as a "theological stance," a statement of belief. He said, "My father feels very justified in poking fun at the whole environment crisis thing. He sees it as kind of a theological stance, that these liberal folks are telling you is a lie because they want to make you afraid of whatever they think . . . I don't know what exactly."

Hunter attributed this divide in his community to the historic separation between the branch of the evangelical church that emphasized pietistic individualism and the groups that followed the social gospel movement. Anthony Leiserowitz observes that "the traditionalist–modernist gap on environmental policy is just one piece of a much greater divide over public policy priorities. Generally, traditionalists give greater weight to cultural issues like abortion and gay marriage; modernists tend to focus more on economic and social welfare issues, such as government programs to help the poor."[20]

---

20. Anthony Leiserowitz, "Climate Change Risk Perception and Policy Preferences: The Role of Affect, Imagery, and Values," *Climatic Change* 77 (2006): 48.

For all American faith-based environmentalists, whatever their tradition, the fundamental spiritual and moral meaning of their work can be lost when the culture wars set the terms of the environmental movement. But, as another leader said, "Once it's a moral issue, then it's okay for churches to do it." Monica from the Reformed group hoped that as the evidence has become overwhelming, the political risk would lessen.

> *Monica: It's undeniable that the earth is failing fast. It's more politically embraced on all parts of the spectrum and therefore it's safer for churches to talk about this and not feel like they are trying to come down one way or another on politics.*

Carol identified the association of environmental causes with politics as a minefield as well. "I think you're asking about when it comes to getting commitment. ... And I think we have issues. With the question of faith, it really matters to people when it seems to be political." As she talked, she felt more sure about the problem with politics. "That's where I think we have an issue. When it seems to be political." She sensed that people strongly resisted being urged to consider the environment if it seemed to be motivated by political leanings. Such urgings came across as an unjustified imposition of one person's personal inclination over against another's. But the shared commitments of faith created a bridge. These shared commitments were highlighted and celebrated in worship. "I think it's easier with worship to get people to come because most of us deep in our heart . . ." My question had been: has it been hard or easy to find reasons in your faith to support or extend what you're doing? And for Carol, when the group reached deep into their hearts for what their faith truly supported, they could find reasons to encourage care for creation. But if the discussion sheared off into the divisive and intrinsically particular trajectories of politics, the cause was lost.

The Divisiveness of Environmental Politics

Framing environmental issues as political fails because politics are so divisive. While the strong social affiliations of congregations are a source of strength and cooperation, the downside of such affiliations is the reluctance to challenge them. All members within a congregation can be reluctant to transgress these groups: individual lay members, committee heads, clergy avoiding hot political issues and declining to "legislate from the pulpit."

The elephant in the room (or the synagogue study or the church hall) when talking about the environment is political affiliation. Researchers recognize that environmental attitudes correlate strongly with political affiliation. Significant relationships between religiosity and environmentalism diminish once demographic variables and political orientations are controlled. In plain language, politics more likely determines a person's environmental attitudes than does faith or attentiveness to a preacher.

I heard this expressed by one of the few conservative voices in the focus groups. The very fact that there were few conservative voices among the sustainability committee members is simple confirmation of the common association of politics with environmental attitudes. Beth, a Presbyterian woman raised Pentecostal, participated in a focus group though not a sustainability committee member. She acknowledged that she didn't think global warming was real. She explained that this was because "perhaps I am a moderate, probably, Republican, who leans to the right, and I see global warming as an ideology of the more liberal people." At the same time, she admitted she didn't really have a reason to identify global warming as an ideological position not worthy of concern, by saying, "Well, truthfully, I don't really have a position on why I'm not [concerned about global warming]. I'm just not."

Beth thus points to the ways Americans are perceived to fall into conservative and liberal camps, with diverging interests in the environment. These camps have been analyzed as representing "six Americas" by sociological researchers.[21] According to a poll on politics and global warming conducted in the spring of 2014,

---

21. Yale Project on Climate Change Communication and George Mason University, "Global Warming's Six Americas in 2012," http://environment.yale.edu. See also Dan Kahan, "Fixing the Communications Failure," *Nature* 463 (2010): 296–97; http://www.nature.com.

"a large majority of Democrats (69 percent, and 75 percent of liberal Democrats) and nearly half (47 percent) of liberal and moderate Republicans, but only 22 percent of conservative Republicans, think global warming is mostly human-caused."[22]

The correlation of environmental attitudes with political affiliation is risky for advocates because political views are divisive, and congregations can be fragile communities vulnerable to these divisions in extremely sensitive ways.

Donors. The divisiveness of political views is especially risky if environmental advocacy alienates significant donors. Chris, a minister's wife, was familiar with such insider dynamics. She noted that there were some very wealthy people "who were involved in supporting churches who make their living not being environmentally friendly. They're of the big industries that don't do that." In response, clergy feared to alienate wealthy donors.

> *Chris (Episcopalian): And then people are afraid to . . . Well, let's say you have a big contributor who happens to be from an oil company or a head honcho or something like that. The people in the church are certainly going to defer to that person, other members of the congregation may defer to that.*

Economically, the defection of five families can destabilize a small and precariously financed congregation. Influential leaders and donors might resist a message of environmental stewardship, and clergy may naturally fear to alienate them. I asked Dr. Hunter about this.

> *Q: Speaking of leadership and boldness in taking a stance, I find it is often very hard for church leaders to do.*
>
> *Dr. Hunter: Do you know why that is?*
>
> *Q. I'd like to know.*
>
> *Dr. Hunter: Because it's the only job that we've been trained for, you know. Many pastors are very sincere people, they*

---

22. Yale Project on Climate Change Communication and George Mason University, "Politics and Global Warming Spring 2014," http://environment. yale.edu.

got in because they wanted to do good; they wanted to shep-
herd their people, but they're very insecure. And if they lose
their job, they've got to put on a hat and say do you want fries
with that?

This kind of job insecurity does explain the ambivalence of a pastor to prioritize in practice what all those official statements from the national polity confirm as essential environmental values. These cross-pulling tensions threaten to undermine the perhaps fragile unity of a congregation.

If leading a strong environmental initiative was too risky for the pastor, the pastor might choose to be the backseat cheerleader, giving permission but not official fanfare. Madeleine raised the issue with her pastor and concluded the message was: evangelize them yourself.

Madeleine: When I have gone and asked about certain issues
and wondered when we would hear thunder from the pul-
pit, there is an encouragement there to just sort of evangelize
your own issue yourself. I am a chair of a committee, so you
can do this yourself. There is a concern to just sort of back
away from the political.

Environmental questions played into financial decisions in other ways besides efforts to maintain the goodwill of donors. The fact is that financial concerns animated many discussions. As a faith-based sustainability consultant said to me, it's amazing how budget issues simplify complex theological questions. When being green pays, economic motivation has a strong voice. Seth, the pastor of a Reformed congregation, used this to his advantage. "I remember including the money word for a couple of folks in the consistory who are going to have to hear that!" For David, some environmental choices were becoming more about cost saving than altruism.

David: The flat-up reality is that oil we're pouring into the
ground out there to heat this place is now $4.25—when it
was 25 cents, we could be more involved in the altruism of
saving it. But now it's cold, hard economics, which happen to
be good for the environment reasons.

Political Issues Trump Doctrine

Furthermore, political views are not easily changed and are often capable of trumping religious teaching. One member of a focus group recalled hearing a fellow church member with traditionally conservative views tell him, "I don't want to be legislated from the pulpit. Don't tell me how to live."

Interestingly, even official statements failed to galvanize a conversion to sustainability, though they prevented unconvinced congregants from claiming that sustainability was irrelevant to faith. For example, after a New Jersey Catholic committee placed notices in the bulletin about climate change, Marie and her committee received an anonymous letter charging that this information did not belong in a Catholic bulletin. In fact, Catholic popes and bishops have written extensively on ecological responsibility as a moral mandate, and the committee shared those statements. But sharing these official teachings did not automatically influence behavior in their parish. For Steve, such teachings merely made people quiet, not convinced.

> *Marie (Catholic): Fortunately, we had a copy of the U.S. Catholic Bishops' "Renewing the Earth" statement, and we put together a statement for the bulletin about why we should, in fact, be doing environmental work, and how the bishops said this is part of our mission, as Catholics, as Christians. We have not heard anything more. Every time ... for example, at our last program, we constantly mentioned that paper, and before that paper came out John Paul II wrote a paper. So we tried to let people know that this in fact is something we ought to be working at, and not something foreign.*

> *Steve: That was more a way of getting them to not be against it, rather than being for it. Because then they couldn't say, "You shouldn't be doing this." Because the bishops said you should. So then they're just quiet. Then you've got to get them to the point of being involved. But we did give away tomato plants.*

The sad truth is that after political views, tomato plants may be more convincing than teachings. Or maybe this is good news: tomato plants are often easier to share than teachings.

For Beth, a traditional social conservative, self-reliance and individual responsibility were among her key values. Government entitlements and large-scale government interventions were not. Thus, even when she chose to do something to support the sustainability values in her church, she chose a project that appealed to her: helping the small business owner by volunteering with the fair-trade coffee table at church.

> Beth: I wanted to do something for the church. I wanted to give my time in doing something, so I had to find something that I believed in that spoke to my values. And it was help the small farmer who is helping himself by selling the coffee. He is not standing there with his hand out, saying (I get a little political here), "My mother and father were on welfare. I want you to hand me my welfare check, too." Because he is helping himself.

She was eager to support charitable practices that affirmed these values, and the fair-trade coffee ministry that supported the working farmer was a sympathetic cause for her. But initially appeals to make sustainable changes in her own life seemed to her to issue from bias, politics, and an ideological agenda that manipulates inconclusive evidence.

Despite the potent tinge of distrust that accompanied political associations with environmental messages, discussions in a faith-based context enabled persons to forge new links between pre-existing political and social values, including assumptions about the environment, and their religious convictions and obligations. Sharing common beliefs enabled persons in the group to risk addressing virtually taboo topics about climate change and developing new views.

The humor and warmth between friends, as well as the leaders' personal invitation, enabled Beth to attend the discussion, maintain her own perspective, and still share in the conversation. In recounting why she was there, Beth said, "I'm here because [the leaders] asked me to be here. I said, 'But you know I'm not a global warming proponent.' And they said, 'That's okay. Come along. We haven't abused you about anything for a while.'" Beth continued the good-natured exchange by adding, "I know that you're going to make a very good presentation and it's probably going to sound good and I'm probably going to believe a lot of it," to general laughter. Because of the way the Earth Corps at her church emphasized worship and celebration, Beth was able to support some environmental initiatives in her own way.

Pastoral Priorities

What are clergy supposed to do?

Ironically, the "bully pulpit" of the clergy makes them effective and necessary leaders, but most ministers are greatly overworked and often feel they don't have the time to lead in new directions. Many congregations faced what Pat from the Baltimore Presbytery called the "distraction of ordination issues," including time-absorbing debates about women's ordination and ordination of gay and lesbian candidates. In her view at least, these ordination issues "sidelined" the mainline denominations, as "a lot of the energy and passion has gone into that." A survey of Presbyterian pastors in Baltimore that Pat's committee conducted found that none had the time or personnel to initiate a program or educate a committee, despite expressed concern for the environment.

When I asked a pesticide awareness organizer in rural Washington what the church did regarding pesticide and health concerns, the response was bitter.

> *Jorge: The first thing [the bishop] said was, we don't have money. We were not there to ask him for money, just his support, and his comments on this pesticide awareness project. After that we went to ask the priests if they have time, the priests they don't have time. I don't know if it's because they're not prepared, they don't get a kind of training or education do to that because their job is to impart the sacraments or to ... I guess that's the business of the church.*

Q: So they're not comfortable with the farm issues, with the workers' issues.

Jorge: They know that there are some problems there, but they don't get involved because I think some of the rich people that support the church, they're going to get upset ... we didn't get a lot of help except from one, he's really good priest.

Jorge was not convinced that the business of the church didn't include workers' welfare, nor that church priorities should be narrowly construed as sacramental ministry. His conclusion that "rich people" would get upset shows how he assessed the priorities of the priest—to maintain the good will of important donors among the landowners. Even more cynically, Jorge pointed to the pamphlets on Catholic social teaching that lay on a table in the church, describing the long-standing support of workers' rights within this tradition.

Jorge: We were in Mass and we found this. These are the principles of social justice, Catholic social justice, but this is in Spanish? Do we have it in English in every single church? We don't have it in English. See, in Spanish, the dignity and the right of the workers, it is talking about the dignity and the right of the workers, but this is in Spanish. But what is the message for the growers? They are coming to Mass, but we don't tell them, because it's in Spanish, describing the personal dignity, the community and participation, the right and duties, the option of the poor.

The influence of powerful landowners to redirect church concern away from workers' issues was evident to Jorge. Another migrant worker advocate, Tito, made an even more damning connection between ecclesial power, economic power, and the implication that piety amounts to submission to these powers. He pointed out that among devoted Catholic migrant workers, the *patron* meant not only the boss, but also the saints. The church taught people to pray, to recognize authority, not to be activist or confrontational.

Other risks for clergy went beyond donor defection to charges of heresy. Rowan Williams, the former Archbishop of Canterbury and a leading advocate for environmental care, noted that historically, the churches focused their concern less on the natural world than on human poverty. Indeed, caring for nature was too often uncomfortably close to heresy, a "pagan" devotion to nature. Annie discussed how the dangerous label "tree hugger" could devastate environmental initiatives.

> *Annie: Tree huggers ... they were different, and I don't think they were accepted into the average church. It was new age, it was labeled, and we're famous for labeling things that make us uncomfortable. I think the church was so caught up in the charismatic issues of salvation and those kinds of things, and they saw no connection between the creating God and the sustaining God. And I think it all had to do with our lack of acceptance. I felt that in my Methodist church.*

But, as Rowan Williams also states, that narrow view of concern for nature is starting to change. People are willing to complain and reject the tree-hugger label. But the potent association of orthodoxy, piety, and power simply offers more explanations for the power of the clergy, who traditionally define doctrine for their local congregations and recognize what is "faithful" behavior.

I emphasize that the role of clergy is beyond the scope of this book, which focuses on the work of lay environmentalists. But the significance of clergy leadership and recalcitrance clearly affects lay effectiveness and requires some mention. The importance of worship necessarily derives from the authority of the clergy. Furthermore, clergy indisputably have the power of the pulpit. Though often the laity evangelized the clergy by first bringing environmental concerns to their attention, most participants affirmed the indispensable role of priests, pastors, rabbis, sensei, and imams.

Clergy have the unique ability to affirm, inspire, and, more to the point, legitimate an environmental ministry. Raymond, a leader in a megachurch evangelical Creation Care committee, affirmed that it was critical to have "the senior pastor at the top who is absolutely in favor of this saying we need to charge on this." Raymond felt the grassroots effort wouldn't take hold otherwise. "Having a senior pastor that is leading that charge is critical for us, and I think if we had started something like this as just a grassroots level without that level of support and leadership I don't think that it would have been as well received."

That senior pastor is Dr. Joel Hunter, a dynamic national leader among evangelical environmentalists. When speaking to me, Hunter characterized his role in supporting the Creation Care Task Force as issuing reminders. He said, "A congregation really needs consistent and periodic reminders in order to build it into their mentality." But in fact he did much more than that. He emphasized that church practice of green teachings is where the rubber meets the road. And, as he said, in his energetic congregation, as with all evangelicals, they do everything "pedal to the metal."

> *Joel: What are we doing as a church? Unless we are doing this kind of thing, then what it sounds like we are asking them to do something but if it's not important for us together, then it's really not important. You know, if it's not our priority as a congregation, then it's really not a priority.*

Clergy were very important sources of validation for Catholic groups as well. I asked Pablo, one of the leaders in the pesticide education program for migrant workers, how do you make that first step to help the workers understand the severity of their expo-sure to chemicals, turn off the TV, and come to the meeting about pesticide safety? What has worked? He emphasized the authority of the clergy and the ability of priests to call attention to issues.

> *Pablo: Well, in the class we have the priest calling everybody when they come to church. During the homily he tells you, there's going to be an important meeting at the school. I want you to go ahead and attend this meeting and all that.*

> *Q: Do you find that they listen more to the priest than to you?*

> *Pablo: Oh yeah.*

Michael, a leader in a different kind of Catholic community, a suburban parish, made the same observation. "I think we've just recently got to the point where the parish is more or less convinced, primarily because the pastor has essentially blessed it. If he didn't, I don't think it would go any further than conversation."

Interestingly, this group believed that local clergy had much more impact than higher profile leaders far away. Bill, also from St. Mary's, felt that "the average person sitting in the pew couldn't care less what the bishops said or what the pope says." While everyone laughed, Bill went on, "They want to hear what their priest has to say." Similarly, the Harlem community organizer gave credit to the Catholic priests who did live in the neighborhood rectories. Those local priests were engaged in the projects that concerned their parishioners, as opposed to the more prominent pastors of high-profile churches often visited by tourists, but whom Charles informed me often did not live in Harlem itself. Raymond of the evangelical church stated the influence of the local pastor bluntly: "I wouldn't be doing this if he hadn't started to speak up and start to address this. You know we might have heard shouts from various rounds within the general public about environmental stewardship, but without having heard my pastor talk about it wasn't necessarily something I'd see as a biblical responsibility."

Thus, very often, people perceived that the environmental work could not go ahead without the clergy's blessing. Often, though, the laity evangelized the clergy on this issue by first bringing it to the clergyperson's attention. Two Presbyterian leaders expressed this feeling, after having surveyed over forty local pastors about their views on the environment and their ministry. As Julie said, "I don't think I encountered a single minister that I talked to for the survey who didn't care about the environment. But at the same time they felt they didn't have the time or the personnel to bring a committee up to speed to do very much at all." Pat echoed this. "Pastors are overwhelmed with so many other things that it's really hard to get them to get their passions stirred. But that's just the nature of the organized church."

In other words, a synergy between clergy and laity was needed. Clergy needed at least to approve projects, and at best to inspire them. An enormous vacuum opens for lay leaders to fill, and they are more than capable of filling it. As a Jewish educator said, "I've always regarded this as a partnership between laity and rabbis. In general I would say we've got enormous talents in our laity, and to say it is underutilized is an understatement. It's hardly utilized at all." But even if environmental committees or projects were started by lay people, and the work done by lay people, there was a clear consensus that clergy needed to validate the project for it to flourish. Cooperation throughout the congregation is essential.

Fortunately, in many places pastors, ministers, lay leaders, and congregants are coming together to this ecological mission. The five dynamics outlined here accelerate personal and communal change, and engage congregations' complicity with the inertia of much of society to act decisively against climate change. But, group dynamics are not the whole story. Social affiliation does not explain pioneers or outliers. Some pioneers are inspired to act in ways their own group does not yet endorse, and their moral originality challenges the status quo. At the same time, the lonely pioneer can rarely work great change single-handedly. Individual leaders must work against the negative power of groups: the widespread inertia of social denial and apathy regarding the environment.

Conclusion: Collective Conversion

Pastors and congregants are coming together to an environmental mission, as individuals and groups engage each other in a positive feedback loop. Groups evolve as individuals press them to move forward; individuals are influenced by group dynamics. Group dynamics energize and accelerate personal change and challenge the inertia of social complicity. The power to support and reinforce environmental values and motivate decisive action is the critical secret of success of congregations. This is all the more critical given the acknowledgment of many participants that religious teachings, statements, and articles do not alone inspire action.

So the answer to the question Is conversion individual or communal? is, of course, both.

However, as the examples in chapter 2, about leadership, showed, group dynamics are not the whole story. There are important ways that religious identity inspires moral courage. Such courage is needed—and authorized from the inside—to critique and expand religious traditions and to challenge unsustainable lifestyles that go unquestioned.

The next chapter further sharpens the fundamental question about what drives or impedes passionate action for the earth. Active religious environmentalists have cleared the knowledge gap; they are on the whole less hindered by cognitive limitations. They have cleared the knowledge–caring gap, usually with explicit reference to religious beliefs. The action gap that remains—among activists, some of the time, and among many others, all of the time—raises the most thorny moral questions. How can we more clearly understand why people act on some of their values, some of the time, to support more sustained environmental engagement?

CHAPTER FOUR

The Courage to Continue

Ann (Catholic): A spiritual center presented a program that I can still remember because they were eliciting ... they were touching things in me that are important. Their program evolved, so that, by the end of the day, it was ... [tears come] Our planet's dying so that's ... I don't know ... Like I said, there's that love there and that's what I respond to.

But then I'm thinking in my mind, "But then what are you doing? How do you live that?" I certainly don't live it as much as I could. That's true, that's definitely true, and I know that.

Why do so many struggle to do what they themselves feel is right? Why is it so hard to act on one's ideals, even when the knowledge and caring gaps are cleared?

Ann is an active member of the environmental committee of St. Mary's parish in Colts Neck, New Jersey. No one would see her as an example of empty talk. That she doesn't live out her love for the earth as much as she could is her own judgment. But others expressed this critical self-judgment as well. For example, Jane, a woman in the Reformed Church, also felt she wasn't good enough at "walking the walk" to "talk the talk." She felt conflicted about the integrity of her own environmental efforts, a conflict that drained her confidence to lead and encourage others. As she said, "It's like I'm not pure enough in my environmental behavior to be able to demand or request actions of others. So I think that's one of the reasons I just do my little private environmental thing. Because

I don't feel empowered. My actions do not empower me to demand it of other people, because what I do is so insufficient."

What I do is so insufficient. I don't live it as much as I could. Many research participants searched their hearts with similar self-scrutiny, trying to understand the struggles they personally experienced. Confronting what they perceived as moral gaps only added to their green blues. Why *do* even passionate people struggle so hard against what they perceive as inaction and as failure? Why is it so hard to be really green—when one *wants* to?

The feeling of failing to live up to one's own ideals is not only a phenomenon I observed in my participants but a perennial topic of existential reflection. Reflections on this seemingly inevitable feeling of failure abound in literature, myth, philosophy, and psychology. This feeling permeates the green blues, and here is where green blues theory focuses its methodological analysis most directly. This method, fusing grounded theory and philosophical interpretation, analyzes the ethnographic data together with philosopher Paul Ricoeur's phenomenology of fallibility to search for clarity about this feeling of failure and deepen our interpretation of the gaps.

The data of the participants' statements has already generated the conceptual categories of the knowledge, caring, and action gaps. Here in this chapter, the green blues that evoke inner conflicts about action and motivation are searched more deeply for an interpretation that may lead to understanding and freedom.

How might Ricoeur help? Ricoeur sees an explanation for this existential reality in the very structure of human nature. He observes a fundamental disproportion between an individual's limited perspective and the infinite wideness of the world. That is, each person is situated awkwardly between her limits—her finitude—and the world's infinite options. This disproportion opens up the gaps between what one might do, might envision doing, might fail to do, and then can actually do.

Disproportion thus becomes the central concept that Ricoeur uses to analyze a problem that is profoundly existential and eminently practical. Practically speaking, this disproportion disturbs the focus needed to corral one's knowledge, love, and action purposefully in a frenetic world. It is easy to become overwhelmed by an infinite flood of facts, priorities, and needs. Becoming overwhelmed is risky, as both participants and decision scientists noted, because, in Ricoeur's poignant phrase, existentially, the "sadness of the finite" can overwhelm those struggling toward the possibility of a better world. "But between this possibility and the reality of evil, there is a gap, a leap: it is the whole riddle of fault."[1]

The testimony of the research participants suggests that bridges *can* be built over the gaps. Knowledge and feeling can be integrated to motivate resolute action. Here is where green blues theory will focus most intently—where observation and philosophical insight converge. Synergistically, Ricoeur's analysis of humanity's limited openness enables not only a richer description of the gaps described by the participants but suggests ways to bridge them. These bridges are intellectual hospitality, prioritized values, and cooperation.

Ultimately, each of these bridges is a necessary form of collaboration within a larger community. Such collaboration both acknowledges human finitude and affirms the multiple dimensions of interdependence that was shown to illuminate environmental spirituality in chapter 1. There is hope for renewal despite one's personal finitude, in the community of other collaborators, together reaching past our limits. As Ricoeur writes, humankind is "the Joy of Yes in the sadness of the finite."[2]

Let us explore more deeply his insights into the gaps and situate his distinctive approach to the finite and infinite aspects of humanity. Our main task is to explore how the central interpretive concept of disproportion may explain the existential unease of failure, of fallibility—of the green blues.

The first section of this chapter explores the existential experience of non-coincidence in the primary approach to the world through knowing. The second section will explore how the idea of

---

1. Paul Ricoeur, *Fallible Man. Philosophy of the Will Part II: Finitude and Guilt* (Chicago: Henry Regnery Company, 1965), 53.
2. Ibid., 140.

non-coincidence sheds light on human limitations in regard to feeling, and the third section turns to human acting.

Fallibility as Disproportion:
A Description of Existential Unease

Introducing Paul Ricoeur. Paul Ricoeur was a French philosopher who focused on philosophical anthropology, or interpretations of human being and activity. As a modern thinker, he is best described as an existential phenomenologist. The philosophical method of reflection called phenomenology observes human experience, thought, and behavior and carefully describes and analyzes them. His philosophical view of human nature offers a rigorous, but not necessarily religious, interpretation of the struggle of human beings to live up to their own moral aims.

One could say Ricoeur is a "recovering Cartesian," attempting to approach human nature through reflection on the self. However, unlike Descartes' famous claim that "I think therefore I am," Ricoeur insists that one's identity is not posited directly by oneself, and still less by one's pure "thinking." Instead, he stresses that one's identity, and one's interpretation of that identity, is mediated through relationships with many others.

Ricoeur's officially nonsectarian philosophy bridges multiple traditions' view of human nature. His status as a secular philosopher has been correctly challenged, as much of his work reflects Christian patterns of thought and Western ideas about the self. Notably, the central concept of self is radically different in Eastern philosophies. Nonetheless, his thought is theoretically accessible to secular discussions of conflict and human limits. His focus on knowledge, feeling, and action parallels classic Kantian categories as well as the cognitive, emotional, and behavioral categories of social psychology and are not necessarily dependent on a religious view of humanity. [3]

---

3. Kant's anthropology is moralistic, beginning with the fallen human passions of possession, domination, and honor. Ricoeur acknowledges the legitimacy of this "pragmatic" or empiric anthropology but is seeking a

Ricoeur's phenomenological method. Though Ricoeur's phenomenological approach is descriptive, it would still strike many as abstract.[4] In this postmodern era, generalizations about universal experiences are often discredited. That is why the evidence of my research participants assessed through field research is particularly valuable. This is not to say their comments can be universalized. Following my approach to grounded theory, however, their accounts of their own conflicts offer a basis for interpretive theory because of the recurring patterns in their testimony.

By using my research participants' reflections on the green blues, the struggle to enact their hopes and ideals about sustainable living, I am blending Ricoeur's phenomenological analysis with an empirical, grounded theory approach that draws on the concrete data of insights from real people into their knowing, acting, and caring. In their own ways they have stated the phenomenon of restlessness, the always striving, restless religious heart of the forever-unsatisfied consumer, the endlessly busy worker, or the distracted

---

purified philosophical anthropology attending to the "unfallen" passions. To imagine humanity in a primordial state of innocent desire is not arbitrary or irresponsible. A valuable discussion of how Ricoeur's view diverged from Heidegger can be found in Patrick L. Bourgeois, "The Integrity and Fallenness of Human Existence," *The Southern Journal of Philosophy* 25, no. 1 (1987): 128; see also John David Stewart, "Paul Ricoeur's Phenomenology of Evil," *International Philosophical Quarterly* 9, no. 4 (1969): 580-85. In Husserl's terms, what Ricoeur does here is imagine humanity in a new way, by pondering an imaginative variation of humanity's observable fallen existence. This imaginative variation "manifests the essence by breaking the prestige of the fact"—and reveals something that is also essential about human existence, by allowing for additional possibilities.

4. Action is a key concept for Ricoeur and one that developed progressively through his work. In his first study of the will, Ricoeur attempted an essential or more formal outline of human willing, an "eidetics of the will"; see Paul Ricoeur, *Freedom and Nature: The Voluntary and the Involuntary*, ed. John Wild; trans. Erazim V. Kohák; Northwestern University Studies in Phenomenology and Existential Philosophy (Evanston, IL: Northwestern University Press, 1966). Later Ricoeur concludes that to study fallibility, an empirical, more observational approach is needed and ultimately identifies human identity with action: "human being *is* acting." See Ricoeur, *Oneself as Another,* trans. Kathleen Blamey (Chicago: University of Chicago Press, 1992), 311.

parent. Their observations provide an empirical grounding for the discussions about conflict and limits in this chapter.

So, as an element of green blues theory, how specifically does the concept of disproportion clarify the gaps?

The ambiguity of innocent limits. In his seminal work *Fallible Man*, Ricoeur suggests that the source of inner conflict, the deepest causes of the gaps, lies in human fallibility. The notion of "fallibility" points to the deeply ambivalent human potential where individual limits both are, and are not, a "fault." Fallibility is a potent, if rarely considered, dimension of human nature: the paradox of innocent weakness capable of becoming fault. Nowhere is the paradox of such self-contradiction more dramatically evident than in the irony of an advanced civilization passively observing its own degradation and potential collapse.

Discussions about fallibility tread a tightrope between insightful diagnosis and moralistic judgment. Fallibility is not the same thing as sin or fault. *Fault* is a convenient untruth accepted; a malicious feeling savored; a concrete injustice committed. *Fallibility* is the human potential to act wrongly. *Fault* is a philosophical synonym for *sin*, which is a religious term for human wrongdoing. Sins or faults "miss the mark," to employ the traditional Hebrew meaning of the term.

Unquestionably, the language of sin can be and has been misused in horrifying ways. Judgmental enthusiasm for blame may overextend the field of sinful acts. Social and ecclesial powers have wielded the word like a weapon. Narrow presuppositions conflate sin with sexuality or rebellion. However, to recognize the existence of sin as a category of behavior is in fact a positive statement about humanity. To call a behavior sinful is to reject it as an intrinsic part of human nature. Sinful acts and thoughts are thus separated from a positive view of the person as fundamentally good, or mostly good.

For Ricoeur, the origins of fallibility lie in a peculiar human experience that is itself innocent but raises ambiguous questions. This is the experience of inward alienation he calls the "non-coincidence of self to self."[5] The non-coincidence of self to self, to

---

5. Ricoeur, *Fallible Man*, 1.

Ricoeur, is a feeling, a felt reality, that can somehow be described as inner disproportion. For example, regarding the knowledge gap, there is a disproportion between one's limited knowledge and infinite knowledge. One's limited knowledge doesn't quite match with the total knowledge available in the world; in fact, it doesn't match at all.

Disproportion suggests an awkward fit, an unjust imbalance. Disproportion also has an uncanny correspondence to the modern ecological crisis of disproportionate ecological exploitation; it echoes perennial philosophical reflection on human experience. The non-coincidence of self to self is an even more ambiguous term, evoking the slippages in purpose and resolution of which the participants spoke. It might mean different things to different people; it might evoke in someone something particular about struggle and frustration.

Ricoeur is trying to seize on the evasive concept of fallibility and snare it using some conceptual net. He proposes an equally slippery and mutable, yet suggestive, concept: the idea of non-coincidence. In his analysis of fallibility, Ricoeur is attempting to draw a picture of human nature that reflects his Western philosophical heritage, but also restates human limits in important ways.

Situating Ricoeur's distinctive approach to finitude. Many theologians and philosophers have also drawn their own pictures of human nature; it is their stock in trade. The classic Western view of humanity as a mixture of the finite and infinite is one attempt to express the experience of human transcendence: namely, that to be human is to transcend finitude. It is, in a sense, to be limited infinitude. The opposite of perfect transcendence, or unlimited openness to the totality of reality, is human perspective—limited openness to reality.

Before beginning the analysis of fallibility in relation to the knowledge, caring, and action gaps, I will compare Ricoeur's description of human nature with two other Western descriptions of human nature. Each follows a different philosophical school, thus comparing Platonic, process, and Aristotelian models. This brief comparison will highlight the particular approach Ricoeur takes to finitude and infinity when reflecting on human fallibility.

Finitude and Infinity Like Oil and Water. The classic Platonic view of the human person is of an immortal soul trapped in a material body. This view deeply influenced most early Christian theologians. So too, early in his career, under the influence of the Manichaeans, Augustine held this negative view of the soul tragically trapped in the material, flawed body.[6]

In this description of the human person, spirit and matter are bound together in uneasy conflict because of their opposite natures. Infinite spirit and finite matter do not easily coincide in the human person. Thus for the Christian Platonist, the spirit seeks to escape the bonds of matter through worship and ultimately in the beatific vision of heaven. Augustine characterizes unworthy concerns and actions as literally heavy, with the power to drag down one's attention, "falling" downward to the heaviness of material concerns or unworthy aims. However, the persistent echoes of Manichaean dualism in Augustine's thought do not reflect an authentically Christian positive view of created matter. A more biblically grounded view of creation follows the Hebrew affirmation that creation is good; indeed, very good.[7]

A contrasting embodied anthropology. By contrast, Marjorie Hewitt Suchocki, a feminist process theologian, avoids both the

---

6. Peter Burnell, *The Augustinian Person* (Washington, DC: Catholic University of America Press, 2005).

7. With Ricoeur, the instability of human nature seems to lie at the source of fallibility. For Augustine, that instability derives from a "nature created out of nothing"; for Ricoeur, it results from the instability of finite perspective opening onto infinite aims—the non-coincidence of self to self. Augustine thus offers another statement of the non-coincidence of self to self, brought about in this view by sinful contraction away from God's being and purposes. "Now nature could not have been depraved by vice had it not been made out of nothing. Consequently, that it is a nature, this is because it is made by God; but that it falls away from him, this is because it is made out of nothing. But man did not so fall away to become absolutely nothing; but being turned towards himself, his being became more contracted than it was when he clave to Him who supremely is. Accordingly, to exist in himself, that is to be his own satisfaction after abandoning God, is not quite to become a nonentity, but to approximate that" (Augustine, *The Trinity*, ed. John E. Rotelle; trans. Edmund Hill, O.P.; *The Works of Saint Augustine: A Translation for the 21st Century*, vol. 5 (Brooklyn: New City Press, 1991), 14.460.13.

classic Platonic-Augustinian conflict of spirit and matter, and what we will see as Ricoeur's post-Cartesian reinterpretation of this conflict in terms of finite perspectives and infinite options. She emphasizes the integrated, organic, physical, nature of the person. Like the CRED researchers, she recognizes the evolutionary patterns shaping human behavior and instincts, patterns that are rooted in biological origins as competitive animals. Human freedom is not thereby reduced to instinctual or reflexive processes. Human freedom emerges from biology, and with freedom humans are able to make choices within the infinity of natural options.

As a process theologian deeply influenced by the post-Newtonian philosophy of Alfred North Whitehead, she emphasizes the network of relationships that truly establish personal existence. This profoundly integrated view of human relationships has parallels in Eastern thought as well. Suchocki holds that when we violate our network of relationships, we risk descending into physical aggression and violence. This applies also to our relationship with the earth.

The finitude of acting. While more classic and abstract than Suchocki's updated model, the distinctive cast and structure of Ricoeur's thought is particularly useful for green blues theory. Ricoeur does move beyond the spirit–matter opposition marking classic Platonism and Cartesian dualism.[8] He shifts the terms of analysis from spirit and matter as metaphysical components of the person to the finite and infinite dimensions of a person's activity. This is an Aristotelian move, as for Ricoeur, following Aristotle, being *is* acting. He thus analyzes the juxtaposition of the finite and infinite dimensions of *action*, which also conflict because of their non-coincidence.

For Ricoeur, finitude and infinitude dovetail in each aspect of humanity's openness to the world; they do not simply coexist like oil and water. It is the tension resulting from this intersplicing

---

8. Ricoeur emphasizes that one disadvantage of Descartes' analysis of the finite and the infinite is Descartes' use of a framework of faculty psychology. Rather than creating a "distinction between a finite understanding and an infinite will," contrasting the limits of one faculty to the openness of another, Ricoeur analyzes the finite and infinite poles of each mode of being: understanding, feeling (will), and action (Ricoeur, *Fallible Man*, 25).

experience of finitude and infinity in how we perceive, feel, and act that generates the possibility of fallibility. Fallibility emerges from the very cohesion of finitude and infinitude formed by humanity's unique openness to a totally expansive world. And in the face of overwhelming environmental crisis, and longings to be "really green," this interspliced tension of possibility and limitation can crumble into action, into the green blues.

Resolution of the conflict comes not from escaping finitude but in seeking balance, a proportionate deal struck between a manic, impossible yearning toward every single possibility life offers and "falling" into a fixed, limited self: the intellectual bias, emotional shallowness, and hardened habits that trap the infinite possibilities of living.

The comparison above is markedly Western, an avowed limitation of this chapter, which cannot comprehensively review how various religious traditions represent the gift of transcendence and the reality of error. Nonetheless, for comparison, a symbol proposed by Latha, a Hindu research participant, enables us to recognize the universality of reflection on limits and literally frame this discussion of human fallibility.

Latha referred to humanity as a mirror reflecting the divinity within. Though she recognized human fallibility, she didn't judge human nature to be fundamentally distorted by sin. "If the mirror has a lot of dust on it, we do not see the reflection, but that does not mean the mirror is not there. So I think the focus is on the mirror and the goodness in Hinduism, and the focus is on the dust in Christianity. ... " Many might disagree with her and cite the diversity of Christian views of humanity's fundamental goodness or depravity, and raise other world religions and their teachings. However, whether the focus is the dust or the mirror, the symbol of the person as mirror underscores the limited reflection any mirror can offer. A mirror is one piece of glass; it has a frame; it is limited. It cannot contain everything.

Latha's image of the limited, dusty mirror from her Hindu tradition could have been a source for this chapter. But this reflection cannot incorporate all the world's intellectual and philosophic traditions. I have chosen Ricoeur as my primary methodological interlocutor because his sensitivity to fallibility echoes the green blues of the participants as they reflect on the gaps. Furthermore, the structure of his analysis of fallibility also maps directly onto the knowledge, feeling, and action gaps that emerge from the participant data.

The root of fallibility. Musing on restlessness and inner conflict isn't just for French philosophers. Ellen, like Ricoeur, notes the curious feeling of being uncomfortable in our own skins. Ellen was a member of the Buddhist group who mused about the "emptiness in our culture," which she felt led to consumerism. "You know, a friend has it so you blindly want it." The competitive nature of consumerism hints at a syndrome that includes both inner emptiness and unsettledness, an uncertainty about one's particular desires that makes it easy to fall into imitation.[9] To Ellen, the real search is the "human spirit grasping for something outside of ourselves."

Her musings on the grasp for "something" uncannily echoes Ricoeur's formal statement of human identity as a "non-coincidence of self to self." While Ellen didn't use the term "non-coincidence," her musings on our lack of connection to ourselves and grasping for some outer reality echo that concept: an uncentered, disproportionate lack of grounding.

> *Ellen (Buddhist): It might be a result of not being connected to each other and not being connected to nature. Looking at that relationship to ourselves: who are we? You know, I think that if more of us were a little more comfortable in our own skins, consumerism itself [might diminish]; there wouldn't be so much grasping for outside things.*

As Ellen suggests, we have the sense of being uncomfortable "in our own skins." She links this empty, uncomfortable grasping with the search for identity. *"Who are we?"* she asked.

The search for identity directly engages how we know, love, and act, which are not coincidentally central themes of philosophical

---

9. The "positionality" of high-end goods means that such affluent consumerism has value only if others don't have the same items; see Robert Frank, *Luxury Fever* (New York: Free Press, 1999).

reflection. Ricoeur, who like many Western philosophers is influenced by Kant, pursues the question of identity and fallibility by exploring knowing, feeling, and acting. Thus non-coincidence—Ellen's uncomfortable feeling of grasping outside oneself—will be seen to pervade the limited openness of cognitive perspective, the particular preferences of conflicted feeling, and the variable desires of one's irresolute motivation to act. How can we struggle to gain a sensible perspective on overwhelming streams of data? How do we process the pain of environmental destruction with a finite pool of worry? Why is motivation so unreliable; why do we act in ways that are less than our goals and aims?

This idea of non-coincidence is central since Ricoeur hypothesizes that it relates to the root of fallibility. He surmises that the root of infallibility is an unstable feeling of being greater and lesser than oneself: a "non-coincidence." Non-coincidence offers Ricoeur a way to explore the "dust on the mirror." The first section of this chapter searches for philosophical terms to explore the existential experience of non-coincidence in a person's primary approach to the world through knowing. The second section will explore how the idea of non-coincidence sheds light on human limitations in regard to feeling, and the third section turns to human acting.

Disentangling feeling, willing, and understanding (theoretically). Despite a possible appearance of clear and distinct analysis, in truth, action, feeling, and knowledge jumble together, they are only separable in theory. Feelings have an original power of their own, certainly, and the heart had primacy for Ricoeur.[10] In his interpretation, feelings are not reducible to thought or willing.

Yet within human experience it is difficult to splice off the pure and separate dimensions of responsiveness. It is hard to dissect thinking from feeling or willing. These human dimensions of responsiveness (cognitive, affective, and volitional) interact. We recognize and conceptualize objects of our desires and other experiences of reality

---

10. It is important to note early feminist writers on affect, including Valerie Saiving, "Human Experience: A Feminine View," *Journal of Religion* 40 (1960), and Carol Gilligan, *In a Different Voice: Psychological Theory and Women's Development* (Cambridge, MA: Harvard University Press, 1982).

(cognition). We feel and desire the fulfillment of what we love (affect). We actively reach for the good things we desire and identify intellectually by responding with choices (volition).

Seth, a Reform Christian pastor, spoke to the connection of understanding and acting in his environmental conversion and ministry.

> *Seth: My theology grows out of doing. I always work backwards. To me you jump in, you plunge in and do stuff and while you are doing it, that's prayer. And I think it was true with the environmental stuff, once we were doing things, whether it was the mugs, or the garbage audit, or having a woman come and help us get rid of all the toxins in our cleaning supplies—doing these things—it then became okay to talk about them theologically. My sermons came after some actions on it.*

Emotional reactions surge up, sometimes inexplicably, sometimes evoked by new ideas. These ideas and emotions may settle into values buttressed by cognitive concepts and provoke responses by the will. Without taking a position about which is primary, this chapter accepts the interrelationship of feeling, thinking, and acting and their connection to responses to the environmental crisis. Action will be taken as an expression of the combined process of all three. Thus, while social science can account for some dynamics of choices and decisions, the course of conflicted choices is harder to chart because of the intermingling of knowing, feeling, and action. It is precisely this problem of the conflicted will, and the intermingled dimensions of fallibility, that benefits from Ricoeur's profound philosophical approach.[11]

---

11. Ricoeur acknowledges two sources of criticism for the priority he places upon feeling, coming from behavioral psychology and depth psychology. Depth psychology objects that feeling is superficial if not deceptive, a symptom of a more significant, latent meaning. Ricoeur argues that even in dissimulation, feeling manifests one's intentionality (*Fallible Man*, 87). Ricoeur cites the objections of behavioristic psychology that feelings do not reveal the whole experience, but only a fragment of behavior, its "silent

Ricoeur captures the paradoxical irony of the conflict of the will, held back with subtle forces, with an image of imprisonment: the will is the *free will bound*. The will does not simply elect an action, and it is done. An impulse has an ambiguous future: Will it commit to decision and become evident in action? Will it yield to contrary impulses and pass away? The seemingly straightforward expression of free choice contains subtle crosscurrents. Free will is neither purely free nor always victorious. "You are what you love," Augustine declared; "love and do what you will." It is not true, though, that one always does what one loves. "For I do not do the good I want, but the evil I do not want is what I do," the Christian apostle Paul said famously (Romans 7:19). In reality, the conflict of interests within each person unleashes an internal drama of battling impulses as potential aims struggle for realization.

Conflict and freedom wrestle in the experience of fallibility, whose central mystery is the *free will bound*. Empowering freedom

---

phase." However, Ricoeur feels that the metaphor of tension, maladjustment, and resolution structuring behavioral psychology describes how drives interact without significantly addressing the content and meaning of those drives. This limited reduction of feeling to a narrowly physical metaphorical vehicle that describes the transfer and regulation of energy fails to represent the entire purpose of drives, which is to express the value that the person intends. Feeling is not a manifestation of tensions but an expression of value. An intentional analysis is necessary to justify behavioristic psychology, without replacing it. Ricoeur places tendencies, tensions, and drives under the heading of action studied by behavioristic psychology. Ricoeur may be proceeding from excessively Freudian assumptions. The behavioral psychology cited in chapter 2 is established on greater empirical foundations. Nonetheless, I agree with Ricoeur that a complementary, and more profound, analysis of conflict requires philosophical and theological analysis; hence this chapter. "Feeling expresses my belonging to this landscape that, in turn, is the sign and cipher of my inwardness. Now, since the whole of our language has been worked at a new dimension of objectivity, in which the subject and object are distinct or opposed, healing can be described only paradoxically as the unity of an intention and an affection, of an intention toward the world and an affection of the self. This paradox, however, is only the sign pointing toward the mystery of feeling, namely, the undivided connection of my existence with beings and being through desire and love" (Ricoeur, *Fallible Man*, 89).

is essential to break the bond of inaction, to transcend the action gap.[12] Thus, in Ricoeur's ethical vision, freedom, fallibility, and bondage are understood in terms of each other. As he writes, "the fundamental motivation of ethics is to make your freedom advance as mine does."[13] The release of the slave-will is enacted in Augustine's famous prayer: "Our hearts are restless until they rest in you." The finite and fallible slave-will finds its freedom resting in the infinitude of God.

Almost all my study participants gave voice to the importance of a sense of freedom in belonging to their faith communities. Free inquiry, openness to discourse, affirmation of exploring new meanings and forms of expressing ancient meanings—these values were shared spontaneously and immediately by almost all. The power of their congregations to affirm free thinking and to support new habits is not incidental.

The inevitably limited nature of each individual's knowledge and activity is not blameworthy. Being one particular individual, with natural limits of knowledge, concerns, and energy—as finite—is not a fault. On the contrary, these human characteristics are part of the uniqueness of each person, a diversity to be celebrated. But along with our limitedness there is the reality that limitations can become weakness, and weakness become failure.

Such limitations impede anyone's resolute action, including the action of environmental leaders. The complexity of climate change science often leaves leaders unable to explain issues; a lack of certainty inspires no one. But, how can we struggle to gain a sensible perspective on overwhelming streams of data? Exhausted feelings cannot motivate. But, how do we process floods of feeling provoked by environmental disruption? Good will expires in irresolution so often as to be cliché. But, why is motivation so unreliable; why do

---

12. The paradox of the free will bound echoes in other images: the free soul enslaved, the seeing sage self-blinded, fear hindering the resolute walk toward one's dearest desire (Orpheus).

13. Ricoeur, *Fallible Man*, xlvi; Paul Ricoeur, "The Problem of the Foundation of Moral Philosophy," *Philosophy Today* (1978): 190.

we act in ways that are greater and lesser than one's goals and aims? The weakness of these very gaps is not yet wrongdoing but a fallible weakness that can stretch and break, leaving open gaps that good intentions can no longer bridge. We start to explore the existential experience of disproportion in the approach to the world through knowing.

Perspectival Knowledge as Limited Openness

The primal finitude of knowing is *point of view*. The finitude of knowing corresponds to my being *here*. One perceives the world through the senses of the body. At the same time, as a particular body, situated in only one place at any given time, one's perception is limited to that which can be seen from that point of view. Perceiving the world is an experience of openness to the world. But this openness is limited just as a camera looks ahead and within its range, not behind or outside the viewfinder. Thus the finitude of knowledge consists in the *perspectival limitation of perception*.[14]

The finitude of seeing and understanding is not immediately apparent. The limitation of perspective is not apparent until my view is challenged by someone standing in a different place, or until I move myself to a new vantage point. By moving my body, I observe that my center of orientation is perspectival, because I can move and make my perspective change.

Furthermore, the sum of all possible different perspectives on the object, its diversity of silhouettes, is not just due to the mobility of my position but also to the complexity of the object. Disproportion in knowledge thus signifies the lack of an infinite capacity to understand. No one can comprehend all possible viewpoints, and it is a rare person who grasps all the complexities of any given object or can see all sides of a thing at once.

Cognitive finitude is what I see from *here*. This relationship of openness and finitude, which is synthesized in perspective, is

---

14. Ricoeur, *Fallible Man*, 23.

the basic theme from which Ricoeur will explore the other ways of being finite. As we shall see, limited openness also shapes acting and feeling. Limited openness is the fundamental theme of the experience of disproportion.

Limitation is indeed arguably the fundamental and profound source of human pain; at least, many great philosophers have argued this. Ricoeur traces a long course of philosophic reflection that echoes the green blues. Plato speaks of the quest of the soul for wisdom, "with time and effort and through a long and difficult process of schooling."[15] Descartes admits to being subject to "an infinity of imperfections." Pascal warns that there is a moral dimension to such imperfections, anticipating Ralph, the Baptist geologist, who strongly condemned willed ignorance. As Ricoeur writes, "Pascal invites us to forgo diversion and to pierce the veil of pretense by which we hide from our true situation."[16]

Pascal inspired Ricoeur's concept of disproportion, as he similarly referred to humanity's existential disproportion: "Limited as we are in every way, this state which is between two extremes pervades all our functions."[17] Pascal believed that human misery is due to the "natural poverty of our weak and mortal condition."

Humanity is caught between the extremes of infinite knowledge. The world offers so much to know! The perspectival limitation of knowledge is a phenomenological restatement of the cognitive limitations specified by decision science, multiplied by the explosion of research and subdisciplines in all fields. Yet we must honestly confront the smallness of our understanding. There is, in short, a knowledge gap. Yet there is a knowledge we are obliged to have: the self-knowledge of humility. We are obliged to know ourselves and avoid the deliberate ignorance that seeks to hide from the pain of our limitations.

---

15. Ibid., 7.
16. Ibid., 12.
17. Blaise Pascal, *Pensées*, ed. Léon Brunschvicg (Paris: Flammarion, 1993), cited in Ricoeur, *Fallible Man*, 13.

Perspectival Feeling as Particular Preferences

"The restless heart [is] the fragile moment *par excellence*."[18]

The second, but by no means secondary, mode of openness to the world is that of feeling. Indeed, Ricoeur felt that the self, the humanly experienced thinking and living self, was centered in the heart. His understanding of the human heart was shaped by conversations among French phenomenological philosophers in the mid-twentieth century. Chief among his influences was Stephan Strasser's *Phenomenology of Feeling* (1956), published four years before *Fallible Man*. While some of their contemporaries emphasized cognition over feeling, Ricoeur agreed with Strasser that the "power of the heart" lies at the core of human experience.[19]

Ricoeur's and Strasser's views of the centrality of the heart prompt key questions with which to query the experience of our participants, aiming for an experientially weighed phenomenology of the heart. For Strasser (and Ricoeur), feeling is the core of human experience.[20] The body's needs and intellectual desires are really lived and expressed in the heart. Through how one understands and chooses to act, feelings take shape as values. Active values become habits, a new being, "achieved spontaneity."

---

18. Ricoeur, *Fallible Man*, 82.

19. Strasser "explicitly places feeling at the center of human existence and recognizes in affectivity the essential core of human being, irreducible to any other consciousness or intentionality." See Andrew Tallon, "The Concept of the Heart in Strasser's Phenomenology of Feeling," *American Catholic Philosophical Quarterly* 66, no. 3 (1992): 342. In Tallon's excellent diagram of the phenomenology of the heart, he identifies two major strands of thought: metaphysicians of the heart, and phenomenologists of the heart. Strasser, he proposes, is a rare example of both.

20. For Ricoeur, the doctrine of *thumos* addresses the role of heart as situated between *bios* and *eros*. "Only with the *thumos* does desire assume the character of otherness and subjectivity that constitute a Self" (Ricoeur, *Fallible Man*, 123). The self, the humanly experienced thinking and living self, centers in the heart. The heart contains the full range of all desires, the darkness of what may be dimly understood, as heart together with thought and will form the real person, the subject and respondent.

Knowing becomes a permanently energizing motivation through conversion to new habits.[21] One's being as an active subject, someone who chooses to respond to others—one's true humanity—centers in the heart. The heart is the "finite spirit transformed by habit."

The primal finitude of the heart originates in one's distinct character and particular loves, which are famously subject to endless conflict. One source of conflict is distraction, that epidemic of our age so often echoed by the participants. The heart is constantly battered by new attractions, digital enticements of micromessages blinking and beeping from smartphones each nanosecond. Conflict also comes from being torn between good things. Many distractions are alluring and wonderful. Just as with the overflowing richness of the knowable, the world offers so much to love.

Though claiming the attention of restless hearts may be the ultimate challenge, participants asserted the centrality of the heart. My conversation with evangelical Christians emphasized this directly. Neither preaching, nor politics, and certainly not sheer pushiness would ever work in the long run. Leaders knew they must reach heartfelt feelings in order to engage people.

> *Paul: I think you have to change people's hearts. I don't think you can solve very many things by a bully pulpit or a bludgeon. I think you have to change people's hearts.*

> *Ted: It really boils down to the fact that it comes down to the heart. You know, until you engage the heart you're not going to find a long-term solution for anything.*

This was also the point made by pioneering environmental advocate and former head of the United Nations Environmental Programme Gustave Speth, when he observed that the professionalization of environmental policy somehow took the battle out of the heart.

How does disproportion explain the conflicts of the heart in a way that illuminates the caring gap? Feeling complements knowing by interiorizing reality, and feeling also has its particular and

---

21. See Strasser, quoted in Tallon, "Concept of Heart," 349.

inevitable limitations. If cognitive finitude is what I *see* from here (perspective), then the limitation of feeling is what I *love* from here.[22] *Here* I find my stance as a person with a history and character. Here is my existence as a character, with a pattern of reactions, responses, and values that motivate or retard action. Just as perspective narrows knowing, character expresses *distinct ways of being open to feeling.* It indicates the traits and preferences that are formed by birth, by parental influences, by life experiences, by all the formative events that are not chosen.

Having a finite perspective on feeling is like peering through a small telescope at the full horizon. In the viewfinder, one's destiny is still complete: it is a full, round picture, if limited and conscribed by the contours of a single lens, a single life. The picture seen through the telescope is simply a part of all the emotional and existential options that exist.

The finitude of feeling often presents a conflict between living shallowly amid numerous aims or pursuing a focused destiny and living it to the fullest. The challenge of finite existence is to find meaning in depth, in deeper appreciation of the decisions and realities of one's particular life, not in exhaustively repositioning the telescope to view an endless horizon.

The conflicts in the depths of the heart, which Ricoeur evokes by the term *thumos*, summon an image of deep water currents.[23] In the depths, there is unseen turbulence: crosscurrents lurk beneath the surface. Limited openness to the rich options for emotional expression in life can surface conflicts in the heart, unprioritized

---

22. My own preferences and loves are the subset of all the possible things one could love—and often I prefer my preferences. This is "affective finitude, difference in love with itself" (Ricoeur, *Fallible Man*, 56).

23. *Thumos* is not an entirely forgotten piece of philosophical arcanery: In his Jefferson Lecture, Harvey Mansfield suggests a key "improvement for today's understanding of politics arising from the humanities [is] to recapture the notion of *thumos* in Plato and Aristotle," a notion that calls us to attend to the power of desires in driving social movements and social justice causes; see Harvey Mansfield, "How to Understand Politics: What the Humanities Can Say to Science," in *2007 Jefferson Lecture* (National Endowment for the Humanities, 2007).

feelings, and restlessness. Likewise, the turbulent conflicts in the human heart are powerful, not bad—just confusing.

But the crosscurrents of ideas and aims and energy can become so distracting and enervating as to ultimately dissipate the energy that sends a current rushing toward its goal. Conflicted feelings drain the power of emotion to motivate action. Among the variable intensities of desire, hidden or background values may gain power to become the operative values, aptly described by Anna Peterson.[24]

Thus the gift of strong feeling is the conviction of understanding how deeply something relates to me, a surplus of value and relation beyond knowledge. Far from being superficial, feeling is more profound because it embraces. Knowing creates separation; feeling restores unity. "Feeling is understood . . . as the manifestation of a relation to the world that constantly restores our complicity with it, our inherence and belonging in it, something more profound than all polarity and duality."[25]

Such conscious emotional connection is the dimension of spiritual interdependence sensed and expressed by so many of the participants. Ann loved her river; Joel loved the turtles; and Carol loved the birds. They knew deeply their belonging to the world, to the world as a whole, through its diverse creatures, and to its wholeness as a family of life. This interdependence is both sensed as a spiritual and dynamic relation and as an aspect of themselves, the one related to all.

For them, being conscious of planetary connections grounded an expansive self-image—and often altruism. The relationship also grounds the pain faith-based environmentalists often feel, the green blues they share. As Joel Hunter points out, the extraordinary global connectivity of the twenty-first century also shifts moral assessment beyond the individual to a much larger plane. No longer is the neighbor the person you knew, and sin was "what you

24. Anna L. Peterson, "Talking the Walk: A Practice-Based Environmental Ethic as Grounds for Hope," in *Ecospirit: Religions and Philosophies for the Earth*, ed. Laurel Kearns and Catherine Keller (New York: Fordham University Press, 2007), 47.

25. Ricoeur, *Fallible Man*, 166.

did that affected you and your family, and maybe somebody else directly, but not really beyond that." For young people,

> Hunter: *The computer screen is the window to the world; they have connectivity all over the place. This new generation is very much defining its own behavior in what affects people all over the world because that's what they see every day, and so it's much easier for them to connect sin or shortcoming or self-centeredness beyond just their personal life.*

For Hunter, this is very good news. Preaching the gospel of caring for the earth "will be easier with one generation than another."

Perspectival Motivation as Variable Desires

The third mode of response to the world is through action. Limited openness marks human acting as well as knowing and feeling. The primal finitude of action relates to motivation. The limited openness of finitude places limits on what one can do, but also what one wills to do. One cannot be open to everything. Furthermore, the infinite range of options presented by the world is overwhelming. Endless choices can make people constantly anxious, called to instant decisions.[26] There is so much to know, so much to love, and no end to the things one might do!

Persons are disproportionately open to all possible action. This description of disproportion captures the experience of confused motivations and ambivalent desires. As Ann said, "I don't live it as much as I should." The finitude of action creates the ambivalence of irresolute motivation.

The ambivalence of irresolute motivation is not the same as moral conflict or ethical debate. Moral conflict and ethical debate occur when one is not sure of the right action. Such debate is more about cognition than motivation. Irresolute motivation rather expresses the experience of varying commitment to different possible actions. In Ricoeur's words, "finitude is here the confusion or opacity which

---

26. Alina Tugend, "Too Many Choices: A Problem That Can Paralyze," *New York Times* , February 26, 2010.

darkens what we might call the clarity of desire."[27] That confusion and opacity darken the clarity to see the hidden values.

The clarity of desire is darkened by all the distractions, habits, and fears by which participants revealed the action gap. "Confused" by these distractions, action is limited because only some things summon feeling strong enough to compel the will to act. Things may be desirable, fascinating, uninteresting, or even unnoticed, and it is these affective responses that motivate action (or not).

From Fallibility to Fault

In this sounding of the deep currents of human nature, the person is thus situated between finite perspectives, particular preferences, ambivalent desires, and the nearly infinite range of outlooks, attitudes, and choices presented by the world. Conflict and confusion are almost inevitable. Choices that veer away from authentic expression of what one knows and feels to be best actions initiate the slide from fallibility to fault.

Ellen described this as an uncomfortable feeling of "grasping outside oneself." That uncomfortable feeling is like hanging in tension between a stable grounding point and swinging out like a trapeze artist for a secure handhold somewhere in the infinity of options. The anxiety of this situation can easily make the swinger retreat back to the secure and narrow starting point, his own small point on the pole, her comfortable perspective.

From Perspective to Bias

Ironically, the very empirical solidity and apparent defensibility of perspective contain the seeds of fallibility. Nothing is more natural than the evidence of one's eyes. Because the finitude of seeing is *not* immediately apparent, one may easily assume one's view is complete. But if this assumption is protected from critique, perspective becomes bias.

---

27. Ricoeur, *Fallible Man*, 53.

Recall Ralph's pointed observation about perspectives that claim to represent self-expression but disguise willful ignorance as a license for overconsumption. "I think we need a change of perspective, which I think is happening. The person who drives the Hummer or whatever at eight miles per gallon, and those who see that person understand that that person isn't being greedy, that person isn't being wealthy, that person is shitting in our swimming pool, all of ours, his too." Willful ignorance is a powerful and recurring force within the tide of denial washing through American society.

Given the complexity of knowledge, humbly acknowledging our limitations is a moral responsibility, even if *being limited itself* is not blameworthy. Limits are not faults per se. That is the generosity of the term "fallible." The innocent fallibility of limited perspective becomes a fault only when it is internalized and dishonestly accepted as unavoidable ignorance. Again, Ricoeur cites Pascal on this critical distinction between unavoidable and willed ignorance:

> It is certainly an evil to be full of faults, but it is a still greater evil to be full of them and to refuse to recognize them, since that is to add the further fault of voluntary illusion.[28]

The evil and injustice of "willful ignorance" was phrased equally strongly by Ralph, who goes on to say, "I'd say we have a great ability to be willfully blind in the consequence of our actions to externalize costs and now see that we are affecting ourselves. I think the ability to change that is one of our great hopes."

Once people see the larger consequences of actions, such as the increased intensity of hurricanes following enormous human forcings of greenhouse gases into the atmosphere, it would seem willful blindness has to recede. Confronting the impacts of climate change locally should make much more of an impact than pointing to far-off glaciers and reefs. Facing hurricane devastation on American shores, or having to adjust planting time as garden zones shift, can bring the reality home. Psychological research confirms that

---

28. Pascal, *Pensées*, 100.

emphasizing local impacts is a best practice in communicating climate change.

Yet even here a willingness to reexamine one's assumptions is essential. Townspeople in Texas that survived massive fires during a season of fierce drought fought back to restore their lives. In the process they held all the tighter to a narrative of self-reliance, a powerful and sustaining narrative that had no room for the destabilizing and self-critical new story of human-induced climate change.[29] Their emotional survival required a self-image of being resilient, not destructive.

A larger narrative that grounds identity in a community helps support honest acceptance of tragedy. Finding a narrative that does not threaten one's core identity as a strong, self-reliant person is essential to support the transition away from bias because the bias is self-protective. The bias, or willful ignorance, protects a sense that one supports others, not harms them through the mystifying process of adding to climate change. Finding a narrative of personal resilience and community support can enable accepting multiple perspectives on climate change and moving past the knowledge gap.

From Preference to Attachment: Identity and Consumption

Though the unique things people love energize and motivate them, the innocent uniqueness of particular preferences can degenerate into biased attachment under the pressure of anxiety and insecurity. Ricoeur describes the sliding path from fallibility to fault as a journey from preference to attachment. Then, what I love is *the* most important thing, and perhaps I feel it is the *only* important thing. This is an extended journey with complex detours into consumerism and social relationships. This journey is intimately connected with establishing the identity affirmed and reflected by links to society and the world.

---

29. Andrew Revkin, "Why Climate Change Disasters Might Not Boost Public Engagement on Climate Change," *New York Times*, November 12, 2012.

Feelings play a powerful role in determining who we are. Through feelings, people determine and affirm their values, choices, and ultimately, their identities. People are distinguishable through the choices of the heart. As Augustine said, you are what you love. Feelings ultimately relate to the ways people experience their connection to the world and confirm identity.

For Ricoeur, the heart governs the search for identity through the very human quest for affirmation. Ricoeur carefully identifies three modes of feeling related that affirm and establish the self: possession, power, and self-esteem. Each of these has a neutral, even positive role in establishing the self. Possession entails industry and creativity. Power originates in the healthy relationships of work and social order. Self-esteem creates an inner identity that integrates and guides one's choices.

But at the same time, these ends can be turned to a fault. When starved for positive affirmation, the heart's desire for these bulwarks of the self is driven to find other nourishment. Instead of finding affirmation for one's identity through positive and healthy forms of possession, power as work, and self-esteem, the self is reduced to a restless quest amid insecurity and vanity. Given participants' comments that frequently connected consumption to the environment, I will focus on the nexus of identity with possession/consumption and esteem/vanity.

The relationship of identity to consumption gives consumerism its particular power. Consumerism permeates identity in two ways. First, consumerism is an engine of economic security, which in the modern age arguably displaces spiritual insecurity and the spiritual quest for identity. Economic insecurity is superimposed on spiritual insecurity, intensifying the anxious quest for identity so eagerly encouraged by a consumer culture. Second, consumerism also confirms social status and thus affects the dimensions of self-esteem established by social opinion.

Consumption and the search for security. Economist Doug Brown traces the modern economic history of insecurity to account for what he diagnoses as a "culture of insatiable freedom." He relates consumption to a habit of insatiability, in which capitalism channels the need for self-esteem toward material fulfillment.[30] The endless drive to have more and to seek unlimited self-actualization creates a "culture of insatiable freedom."[31] This culture of insatiable freedom is made possible by the modern age. Drawing on economic historians Karl Polanyi and Karl Marx, Brown argues that the roots of insatiable living reach back to the emerging capitalist society of the sixteenth century.

In early Christendom, Brown argues, people felt insecure primarily by apprehending their mortality and sinfulness in a religious cosmos. Then, personal insecurity shifted onto an economic base. The great transformation from a feudal agrarian society to modern capitalist economy resulted in a system driven by markets and competition.[32] Individuals could no longer count on the stability of inherited land and traditional roles, nor the protection of social class.[33] The freedom created by market competition enriched suc-

---

30. Helen Alford, Charles Clark, S. A. Cortright, and Michael J. Naughton, eds., *Rediscovering Abundance: Interdisciplinary Essays on Wealth, Income, and Their Distribution in the Catholic Social Tradition* (Notre Dame, IN: University of Notre Dame Press, 2006); Doug Brown, *Insatiable Is Not Sustainable* (Westport, CT: Praeger Publishers, 2002); John Cobb, *Sustainability: Economics, Ecology, and Justice* (Maryknoll, NY: Orbis Books, 1992); Gary Cross, *An All-Consuming Century: Why Commercialism Won in Modern America* (New York: Columbia University Press, 2000); Stanley Lebergott, *Pursuing Happiness: American Consumers in the Twentieth Century* (Princeton, NJ: Princeton University Press, 1993); Ernest F. Schumacher, *Small Is Beautiful: Economics as If People Mattered* (New York: Harper & Row, 1973); Mark Stoll, *Protestantism, Capitalism, and Nature in America* (Albuquerque: University of New Mexico Press, 1997).

31. Brown, *Insatiable Is Not Sustainable*, 2.

32. Ibid., 68. See Karl Polanyi, *The Great Transformation* (Boston: Beacon Press, 1944), 43.

33. These are the characteristics of an "embedded economy," in which social norms and customs governed economic activity (Polanyi, *The Great Transformation*, 1944, in Brown, *Insatiable Is Not Sustainable*, 6). In such an embedded economy, a "culture of security" prevails. Relationships between serf and lord obliged both to provide (nonreciprocal) services and protections in a stable social order. Economic activity was subordinate to social roles, controls set by guilds, and church influence; see Brown, *Insatiable Is Not Sustainable*, 55. But in the sixteenth century, under pressure of great population

cessful entrepreneurs. At the same time, the market economy created new insecurity and unlimited wants. Surviving economic insecurity demanded ambition, and the new possibilities of class mobility amply rewarded ambition.[34]

> *Alok: So that is why there are reasons why global warming, or whatever is happening to the earth, because the desires of people, the desires of people are growing so much, and they're wanting everything on this limited earth, on this finite amount that's there.*

Restlessness is an enduring quality of human existence, which energizes great discovery and achievement. The achievements of capitalism and industry and invention are not to be cast aside. But Brown's study enables a new look at excess consumption as a modern distortion of natural human restlessness leading away from spiritual transcendence. Brown argues that amid the secularity and social mobility of the early modern age, insecurity became primarily experienced via economic life and sought an economic resolution.

Consumption and the search for identity. Consumption thus becomes a proxy for identity. As production became culture's dominant activity, it became a source of identity, as consumer goods "create a subject for the object."[35] Production defines the subject who is the consumer, shapes the way we fulfill our needs, and choreographs the behavior of consumption. Capitalism, Brown argues, also emphasizes needs fulfillment through the purchase and consumption of commodities. Thus, insatiable freedom turns

---

growth and the opportunities of the colonial era, landless workers found their labor salable, and economics began to "disembed" from culture. John Kenneth Galbraith similarly writes about the insecurity of the modern competitive economy (*The Affluent Society* [Boston: Houghton Mifflin, 1958], 98).

34. "Insecurity is a collective motive in the embedded economy but an individual motive in the disembedded economy" (Brown, *Insatiable Is Not Sustainable*, 72).

35. Karl Marx, *Grundrisse*, trans. Martin Nicolaus (New York: Vintage Books, 1973), 92, cited in Brown, *Insatiable Is Not Sustainable*, 83.

to economic activities for its actualization.[36] The economic coopting of insatiability diverts restlessness from its spiritual quest for peace and wholeness.

The destabilized early capitalist society created a condition of insecurity and anxiety in the economic realm. Status and security are means to confirm identity via consumerism that risk falling prey to attachment. The potentially innocent structures of power, possession, and worth are enmeshed in an economic and social structure that bonds identity and security to consumerism. Existential and economic needs merge; this threatening insecurity must be confronted. Yet the economic coopting of desire diverts even noneconomic restlessness from its spiritual longing for peace and wholeness. All restless energy is channeled into economic activity.

Brown thus argues that personal identity has been coopted by economic insecurity. Insecurity, anxiety, and attempts to escape them are perennial topics of ethical and theological reflection.[37] My aim is to bring into dialogue the shared focus of Brown and Ricoeur on consumption and identity to illuminate the comments of the participants. Ricoeur offers a complementary existential analysis of the ways the quest for identity passes through the detour of insecurity. In so doing he delves into the nexus of consumption and identity.

---

36. The ecological crisis underscores that insecurity is again a collective, indeed, planetary experience. Security now demands a revision of purely market-driven competition for resources that balances the needs of humanity and the biosphere. There are natural boundaries in human energy as well, and have always been. Even with restrained and sustainable consumption, humans must make choices about our ecological, economical, cultural activities and expressions. Even if solar powered, these actions take finite human energy, which is renewable, not inexhaustible. Hence perennial teachings on the difficult spiritual lesson about accepting finitude remains; the restless heart cannot roam ceaselessly without collapse. History shows that the hyperconsuming society also collapses; see Jared Diamond, *Collapse: How Societies Choose to Fail or Succeed* (New York: Penguin Group, 2005).

37. Niebuhr also critiques the anxiety that seeks a resolution through sensual excess (Reinhold Niebuhr, *The Nature and Destiny of Man*, vol. 1, *Human Nature* (Louisville: Westminster John Knox Press, 1941), a parallel to Brown's lament for the coopting and loss of spiritual wholeness.

Augustine would easily view materialism as the literally heavy concerns that drag one's attention away from higher pursuits. Modern critics have labeled the heavy drag of materialism as a disease, calling it "affluenza."[38] Following Elizabeth Johnson's critique of the market as religion described in chapter 2, this affliction becomes the sacred disease of idolatry. Society is caught in a superdeveloped dream blissfully (or willfully) ignorant of the costs of routinized luxury. Yet superdevelopment is bitterly critized by Pope John Paul II and by Pope Francis, who sharply reject neoliberal capitalism as an "economy that kills."[39] Perfectly in tune with Catholic social teaching, musicians mock obsessive consumption in old classics like the Monkees' "Pleasant Valley Sunday" and new statements like the ironic teen rap "First World Problems."[40] In this Youtube rap, rapper Funny Z flushes a dollar down the toilet while chanting, "I killed a spider with a dollar 'cause I didn't have a tissue . . . it's a first world issue."

From self-esteem to vanity. The second link in the nexus of consumerism and identity involves the dimensions of self-esteem established by social opinion. Identity is not established by possession, economic security, or power alone but by the recognition of relationships. For Ricoeur, the other recognizes my worth through the gift of *esteem*. This quest for esteem is markedly interpersonal.

Oneself is a reality created by relationships with others, and confirmed by the promises and commitments made to them. Feeling bonds us to other people and establishes the foundations of identity, as Ricoeur details in his later ethical treatise *Oneself as Another.*

Being a person in relationship with others is a mutual bond. One's promises and commitments confirm the relationships to which one will give one's heart and one's time. In those

---

38. John de Graff, David Wann, Thomas H. Naylor, *Affluenza: The All-Consuming Epidemic* (San Francisco: Berrett-Koehler Publishers, 2005).

39. John Paul II, *Sollicitudo rei socialis,* www.vatican.va; Francis, *Evangelii gaudium,* http://w2.vatican.va.

40. Funny Z, "The First World Problems Rap," 2011, https://www.you tube.com.

relationships, one also receives and responds to the needs of others. These are the fundamental platforms of the self in Ricoeur's intersubjective view of personhood. On a more superficial level, one's identity is reflected back by the opinions and judgments of others. "My 'Self,' it may be said, is received from the opinion of others that establishes it. The constitution of subjects is thus a mutual constitution through opinion."[41] In the slide from fallibility to fault, the positive affirmation of self-esteem can become the shallow mirror gazing of vanity.

It is this dependence of identity on "fragile opinion" that gives consumption the power to bolster identity with status and glory. Ellen directly linked a feeling of emptiness to the pursuit of consumerism and social pressure. Social affiliation plays a strong role in social goals and the decisions and purchases one makes.[42] Consumerism is partly driven by social bonding ("a friend has it so you blindly want it") in quest of identity. "Who are we?" Ellen asked. In the modern world, consumerism and globalization play an outsize role in shaping identity, not simply in terms of the economic system and resource exploitation but in the very construction of identity. Being globally connected to "each other and nature" is an opportunity too often lost; the resultant emptiness leaves people relegated to retail therapy, turning to consumerism for identity, "grasping for outside things."

The research participants recognized the enormous pressures for unsustainable consumerism, the "onslaught" of consumerist pressure Latha described. As a counteroffensive, participants found motivation to care for the environment, despite the enormous consumerist pressures, from their spirituality rooted in scientific knowledge, a sense of spiritual interdependence, and a concern for social justice.

---

41. Ricoeur, *Fallible Man*, 121.
42. David. H. Krantz, Nicole Peterson, Pooman Arora, Kerry Milch, and Ben Orlove, "Individual Values and Social Goals in Environmental Decision Making," in *Decision Modeling and Behavior in Uncertain and Complex Environments*, ed. T. Kugler, J. C. Smith, T. Connolly, and Y.-S. Son (New York: Springer, 2008), 177.

This spirituality led to a consciousness of moral globalization in which other and self are intimately linked. By perceiving oneself in an interdependent planetary community, self-preservation converges with conservation of the "other." Planetary "affiliation" can reconcile the disproportion of self and its greater self, the cosmos. The impact of social pressure on identity prompts reflection on the buffering power of a faith that honors each person and each creature as beloved. Furthermore, the larger religious vision that places personal identity in the context of the whole cosmic community fosters a commitment to the common good, where concern for self and other converge. What seems to be legitimate consumption in one context is easily displaced by connections with global neighbors in greater need.

From Will to Whim

Innocent openness to different possible actions becomes faulty when irresolution fails to do anything. Ricoeur called the unreliable power of decision the *free will bound*. Yet too often the will is not captured after a valiant struggle, or vanquished by oppression, but undone by the weakness of merely moderate inclination.

As ethicist Daniel Maguire writes, "Superficially good motives are like playful flirtations. They lack the strength needed for follow-through. Yet they can serve a devious purpose by making us feel that our heart is in the right place." Maguire observes the distinction between the will and the little-used but perceptive term velleity. Will derives from volition, which is derived from the Latin *volo*, "I will." Velleity derives from *vellem*, meaning "I would like." Thus, velleity shifts action "from the forthright indicative to the hedged subjunctive."

Precisely this hedging and thumb twiddling weakens the "really green" to merely "ideally green." As Maguire shrewdly states, "volition refers to what you *really* will; velleity, to what you *would* will, were things more to your liking and less taxing."[43] Paul's

---

43. Daniel C. Maguire, *Ethics: A Complete Method for Moral Choice* (Minneapolis: Fortress Press, 2010), 98; emphasis added. Augustine reflects

self-accusation about failing to act—"what I will to do, that I do not do"—becomes the permissive, "what I can easily do, that I will do. And that's OKAY." Ogden Nash also uses the sharp power of the word velleity to skewer vanishing commitments. "It's not laziness, it's velleity I've got!" Naming velleity is the damning indictment of the progress of varying commitment to vanishing commitment.

Evon Peter, a Gwich'in chief who frequently speaks about environmental issues and advocates for his people in the Arctic Circle, spoke with similarly discomfiting authority about people's inability to follow through with spiritual growth. In his experience, few can persist in any new spiritual practice for very long. I asked him, what are the reasons it may be hard to either come back to a sustainable way of life or pick up new sustainable practices? What's the lure backward, so to speak? He replied,

> *What I'm asking, what I'm suggesting, I should say, is no small task by any means.*
>
> *Simply to ask someone to say a prayer each morning, for another day of life, to say thanks for the air that we breathe, for our connections, for our families, it's too difficult for most people to sustain. Try it. Ask one of your friends to just put aside three minutes each morning. I've done this many times. Two or three days are the longest most people can last with this. We're so distracted by the media, other voices coming at us, saying, No this is just the way it is, we have to accept it. That's really common language.*
>
> *It's so challenging to really begin to face ourselves and to begin to live a life of greater integrity. And this is as true for*

---

that the will is the helm of the whole person, steering the thoughts, emotions, and desires common to both and soul. Augustine acknowledges "that the soul is not only moved to desire, fear, joy, sorrow, by the flesh, but that it can also be agitated with these emotions at its own instance" (*On the Trinity* 14.447.5). It is the will's critical responsibility to shape these impulses of the human person: "if it is wrong, these motions of the soul will be wrong, but if it is right, they will be not merely blameless, but even praiseworthy" (14.447.6). The right will is "well-directed love" (14.449.7), which is love of God and neighbor as himself (14.448.7).

indigenous people as it is for all other people. Not only that but the decision to face something that's very challenging for us to face.

This is a real crisis if, as the participants emphasized, persistence is one of the most needed qualities of leadership. Spiritual intentions become passing whims.

How does anyone escape the bias, selfishness, and irresolution of fallible perspective?

In the field of knowing, perspective can be changed. One can, in fact and metaphorically, move one's position and see differently. By contrast, the *origin* of one's values and characteristic feelings cannot be changed, which accounts for the difference between education and conversion. Nonetheless, while deep emotional habits are hard to change, a shift in mental perspective can transform attitudes.

> *Seth: I pretty much stopped eating meat, and it was pretty much because of this church, and wanting to eat further down on the food chain, and a comment someone in the church made about how much it takes to feed a cow. That was all it took.*

> *Q. Was that hard?*

> *Seth: No, it wasn't hard. And I'm not a purist on this at all, and we eat enough meals at other places, it's a good thing I'm not a purist, but I don't cook meat at all, and I don't get meat at restaurants.*

This may seem like a trivial example, but converting to vegetarianism is a real and reluctant struggle for many. Moral guilt has invaded the comfortable memories of family recipes and holiday feasts, as well as convenient grills and carefree barbecues. In Seth's case, his commitment to social justice and previous habits of discipline acquired in a separate effort to eat healthily enabled him to make a consistent change in habits. He knew he lives in an interdependent system, and the full realization of the impact of his food choices worked with love to motivate total, immediate action. There is a power of identity within the cosmic family to promote "irrational" sacrificial behavior.

To summarize: being human is a blues-inducing experience of many limitations. The finitude of knowledge consists in the perspectival limitation of perception, the limited openness to total understanding. The finitude of feeling presents inescapable conflicts. One either lives shallowly amid numerous aims, seeking to avoid commitment and depth, or chooses a single destiny and lives it to the fullest. The finitude of action creates the ambivalence of irresolute motivation.

So the Arctic chieftain's pointed remark about how people fail to persist in spiritual practice, to keep their intentions, demands an answer. How can limited perspectives, narrow priorities, and irresolute commitments—natural fallible responses to an overwhelming world—be transformed?

Ricoeur's interpretive model of limitation, of disproportion, suggests that complementing those limits is a path toward empowering leadership. First, cooperation with finite perspective through intellectual hospitality, or a willingness to consider other perspectives, completes and expands the limited knowledge we all have. Second, prioritizing finite loves accepts the reality of conflicted feeling and has the courage to embrace the most important ones. Third, accepting the reality that we have a finite ability to act empowers a focus on the gift of the possible through collaboration. The community itself offers gifts and solutions: the support of others brings the joy of "yes" in the sadness of the finite. The three-part analysis of knowing, feeling, and acting describes the process of transforming to living in a way that is really green, expressing the green intentions of the heart in action.

Bridging the Gaps:
The Balancing Act of Cooperation

Intellectual Hospitality: Connecting Limited Knowledge

The alternative to bias is cooperation with our limited perspectives. How? Each can accept and seek the truth of multiple perspectives; learn, listen, and be corrected. Cooperation with one's limited perspective exchanges certainty for humility and the ideology of assurance for intellectual hospitality. Hospitality frees one from paralysis by granting a willingness to listen. Pretending that our limitations are not really so blinding is a strategy to lessen the pain of limitation, to ignore the disproportion. But justice demands honesty, a confrontation with reality as clear as current understanding allows. Honesty drives the search for greater understanding, and avoids the harm made possible by willed or pretended ignorance of the ways our actions harm others.

Willful ignorance, the stance of the passive bystander in the Holocaust, is not an ethical excuse. A theology of intellectual hospitality can be borrowed whole cloth from the Jesuit philosopher Bernard Lonergan, whose broad theology exemplified intellectual hospitality by including economic thought. Lonergan taught the imperative to be aware; be attentive, be intelligent: then judge what one must do.

Intellectual hospitality in environmental discourse must seek solutions on an adequate scale, which requires new kinds of dialogue. Jeffrey Sachs of the Earth Institute, and a Millennium Development Goal advisor, is nothing if not the prophet of scale, advocating ways to multiply sustainable ideas on globally effective levels. Society needs the multiplication of ideas and implementation. Environmental leaders must engage with diverse jargons, philosophies, and partners. They need not become scientists but must accept the challenge of becoming conversation partners in order to become meaningful ethical interpreters. The subject of justice broadens to include kilowatt calculations, watershed geology, aerosol dispersal, disaster housing. Different jargons arise in interdisciplinary work.

Interdisciplinary environmental ethics also engages diverse philosophical frameworks. An interesting project funded by the National Science Foundation has analyzed the various philosophical frameworks employed by researchers in different disciplines. This project helps identify the barriers to communication that often plague interdisciplinary work.[44] Sociologists, decision

---

44. Sanford D. Eigenbrode, Michael O'Rourke, J. D. Wulfhorst, David M. Althoff, Caren S. Goldberg, Kaylani Merrill, Wayde Morse, Max Nielsen-Pincus, Jennifer Stephens, Leigh Winowiecki, Nilsa A. Bosque-Pérez,

scientists, soil scientists, and oceanographers may hold strongly diverging views of objectivity, reductionism, evidence, and the role of values in research. I listened to a fascinating disagreement between two expert agronomers on the capacity of organic farming to meet worldwide food needs. Ecological ethics, such as food issues, requires the willingness to work through, or simply accept, conflicting epistemologies, while committing to finding solutions.

Lastly, diverse partners participate in this dialogue. Window repairers and insulation experts, as well as hydrologists and climate scientists, become essential partners. Environmental leaders must engage what is practical to be honest, hospitable, and effective.

Prioritizing Values: Embracing the Conflicts of Feeling

Given the environmental implications of a distorted quest for identity, cooperation with our finite capacities for concern demands that we prioritize time, spending, and resources. Cooperation with finitude calls for assessing feelings, values, and needs, and prioritizing them justly. A theology of prioritization must follow.

Many things start the cascade of events leading to committed action. First, there is the simple act of *noticing something*. Conflicted feelings gain integrity in prioritization, ordered by significance, by relationship to others, to what we give most attention and support—what we notice and attend to. The priority of feelings thus develops from attention. Clarity regarding one's priorities is the fruit of attention. Prioritization is part of an unfolding relationship between myself and the objects I notice.

Second, I choose to value different objects more or less, in part based on my reactions to them. Through affect the object brings forth a reaction in me; then, I can prioritize its significance. Without prioritization, feelings are not yet values. Unprioritized feelings are initial emotional responses, what Ricoeur calls "preliminary signs of being affected." Feelings become values when compared with other feelings and prioritized. Through this process values are

---

"Employing Philosophical Dialogue in Collaborative Science," *BioScience* 57, no. 1 (2007): 57-58.

confronted with other values in a "preferential outlook." This is not pure feeling, but not yet objective knowing either.

Comparing values engages feeling and knowing. It is thought about feeling, reflected feeling, recognition of what I feel to be important about my feelings. And critically, it is *communally processed* reflections on feelings.

> *Vinay: To understand how the environment is doing, basically it boils down to your needs; if you can reduce your needs, it is the single most important issue to reducing impact.*

> *Q. How do we do that? How do we convince people that they don't need things that they are very convinced that they do need?*

> *Ari: First you convince yourself!*

Third, the process of prioritizing often includes *conflict* as I weigh equally compelling values. The reality of valuing many things opens an acute mode of inner conflict, revealing the turbulence of multiple values. "Indeed, feeling alone can reveal fragility as *conflict*," writes Ricoeur, as opposed to the fragility of cognitive limitation or partiality. By contrast, cognitive limitations proceed from one's perspective on an exterior object. The conflict within feeling expresses the fragile duality of limited openness felt internally and experienced as conflict.

This conflict must be endured, as a judge hears and weighs competing claims. For the participants, hearing and seeing suffering ecosystems and persons reweighted the evidence and reprioritized their claims. *Aha—paper is precious! That one flush is water for a whole day to us!*

For Jane and Nancy, a cognitive reevaluation of the value of a resource prompted emotional reevaluation, and new commitments to action followed. "Paper is precious!" Roshan expressed the fusion of cognitive and affective reprioritization powerfully. Both are essential; conscious knowing transforms values and action.

> *Roshan: The question is on the plane of action. The value of taking the action has a price higher than something else. So*

*it's not only its value, it's rising in personal life, bringing it
to a higher level not only of consciousness, but value too. I
think that is where the question is. Not in the awareness. The
question is somehow now changed. It's the alteration of the
value of taking action which is the necessity.*

Prioritization is exactly altering the value of taking action that
derives from a heightened, conscious love of the earth. A broader
identity as a global citizen expands not only one's view of God but
a noneconomic relationship to the earth.

While prioritizing is itself a morally neutral process, prayer and
discernment—community conversation—order the valuing of
goods. For many, religious convictions make that choice to shift
priorities simpler. Asked if caring for the environment was a choice,
a kind of personal spiritual expression, or a widespread religious
mandate, one member of an evangelical church responded: "I think
there are some folks that have misinterpreted it as a choice. Someone said to me, 'I don't know if that's a priority of our church this
year.' As if you could prioritize what year you're going to follow
certain mandates from God."

Recall Ricoeur's interest in the heart as the seat of values. Values are confirmed by habits. Feelings take shape as values. Active
values become habits, a new being, "achieved spontaneity." Knowing becomes a permanently energizing motivation through conversion to new habits. One's being as an active subject, someone who
chooses to respond to others—one's true humanity—centers in the
heart. The heart is the "finite spirit transformed by habit." The
heart desires the absolute: it is transcendent, even insatiable.

Habit partially transcends finitude, as the strength of good habits releases one from the constant struggle to choose. The needs
of the other may call us beyond our finitude, as restlessness leads
us out to the divine. If we absolutize instead the finite other, most
commonly in consumerism, transcendence fails, and succumbs to
idolatry. "Our capacity for 'bad excess' is an excellent proof of our
capacity for 'good excess.'"[45]

---

45. Tallon, "Concept of the Heart," 357.

The Gift of the Possible: Empowering Action

Tom (Baltimore Presbytery): I think we can only achieve our goals in that sense if our goals are very limited, because the size of the task is infinite and I think our goal can just be to be faithful, and if we're being faithful then we've achieved our goal. What we've achieved in terms of measurable objectives that will always be expanding because the goals will always be moving further away.

People can only handle reasonable goals. One task to focus on, one target in the viewfinder of our limited perspective, is enough. Taking on too much leads to despair, draining away motivation.

The Belgian theologian Edward Schillebeeckx recognized the painful conflicts inherent in being created, bodily, and mortal—a conflict that calls for a "reconciliation with finitude." Simply as finite creatures, humankind will experience more demands than can be met, more needs than can be satisfied, and conflicts of preferences that are equally valid. Part of the task of humanity, precisely as finite creatures given autonomous responsibility for history, is to respond creatively to conflicting needs. The risk of failing to resolve this conflict is to fall into bitterness and despair.

Still, there is hope that the negative, the listlessness, and despair of achieving anything can change into the positive: little by little.

Carmen (Catholic): I have a great deal of hope because God works with us, and that we are coming little by little to know more about what our faith is. And to know more about self-love. And when these things happen it will be even better, because all the news and everything in the world talks about what is negative, negative, and many times the negative, we imagine that everything is negative, and then I start to speak negatively. But we have to begin to change toward the positive. I have a lot of faith in that everything that is negative is going to change into the positive.

Carmen expresses the powerful hope that people can do things, that we can create new habits, and change everything negative "into the positive." She challenges us to self-love—to a healed and positive view of identity within one's community. Accepting one's finitude, yet not abandoning the highest priorities of seeking for a radically transformed, sustainable world, one can cooperate with finitude through collaboration. Self-love and other-love hear the cry for a healed world, and, hoping for that, the injustices that poison communities can be healed.

Life is a particular existence, bracketed by one's unique perspective. It is situated, but not thereby paralyzed. Experiences lie within channels like Tennyson's narrow brook, overflowing with "torrents in summer"—the rising flood of God raining into their sources.

A religious analysis of fault and fallibility should be followed by a message of healing and reconciliation. In secular terms, identifying the source of fallible transcendence may offer release and rest. Chapter 5 examines the insights of diverse religions into inner conflict and their hopes for finding *shalom*.

Is Carmen's hope realistic? In the next chapter, we consider the insights, and consolations, of religious thinkers who know the conflicts all too well.

> *Like torrents in summer, half dried in their channels*
> *Suddenly rise, suddenly rise, though the skies are still*
> *cloudless, the skies are still cloudless.*
> *Still hearts that are fainting may full to o'erflowing*
> *For rain has been falling, far off at their fountains ...*
> *God has been raining.*[46]

---

46. Henry Wadsworth Longfellow, "The Musician's Tale," from the *Saga of King Olaf.*

CHAPTER FIVE

Renewal and Community Spirit

"Love Your Mother," urged a bumper sticker I saw while in Flagstaff, Arizona. The bumper sticker was marked with an image of the earth and lay stacked among piles of brochures and books describing the water crises caused by coal extraction on the Navajo nation's Black Mesa mountain. The Black Mesa was home to Shonto, Tony, Gabe, and other sustainability leaders I met in Flagstaff. As the mother of two, I agree that loving your mother is good advice, whether she be a human person or Mother Earth. Admittedly, many have conflicts with their human mothers, as well as with caring for Mother Earth. In this complex world, love often involves conflict.

Ann, of the St. Mary's environmental committee, loved a river in a way that brought her to tears, as she felt that she did not "live" her love of the earth as much as she could. As she said, "I grew up on a river and I was enthralled with nature as a kid. I just loved it. I guess I could say I probably had a relationship with it." But despite her relationship—a love affair, as she described it—she was disturbed by her perception that she wasn't putting that love into action rightly. Ann's sense of not "living" her love of this river had spiritual depth. That is, she linked her love of the river to her spiritual identity, to a sense of belonging to the cosmos—to a dying planet that needed her. Her recollections of the river she loved started by recalling a lecture on the earth crisis. This lecture started "with the Big Bang theory and all the wonders of that; how the things that exploded make us up. By the end of the day, the message was . . . our planet's dying, so that's just . . . I don't know . . . Like I said there's that love there, and that's what I respond to." Again, I do not share her perception, nor is the aim of this analysis to be judgmental. The point is to explore the conflicts reported by the faith-based environmentalists themselves.

When Ann asked herself, "What am I doing? Why don't I live it as much as I could?" she judged that somehow her commitment betrayed ambivalence, her actions were insufficient, and her integrity was lacking. In addition to the existential unease resulting from the conflict between humanity's inevitable limits and the world's infinite options (the non-coincidence of self to self), the painfully honest faith-based environmentalists seemed to experience a non-coincidence of self to community, a rupture between themselves and the earth. To them, exploiting the earth was not simply unwise and imprudent: it was a fundamental self-contradiction because of their spirituality of interdependence, which perceives divine concern to be ever more linked to the cosmos.

Broken relationships with the earth were thus spiritual crises, which they articulated in terms of what wholeness and salvation meant for them. Amid feelings of conflict, imbalance, disproportion, regret, there is a deep desire for peace, wholeness, and completeness. These words all echo in the religious terms *shalom* and "salvation." Religious traditions answer that desire by inviting the seeker to find spiritual integrity through peace with the divine and good relationships with the neighbor and the earth community. The desire for spiritual integrity includes the desire to feel at home in the cosmos and at peace with one's neighbor and all earth's living communities through right relationships.

The task of this chapter is to search for this balance, this peace with the neighbor and the cosmos, a balance that I am calling "spiritual integrity." The term spiritual integrity deliberately invokes a counterpart to disproportion. Integrity fits the pieces of one's life and values together proportionately, in harmony: it answers a deeper need than survival on a degrading planet. For faith-based environmentalists, seeking to heal the earth is a way toward their own salvation.

For example, Erik, a young member of a progressive Baptist church, recast the central Christian concept of salvation into terms of wholeness. For him, wholeness suggests the interdependence and integration of an ecological perspective.

> *Erik: I used to think in terms of redemption all the time, the act of being saved. And that was always in the context of confessing sin and being good enough and being worthy of Christ's sacrifice. Instead of thinking of being redeemed I think of being brought into the wholeness that God has for me . . . God's interest is for me to be a whole integrated person. And I think that kind of directs my environmental perspective as well, that the earth was meant to be an integrated system of life and it's all a cycle.*

Being out of tune with the "integrated system of life" was experienced as religious dissonance by the participants. This dissonance touched the core of their being as persons with a worldview that profoundly integrated their lives and communities with God, or the holy, or the interconnection of reality. That spiritual dissonance is the spiritual dimension of the green blues, which seeks a resolution in spiritual integrity.[1]

Moving from the Green Blues toward Green Possibility

Our analysis of the conflict of the green blues has proceeded *with the suspicion that the conflict is revelatory.* The conflict forces us to confront our natural, fallible limitations. But natural limitations of time and energy did not justify inaction for the faith-based environmentalists. They searched for ways to work smarter, together, and without letting obstacles become excuses. We have observed their search through this analysis as part of an ethnographic phenomenology, a hermeneutical circle that questions how to resolve the green blues.

Recall the steps of this method. We have explored the inner conflict of action and motivation, the self-reported descriptions of the

---

1. Readers of critical theory and Edward Schillebeeckx will recognize this as discernment through negative contrast. See Philip Kennedy, *Schillebeeckx* (Collegeville, MN: Liturgical Press, 1993), 128.

green blues, by correlating the ethnographic data with Ricoeur's phenomenology of fallibility and employing environmental decision theory. That was step three—the need for new data, which the participant testimony about the gaps supplies.

Now, the phenomenon of conflict is interpreted with classic religious texts according to step four—an "exegetical suspicion" that calls for a new reading of texts. Many great spiritual thinkers have also struggled with inner conflict. A selection of classic texts that chart those struggles are brought together here not as an exercise in comparative theology but as resources for an ongoing step in the hermeneutical method of green blues theory.[2] The texts continue the hermeneutical circle by offering deeper ways to diagnose and cure the green blues. Their spiritual visions not only analyze but offer pathways to resolve conflict. Their visions lure us forward and renew the energy for the work ahead.

This fourth step, the new interpretation of conflict and faith, will begin to bring forth the outlines of a theology of green possibility: a more hospitable and interdependent view of the world. A new set of core concepts correlating to the knowledge, caring, and action gaps will emerge. These concepts establish the construct of spiritual integrity, an answer to the gaps. We start to see a vision of green possibility, rooted in recognizing and accepting our limits— and the limits of the earth—realistically and critically assessing our choices as they affect the earth, and prioritizing our values in order to act decisively and peacefully.

First, interrelation is seen as the depth of self-knowledge—knowing oneself as related to all life—and this unity motivates action for others and the earth. Pondering Buddhist notions of interrelation can heal the divorce between humanity and the earth, invite deeper relationship, motive and inspire action.

Second, priorities are seen as the depth of feeling, the core feel-

---

2. For models of comparative theology, see Francis X. Clooney, *Comparative Theology: Deep Learning across Religious Borders* (Chichester: Wiley-Blackwell, 2010). See also Leo D. Lefebure, *The Buddha and the Christ: Explorations in Buddhist and Christian Dialogue*, ed. Paul F. Knitter; Faith Meets Faith Series (Maryknoll, NY: Orbis Books, 1993).

ings that endure despite conflicts. Prioritizing is the tool that finds one's deepest values amid conflicted feelings, and the simplicity of priorities liberates action. The ancient Christian monastic Evagrius wrestled with inner conflict, and his struggle yields fruitful insights about the power of prayer and the gift of prioritizing one's passions.

Third, fairness is the measure of conflicted action, balancing the needs of the other and the self, and this balance enables one, when justified, to decide *for* the other—and recognize that the other is not isolated from oneself. Rabbi Joseph Soloveitchik's reflections on humanity's creaturely vocation to the earth offer valuable clarity about the nature of humanity's covenantal responsibilities. In short, spiritual depth of knowing, caring, and acting helps motivate, liberate, and guide.

Religious visions of the person and community can illuminate the spiritual conflicts of the fallible person trying to care for the earth without necessarily casting a judgmental glare. In fact, monastic traditions, which safeguard some of the most ancient spiritual practices, speak with great compassion and forgiveness about human weakness. "In the monastery, we fall down and we get up, we fall down and we get up."[3] There is salvation in accepting limitations and then trying to be the best limited person one can be.

Because each religious tradition offers rich resources, it is impossible to attend in appropriate depth to all traditions. This section does not attempt even to sample the overflowing wisdom in religious writing relevant to theology and ecology. Still, in our pluralist context, the attempt to listen to even a few voices from the great world wisdom traditions is necessary and rewarding. The doctrines have a clarity and imaginative power to transform one's self-understanding. They are thus practical resources that can catalyze useful attitudes and support spiritual integrity.

Drawing on these religious resources thus enables the thinker and spiritual seeker from any tradition to expand his or her own assumptions, and find new answers to shared questions. Precisely because teachings from other traditions come in unfamiliar

---

3. Joan Chittister, *Wisdom Distilled from the Daily: Living the Rule of St. Benedict Today* (San Francisco: HarperOne, 2009), 55.

symbols, they may more effectively jar loose settled notions and spark creative responses. To borrow such teachings need not be the violent raid of a pirate looting foreign treasures, wrenching them loose from their original context. Rather, like a museum visitor, the reader encounters great art and comes away with a wider vision, and greater capacities for expressing her own worldview.[4] As Donald Swearer acknowledges, the contextuality of religious traditions is essential to their power and ability to speak directly to their own adherents. Nonetheless, "those of us engaged in the religion and ecology movement also believe that particular traditions may embody principles and practices of more general applicability." One of my research participants, Mohamad, put it colorfully: "Every good teaching from any tradition is a lost riding beast of the Prophet." Let us see how these select beasts, these resources from world religions, offer insights for healing the conflicts, finding peace, and inspiring action—taking "care of the environmentalist," as Thich Nhat Hanh urges.

The Depth of Hospitable Knowing: Knowing Oneself as Related to All Life

The question regarding Buddhist notions of interrelation is simple: how do such ideas help my research participants with their conflicts about action? The point is clearly not to encourage all environmentalists to become Buddhists; nor did all my participants encounter Buddhism explicitly. But a focused exploration of one of Buddhism's most characteristic teachings shows how pondering one's kinship with all life invites empathy and diminishes egoism. Regardless of one's specific religious views on karma, sin, grace, or rebirth (to jumble together Christian and Buddhist terms), pondering a philosophical model of interrelationship invites compassion

---

4. Roland Faber and and Catherine Keller, "A Taste of Multiplicity: The Skillful Means of Religious Pluralism," in *Religions in the Making: Whitehead and the Wisdom Traditions of the World*, ed. John B. Cobb, Jr. (Eugene, OR: Cascade Books, 2012), 186; Donald Swearer, "Principles and Poetry, Places and Stories: The Resources of Buddhist Ecology," *Daedalus* 130, no. 4 (2001): 225.

and highlights the consequences of one's action within an inter-related system.

As Madeleine said, "I'm not Buddhist, but I think my connection to the environment is sort of Buddhist-like with the Incarnation added." Madeleine had grown up Catholic and now worshiped in a Presbyterian church; she was a one-person interfaith dialogue. While Madeleine did not acknowledge any focused study of Buddhism, her comments reflect a personal appropriation of Buddhist ideas as she grasped them. Even the Buddhist participants I met may or may not have studied academic doctrines and readings. This discussion is about their personal appropriation of those ideas.

In addition, classic Buddhist doctrines do not neatly map onto modern environmentalism. Ken Jones and Kenneth Kraft, contemporary scholars who study Buddhist environmental practice, both note the ambivalent application of traditional Buddhist teachings to contemporary contexts. Often modern forms of Buddhism read contemporary concerns back into classical Buddhism.[5] This interpretative freedom is not unique to modern Buddhism; interpretive freedom belongs to the organic evolution of religious forms in new contexts. Adoption and adaptation are inseparable from religious identity as old religious forms grapple with new earthly realities.

But reflecting on the Buddhist concept of interrelationship shines a light on similar themes of solidarity or unity in other traditions and highlights the ethical consequences and responsibilities each tradition stresses. And spiritual thinkers inevitably bring new life to the teachings themselves. Melanie, an African American woman, was the leader of the Buddhist group, who called her their sensei. When I asked what people liked most about being Buddhist, she responded: "Perhaps a better question is, do you consider yourself

---

5. Ken Jones, *The Social Face of Buddhism* (London: Wisdom Publications, 1989), 271. This discussion highlights the Buddhist tradition among the Dharmic tradition, though Jainism and Hinduism have similar teachings on suffering and impermanence, though important differences regarding the idea of the soul. I thank Leo D. Lefebure and Linh Hoang, O.S.F., for reviewing this chapter.

Buddhist?" Her comment points to the intermingled interpretation of self and tradition.

First, a note on terminology. Interdependence was repeatedly discussed as a key dimension of the participants' spirituality and their commitment to environmental advocacy (recall chapter 1). While interdependence, interconnection, and interrelation express similar ideas, I will here use interrelation to signal how a sense of relation is a form of self-knowledge, a spiritual kinship that informs one's attitudes to others. By contrast, interdependence evokes the social and physical exchange of impacts in the linked ecologies of the earth. This term connotes both physical needs and vulnerability and thus an ability to harm or be harmed. Likewise, interconnection suggests physical contact and causality, social interactions, the chemical permeability of toxins—all the links of causality within material systems. Interrelation looks beyond the exchange of impacts, the effects of the exercise of power within chemical, ecological, social, and political systems, to the underlying reality of relationships and identity. So while my participants used all these terms, as do many writers, I will use the term interrelation here to mean the spiritual depth of interconnection and interdependence. To see oneself as related is a spiritual choice. It is a deliberate way of looking at the connections and dependencies within the natural and social world.

I will explore three related points. First, Buddhist teachings invite a deeper awareness of interrelationship with all life. The particularly explicit Buddhist explanation of interrelation renders an initial awareness more vivid. Then, this more vivid imaginative conception of interrelation gives the idea traction: a more vivid notion of interrelation spurs action because it is more easily imagined. Second, after pondering interrelation, one finds the ethical consequences of interrelation become more easily understood. Together, awareness and understanding lead to compassion. In short, a deeper awareness of life's interrelation clarifies the consequences of environmental exploitation and highlights the need for kinship, empathy, and active engagement. Third, Buddhist doctrines diagnose the problem of greed, hatred, and delusion and recommend simplicity and connection.

Invitation to Deeper Awareness of Interrelation

Pondering Buddhist teaching and engaging in intentional meditation invites the practitioner, like Dick, to consider the interrelation
of life more deeply. His self-knowledge was expanded by the ideas
of kinship and compassion.

As in Dick's case, the teachings generated a fruitful conflict in the
first place: by creating a new awareness of the needs of the earth for
his action and then summoning him to ponder what to do. I met with
a group of Western Buddhists who were working on a shared garden. None were ethnically Asian or from Buddhist cultures but were
variously raised Catholic, Pentecostal, Jewish, Congregational, and
Reform Christian. During our discussion, Dick shared how his meditation practice brought him to greater environmental awareness.

> *Well, interestingly, I don't feel like I've had very much of an
> environmentalist view since before I ventured into this prac-
> tice. It's had a big impact. I feel like I have a little bit of con-
> nection with nature, and I think the connectedness has really
> come through this. It's kind of a new thing for me.*

At this point the threat of rain issued by the gathering clouds
became real, and we regrouped inside the church near the garden,
where the group conducted their Wednesday night sitting practice.
Dick continued, "I think it's kind of a new experience. I really feel
compelled, a real sense of connectedness with people, and that's
how it expanded to life in general and so forth. As I was reading
more, about Buddhism and meditation and Zen Buddhism, that
apparently is a common feeling."

Doctrines of Interrelation. The awareness of interrelation Dick
noted is indeed a profound part of Buddhist philosophy. While multiple religions express kinship in their own ways, Buddhism offers
a particularly profound doctrine of relationship, a metaphysics in
which existence and nonexistence fluidly interact. The Buddhist
vision of interrelation is not just mutual reliance, but the vision
of existence as the very interaction between things. The popular
Buddhist teacher Thich Nhat Hanh expresses these ideas as "interexistence," or "interbeing." Thus, interbeing is the mode of existence

through interaction itself. There is no fixed, tightly bounded individual reality to a separate "self." In fact, there is no self at all, no distinct, permanent, somehow substantial or material identity.[6]

More technically, interdependence or interbeing may be called "conditioned genesis" or "dependent origination." Walpola Rahula, one of the foremost scholars of Buddhist teaching, writes,

> According to the teaching of the Buddha, the idea of self is an imaginary, false belief which has no corresponding reality, and it produces harmful thoughts of "me"and "mine," selfish desire, craving, attachment, hatred, ill-will, conceit, pride, egoism, and other defilements, impurities and problems. It is the source of all the troubles in the world from personal conflicts to wars between nations. In short, to this false view can be traced all the evil in the world.[7]

The truer understanding of existence is based on the "principle of conditionality, relativity, and interdependence," which explains "the whole existence and continuity of life."[8] The doctrine of *anatta*, or "no-self," is the natural corollary to the principle of conditionality and relativity.

---

6. Thich Nhat Hanh, *Call Me by My True Names: The Collected Poems of Thich Nhat Hanh* (Berkeley, CA: Parallax Press, 1996). According to core Buddhist doctrine, there are three marks of existence. These are impermanence (*anicca*), suffering (*dukkha*), and "absence of permanent identity or a soul (*anatta*)." See Huston Smith, *The World's Religions* (San Francisco: HarperOne, 2009), 117. The classic explanation of Theravada Buddhist views is Walpola Rahula, *What the Buddha Taught* (New York: Grove Press, 1959). For explanation of Theravada practice, see also Bhante Bunaratana, *Eight Mindful Steps to Happiness: Walking the Buddha's Path* (Somerville, MA: Wisdom Publications, 2001). The great Self or True Self are Mahayana notions that are explored by Thich Nhat Hanh.

7. "Conditioned genesis" is Rahula's term, while Ajahn uses "dependent origination" (Rahula, *What the Buddha Taught*, 51). "The doctrine of *anatta* or no-soul is the natural result of, or the corollary to, the analysis of the Five Aggregates and the teaching of conditioned genesis (*paticca-samuppada*)."

8. The principle of conditionality and interdependence are explained in the detailed formula of *paticca-samuppada*, or "conditioned genesis," consisting of twelve factors. See ibid., 54.

The doctrine of *anatta*, the "no-self," can challenge and disorient Western readers. I am not espousing any metaphysical position on the self but exploring how the theme of interrelation expands views of self and other, the interdependence so often discussed by research participants.[9] Indeed, Rahula also states that the teaching is meant to lead to peace and tranquility but not to cling to; it is a "raft" to abandon.[10]

Ajahn Sona, a Buddhist participant in the Gethsemani inter-religious dialogue that specifically addressed environmental themes, helpfully breaks out this metaphysical explanation into the discrete level of atoms and thought. His concrete explanation makes the concept of interdependence more vivid: "We may naively conceive of ourselves as independent beings, but the atoms of our physical form are constantly exchanged with the outer world and the contents of our minds are filled with ideas and thoughts originating in other minds. There is no real self-substance (*svabhava*)."[11]

Reverend Heng Sure also emphasizes that along with resisting greed and living nonviolently, interdependence is a foundational theme that underlies specific monastic precepts.[12] Reverend Sure

---

9. Bruno Barnhart and Joseph H. Wong, "Introduction," in *Purity of Heart and Contemplation: A Monastic Dialogue between Christian and Asian Tradition*, ed. Bruno Barnhart and Joseph H. Wong (New York: Continuum, 2001).

10. Rahula, *What the Buddha Taught*, 13.

11. "Later Buddhist thought elaborated these ideas considerably, particularly in the Mahayana tradition, with its great emphasis on the emptiness principle (*sunyata*). The 'matrix' of mutual dependence was developed with the metaphor of Indra's net in the Avatamsatka Sutra"; see Ajahn Sona, "Birken: The Tradition of the Green Forest Monastery," in *Green Monasticism: A Buddhist-Catholic Response to an Environmental Calamity*, ed. Donald W. Mitchell and William Skudlarek (New York: Lantern Books, 2010), 41.

12. These precepts in the monastic code known as the Pratimoksha are meant to lead to compassion and virtue. The Pratimoksha is a list of monastic precepts honored by all Buddhist traditions. The Theravada tradition additionally honors the Patimokkha code, and the Mahayana traditions also follows a code called the Bodhisattva Precepts. See Heng Sure, "The Monastic Rules of Theravada and Mahayana Buddhism: The Bhikshu Patimokkha

links these themes to environmental practices today. Simplicity resists greed and gratefully lives with limited, sustainable resources. Nonviolence links to the sustainable practice of vegetarianism. The classic image of Indra's net models the globalized networks of society and ecology today. Indra's net is a "net of interlaced pearls cunningly contrived so that the totality of the net appears by reflection in each and every single pearl. In one, you see all." Reverend Sure emphasizes the connection of compassion and interdependence: "same body, great compassion." The kinship of all life underscores unity and compassion for all.[13]

Similarly, Rev. Eko Little expresses the theme of interdependence by highlighting Dogen's vision of all life and the entire physical world as the living essence of the Buddha: everything is Buddha nature.[14] Dogen was a thirteenth-century Japanese Zen Buddhist teacher who founded the Soto school of Zen. The corollary of Dogen's religious vision of everything and everyone as Buddha nature has profound environmental implications, which Rev. Little brings forward today: we must treat everything with "reverence (love), renunciation (lack of greed), gratitude, and generosity." Thus, interdependence is a natural foundation for love and compassion, for prioritizing care for the earth's communities, and the kind of renunciation that permits prioritizing.

The challenge of seeing interrelation. Nonetheless, as Melanie stated, being interrelated is not an easy notion to grasp. "Many people are able to feel that certain results can occur and somehow they won't be affected. Or their children won't be affected. Or their grandchildren—and they're certainly not thinking about great-grandchildren." Illuminating this obstinate sense of isolation, Ken-

---

and the Ten Major and Forty-Eight Minor *Bodhisattva* Precepts from the *Net of Brahma (Brahmajmala) Sutra*," in *Green Monasticism: A Buddhist-Catholic Response to an Environmental Calamity*, ed. Donald W. Mitchell and William Skudlarek (New York: Lantern Books, 2010), 62.

13. Ibid., 68.

14. Eko Little, "The Monastic Instinct to Revere, to Conserve, to Be Content with Little, and to Share," in *Green Monasticism: A Buddhist-Catholic Response to an Environmental Calamity*, ed. Donald W. Mitchell and William Skudlarek (New York: Lantern Books, 2010), 91.

neth Kraft shares a Zen koan, a paradoxical teaching about sensing our relation to the earth:

> The master says to the student, "See that boat moving way out there on the water? How do you stop it?". . . An increasing number of practitioner-activists believe that the only way to stop the boat of ecological disaster is to deepen our relationship to the planet and all life within it.[15]

It is not easy to grasp the paradox of one's ties to a far-off boat or to seemingly unstoppable climate trends. But without an awareness of interrelationship, the earth's problems were easily sealed away. One's true impact through time and space was sealed off from consciousness. The ethical consequences of one's actions were also hidden, and the true vastness of one's identity was lost. Melanie identified this as "an aspect of what we call ignorance. This meditation practice addresses just how easy it is for us to see ourselves as separate and not connected—but we *are* connected." Asserting one's isolation is a delusion that enables denial and alienation from nature.

For Melanie, meditation addressed the false sense of an isolated, separate identity. Her practice contributed to her own self-knowledge as kin to all, related to all, and able to impact all through her actions. Being kin meant affecting others through her actions. Actions had consequences that carried into future times and future relationships, and all of this comprised one's true, vast identity. She explained that ignorance was "not being able to understand how vast you are in that sense." Interrelation is thus a depth dimension of identity. For Melanie, the idea of interrelation simultaneously reveals the vastness of one's identity and demonstrates the ethical implications of "being connected."

Her use of the term "vast" is fortuitous. Vastness has a particular meaning in a school of Tibetan Buddhism known as a philosophical "middle way" between the extreme views of existence and nonexistence. In interpreting a classic text of this tradition,

---

15. Kenneth Kraft, "The Greening of Buddhist Practice," *Cross Currents* 44, no. 2 (1994): 2.

"The Adornment for Nagarjuna's Thought," Gendun Chopel, a Buddhist monk, discusses the practices that lead to buddhahood. These practices are labeled either "profound" or "vast." The profound set of practices attends to the nature of reality, and the vast practices focus on the deeds that are motivated by compassion.[16] In this context, then, vastness signifies compassion. And, grasping one's vastness—one's true interrelation—leads to compassionate, ethical action.

From Understanding Interrelation to Compassion

The second way Buddhist teachings on interrelation deepen any spiritual meditation on unity and ethics is that after pondering interrelation, one finds that the ethical consequences of interrelation become more easily understood. Kenneth Kraft observes how the traditional meditation Dick and Melanie practiced can develop attitudes that are essential to environmental awareness in several key ways. Meditation is "supposed to reduce egoism, deepen appreciation of one's surroundings, foster empathy with other beings, clarify intention, prevent what is now called burnout, and ultimately lead to a profound sense of oneness with the entire universe."[17]

Reduced egoism. Appreciation of one's surroundings. Empathy. Intention. Preventing burnout. Oneness. Kraft thus clarifies the specific attitudes that result from meditation and catalyze awareness of spiritual and environmental interrelationship. Like deep cold water currents that rise up to the ocean's surface, full of nourishing oxygen, then sink down again to the depths, these attitudes emerge from and further energize an oceanic awareness of spiritual interrelation.

Interrelation coexists with moral choice. In Buddhist teaching, all life is linked existentially and morally. Existentially, life is interlinked by virtue of the universality of suffering. Morally, all life is linked over the course of time by the cycle of rebirth conditioned

---

16. Donald S. Lopez, *The Madman's Middle Way: Reflections on Reality of the Tibetan Monk Gendun Chopel* (Chicago: University of Chicago Press, 2006), 122.

17. Kraft, "The Greening of Buddhist Practice," 2.

by karma. Thus "the concepts of karma and rebirth (*samsara*) integrate the existential sense of a shared common condition of all sentient life forms with the moral nature of the Buddhist cosmology."[18] Thus, existential and moral links are transmuted by environmental concern to emphasize the ethical and causal links. Swearer notes that interdependent causality evolves in later schools of Buddhist thought into visions of ontological unity conveyed by the Buddha-nature of all things. This unity is beautifully imaged with the metaphor of Indra's net, a web of many jewels linked together and imaging all the world. All entities share a common sacred universe.

Each life exists in its present condition due to the causal sequence of actions and influences that leads to the present moment. Huston Smith selects the Buddha's image of a flame passing between candles as the clearest description of causality. The flames are linked by a chain of causation, but none has a truly separate material existence. Nonetheless, crucially, despite and throughout the chain of causality, interrelation does not erase ethical responsibility or causality. The will remains free and thus has moral choice.[19] Within that universe, humans retain particular ethical responsibility for causing the ecological crisis and are obliged to address it. Human responsibility will be especially relevant to the discussion of roles in Jewish thinking below.

Diagnosing Delusion, Prescribing Simplicity

A third way Buddhist doctrines contribute to the sense of unity, empathy, and ethical urgency felt by many participants is the Buddhist diagnosis of greed, hatred, and delusion as a source of trouble, with the recommended cure of simplicity and reconnection.

---

18. Swearer, "Principles and Poetry," 227, 230.

19. The discourse centers on compassion rather than the rhetoric of rights, reflecting Chopel's discourse on vastness as compassion, and non-individuation as an embrace of compassion. Swearer notes this emphasis on mindfulness and moral transformation to refute critics who imply that a distinction between self and other is necessary for an ethic that cares for the other. Rather, mindfulness has the capacity to challenge oppressive structures (ibid., 236-39).

Buddhism traditionally teaches that suffering is caused by desire or hatred, greed, and delusion. Katrina acknowledged how interconnection fueled her desire to act on her awareness but also surfaced a feeling of frustration. "Looking at the environment it's hard to deny that the crisis is not there. It kind of creates a sense of wanting to act on that awareness. Also, I begin feeling an interconnectedness, and with that feeling maybe a sense of responsibility arising. I do sometimes have frustration."

Hatred. Attachment to one's views can demonize people whose views are different from one's own, an anger that may intensify to hatred when those views appear to endanger the earth and oneself. This is the very opposite of hospitable knowing. But Buddhist interdependence challenges the oppositional mindset that permits an ideological attachment to one's own viewpoints. Rather than radically opposing the good and true from the evil and false, reifying and despising the views of the "enemy," the practitioner is challenged to acknowledge these oppositions as part of the whole. Ultimately, the oppositions are themselves false. Instead, one is challenged to see and embrace those views somehow related to oneself.

Jason reflected on the problem of blaming someone else instead of himself. He said, "Your natural action is to be angry about what people are doing there, but I think we're taught to develop a sense that we're responsible for everything that happens. I'm responsible for what's happening in the environment. A big garbage dump down the street from me: I'm partially responsible for that. I want to blame someone else, but I need to take responsibility." Even if he wasn't sure how to take on his responsibility, he felt acknowledging it more truly reflected the reality of his links to garbage in the world.

Greed. Contemporary socially engaged Buddhists such as Ken Jones translate the analysis of suffering and desire within the individual psyche to social, economic, and political systems. Within these systems greed and attachment drive inequalities and violence, resulting in militarism, ecological degradation, and the misery of poverty. Melanie also commented on how greed and the desire for instant gratification obscure one's awareness of personal impacts through time, the relationship to the generations of the future. As she put it bluntly, "The other thing is greed and wanting what we want when we want it. Not thinking so much about the future."

Delusion. As Ajahn writes, "Buddhism identifies three primal roots of all ill: greed, hatred, and delusion. If we can agree that greed for material objects to please the senses is the primary root of climate change, I think we can also identify delusion as a major secondary cause. One form this takes is the widespread denial of the problem."[20] Delusion is a false knowing that includes alienation from nature. This model of reality with its strong awareness of interrelation counters the often reductionist Western model of reality, a model that has achieved many technological triumphs but lost sight of greater wholeness and integrity of the world.

Denial is partly rooted in preferential bias for one's own limited perspective, as was emphasized by the discussion of fallible knowing in chapter 4. It is a form of egoism. Thus, while overcoming egoism is easier said than done, it heals the tendency to bias inherent in fallible humanity's limited perspectives. Accepting one's interrelation releases one from clinging to finite perspectives and grounds the respect for others that enables intellectual hospitality. For Melanie, this meant ensuring that her concern for the environment was truly an act affirming her relationships with all life, through time: "I don't feel discouraged, I just don't know what's going to happen. And I guess I want to make sure I'm not just indulging my own ego." Even living one's own values contained the risk of being driven by ego-fulfillment. Melanie went on to explain the "indulgence," saying, "Well, it's nice to live by one's values. But even that can be ego driven. This is a bigger question than just me and what I do—whether I use plastic or I don't use plastic."

The monk Chendun spoke pointedly to bias and limited perspectives in a way that reflects both Melanie's comments and Ricoeur's discussion of fallible perspectival limitation. Chendun observes that though we seek awareness, knowledge is still marked by perspectival limitation. Chendun gives the example of looking at a white conch with jaundiced eyes. This does not make the conch yellow—even if the entire community has jaundice. Thus, Chendun

---

20. Sona, "Birken," 45.

concludes that regardless of the limits to knowledge, there is at least the other path, the path of vastness, of compassion borne of being interlinked with the vastness of life.[21]

Egoism erodes a sense of being at home in the universe by reducing a feeling of kinship. In turn, meditating on kinship diminishes egoism; the resulting sense of connection to all communities of life creates a fruitful ground for action.

For the faith-based environmentalists, reflecting on kinship frees them from a self-centered perspective, fixed upon the perspective of the individual self, to hospitable knowing. The depth of hospitable knowing is recognizing the world as kin in a way that grounds compassion for creation and inspires action.

Evagrius and Prayer: Prioritizing the Passions

During an interfaith dialogue held at New Camaldoli Hermitage, in Big Sur, California, a group of scholars and practitioners proposed that Buddhist contemplative awareness and Christian monasticism are linked by the theme of "purity of heart." This theme links the unity and compassion discussed by Buddhist phi-

---

21. For Chopel, the question of truth relates to the philosophy of valid knowledge. He observes, "All our decisions about what is and is not are just decisions made in accordance with how it appears to our mind" (Lopez, *Madman's Middle Way*, 129). Knowledge of existence is perspectival, and perspective is fallible. Even if all persons share the same incorrect perception, their view is not correct. Chopel gives the example of looking at a white conch with jaundiced eyes. This does not make the conch yellow, even if the entire community has jaundice. Thus, "there is no confidence whatsoever in our decisions concerning what exists and does not exist." Lopez echoes Ricoeur in calling this the "the fallibility of humans ... a defining characteristic of samsara, the beginningless cycle of birth and death" (130). The comparison persists as Chopel considers the physically grounded origin of perspectival limitation. The limits of perception relate "not so much on the mind but on the body, on the physical form as the container of consciousness, and how the size and shape and configuration of that container color the experience of the world, or perhaps more precisely, how that container creates the world" (133). For Ricoeur and Chopel, consciousness is limited by embodiment in its larger context, its geographical and historical situation: by its originating perspective.

losophy to the Christian ideal of *apatheia*, exemplified here by Evagrius of Pontus, the fourth-century monastic whose theory of inner struggle can illuminate the green blues and how religious environmentalists might overcome them.[22] Evagrius offers a bracing diagnosis of inner conflict, insists on confronting the conflict, and suggests how to heal it with peaceful practices. His most useful prescription is his attention to integrating the passions and finding peace through what I will call prioritizing. As Kevin Hunt writes, "The whole of the teaching of Evagrius is devoted to setting forth a method for attaining purity of heart, *apatheia*, through the right ordering of the passions that are so much a part of being human."[23] Again, the purpose is not to suggest faith-based environmentalists need become ascetics, or adopt his particular understanding of the passions (just as the last section didn't mean to imply one must be Buddhist). The gift to borrow is the aim and method of Evagrius's ascetic practice—peaceful release from conflict and union with God.

Like Ann, torn by self-accusation, feeling she betrayed the claims of her river despite her best intentions, the hermit Evagrius also knew keenly how easily good intentions drain away. Evagrius's understanding of the distracted person becomes a moral assessment, acknowledging personal priorities to be the result of choice. For Evagrius, the battle of conflicting feelings takes on moral color.

Evagrius's self-accusation resulted from the painful temptation of his passion for a married woman, leaving him tormented by depression and self-doubt. Born in Asia Minor in 384, Evagrius became a radically ascetic monastic and "the most accomplished theorist of the monastic life" in his search for "radical therapy for the tempted self." He developed his theory from the crucible of personal experience and described his conflict as battling thoughts,

---

22. Barnhart and Wong, "Introduction," 5.

23. Kevin Hunt, "Doubt and Breakthrough in the Desert Fathers," in *Purity of Heart and Contemplation: A Monastic Dialogue between Christian and Asian Traditions,* ed. Bruno Barnhart and Joseph H. Wong (New York: Continuum, 2001), 171.

envisioned as the onslaught of attacking demons.[24] While demonic temptation seems quaint and strange, this way of thinking belonged to the ancient world and expressed Evagrius's real sense of torment. As a perceived reality or a metaphor, demons continue to exist as a label for mental misery, as the bestselling contemporary account of depression attests, titled *The Noonday Demon*. His monastic weapon was the prayer that sought freedom from conflict and inner peace, the resolution he called *apatheia*.[25] Let us see how he understood the conflict of emotions that defeats good intentions, provided his own spiritual interpretation of the action gap, sought help with the weapon of focused prayer, and found refreshment and guidance in the community.

The Battle: Thoughts and Demons

Conflicting feelings and thoughts are almost inevitable in the model of the self that Evagrius inherited. Educated by the great Cappadocian theologians Gregory of Nazianzus and Basil of Caesarea, he inherited the Greek view of a tripartite soul and Origen's doctrine of the soul as a fallen rational being.[26] This ancient psychology facilitated a mental model for inner conflict. In this model, human beings are identified most with the rational mind. Yet, having fallen away from knowledge of God, they became easily dominated by passion and subject to the demons of aggression and desire, dominant in the "lower" parts of the soul.[27]

For Evagrius, thoughts and demons were the same reality—a modern psychological insight from an ancient thinker. Even the

---

24. David Brakke, *Demons and the Making of the Monk: Spiritual Combat in Early Christianity* (Cambridge, MA: Harvard University Press, 2006), 49.

25. Evagrius Ponticus, *Ad Monachos*, trans. Jeremy Driscoll, O.S.B., in *Ancient Christian Writers: The Works of the Fathers in Translation*, ed. Dennis D. McManus (New York: Newman Press, 2003). Robert Van de Weyer, ed., *On Living Simply: The Golden Voice of John Chrysostom* (Liguori, MO: Liguori/Triumph, 1996).

26. The tripartite soul is a Platonic model, envisioning the soul with a mind, spirit, and appetite or passions.

27. Brakke, *Demons*, 54.

terms for demons and thoughts are used interchangeably in his writing to describe the "outer forces that work upon the [person's] mind."[28] To master these conflicting thoughts, emotions must be first understood, then directed to good ends. To understand the emotions, Evagrius developed a complex science of the nature, origin, interaction, and effects of thoughts. As the theologian David Brakke writes, "For the Evagrian monk, knowledge was power."[29]

Evagrius's systematic psychology armed the disciple to master the "thoughts," or demons of passion. Then, battling emotions must be pacified and prioritized to serve their proper roles, energizing the quest for God. Evagrius listed eight sins whose energies could be redirected to good: gluttony, lust, greed, anger, melancholy, sloth, vainglory, and pride. For example, anger can be a force for good, blazing in a rage for justice. In its proper role, anger provides courageous energy for redressing wrong. Likewise, the consciousness of lack that might breed resentment should instead be directed to patience. Similarly, the energies of lust, gluttony, and avarice should seek holy ends and desire continence, charity, and temperance.

Yet the power of the energizing emotions easily dissipates, leaving both a caring and an action gap, as seen so often in the stories of religious environmentalists and in the larger culture. Anger ebbs into resentment. Sadness blocks prayers. Being overwhelmed inhibits creative thinking, energy, and attention to the problems that really require our focus. If the primal energies of emotions and feelings are not properly directed into action by a deliberate will, the "volition of low degree" that Ogden Nash pointedly described, the seemingly mild vice of velleity, robs good intentions of their power.

Battling the distracting demons of the gaps. Many participants would resonate with Evagrius's imagery of weapons and temptation. Chapter 3 described how Latha admitted feeling embattled by

---

28. George Tsakiridis, *Evagrius Ponticus and Cognitive Science: A Look at Moral Evil and the Thoughts* (Eugene, OR: Pickwick Publications, 2010), 4. Modern psychological theories are scarcely more definite about the origin of evil, whether it be an external force, the objective existence of an evil power, a subjective creation of social pressure, or an inexplicable mental choice.

29. Brakke, *Demons*, 52.

the "onslaught of consumerism." With perfect Evagrian sensibility, Nancy called consumerism "a seduction." The Big Sur monastics cite the same obstacles as those in the caring gap: distraction, dullness (acedia), laxity, and, agitation (which parallels being overwhelmed). These obstacles require mindfulness and attention to overcome, practices to which Christian monasticism, like Buddhist monasticism, is dedicated.[30]

Evagrius's distinctive and profound analysis of acedia has received interesting modern attention from the spiritual writer Kathleen Norris. She has seized on this vice of acedia in a popular spiritual book of the same name, *Acedia and Me*. In this book, she reflects on her own struggles with listless, unmotivated, depressed dullness. As she writes, acedia results from distraction more than actual laziness. It is the guaranteed failure of boredom, restlessness, or impossibly large projects.[31] She has captured the risk of taking on too much in her canny assessment of acedia, the ancient vice of listlessness and ennui that evolved into the medieval vice of sloth. This is precisely the risk of rejecting what is possible for what is perfect by underestimating one's finitude.

Fighting back with persistence. To fight back, to regain one's self-possession, to assert one's personal priorities against the onslaught and the seduction require the focus of a driven athlete and the cheering support of one's team. Consumerist onslaught, life's 24/7 distractions, throwing up one's hands: these feelings are easily normalized. But Norris reminds us that the sluggishness of acedia is rooted in despair, a lack of faith that must be resisted. Likewise, the metaphor of passive distraction, literally being pulled away, grants too much power to those seducing "demons." The demon of velleity, profiled by poet Ogden Nash and ethicist Daniel Maguire, returns, taunting us with what we *would* will, if only it

---

30. Laurence Freeman, "Purity of Heart: Discovering What You Really Want," in *Purity of Heart and Contemplation: A Monastic Dialogue between Christian and Asian Traditions*, ed. Bruno Barnhart and Joseph H. Wong (New York: Continuum, 2001), 255.

31. Kathleen Norris, *Acedia and Me: A Marriage, Monks, and a Writer's Life* (New York: Riverhead Books, 2008). See also Tsakiridis, 28.

were easier. One does have a choice. In the end, focusing on one's real goal only occurs as an act of will. And, as Benedictine Judith Sutera wisely observes, finding the stability that is the true resolution of acedia's restlessness is the way to "deep peace and inexpressible joy. Isn't that worth a look?"[32]

Willingness is a key recognized by many traditions. I asked the Buddhist group, What would be the one thing you could make go away to make this problem better? Melanie headed straight to the heart of the matter. She said, "I don't know what kind of miracle it would take, but I would make it so we were all willing to work on it and resolve the problems." Mohamad from the DC Muslims referenced the Islamic scholar Seyyed Hossein Nasr, who also reflected on how the will must consciously and strenuously lift its focus past the barriers of ignorance, deception, distraction, and rebellion.[33] The will remains free and responsible, despite all the demonic barriers of ignorance, deception, distraction, and rebellion—the knowledge, concern, and action gaps. One of my Jain participants said something similar. "What I like about Jainism is that it emphasizes one's efforts, where other religions might empha-

---

32. Judith Sutera, "Acedia Revisited: New Case for an Old Sin," *American Monastic Newsletter* 29 (October 1999); http://www.osb.org.

33. While Seyyed Hussein Nasr has been critiqued for his links to the perennialist movement (see Mark Sedgwick, *Against the Modern World: Traditionalism and the Secret Intellectual History of the Twentieth Century* [Oxford: Oxford University Press, 2009]), his thought was discussed by my participants. Nasr teaches that to be created in "His own form" means being endowed with divine qualities in humanity of intelligence, free will, and the gift of speech. Nonetheless, the will is limited. Persons are able to choose freely between alternatives to the extent they share in God's absolute freedom of will. Nasr acknowledges that this is not a logical premise, but a truth only "comprehended through that intellectual intuition which alone can realize the *coincidentia oppositorum*." Habit is built and dismantled by these conscious acts of the will, strenuously combatting demonically persistent distractions. For Nasr, humanity "as theomorphic . . . shares in the freedom of the will which really belongs to God" and so must choose it (Seyyed Hossein Nasr, *Ideals and Realities of Islam* [Boston: Beacon Press, 1966], 20). This discourse on habit reflects Ricoeur's and Strasser's discussion of the renewal of the person in creating new, chosen habits.

size grace from God, a deity, or that you need some blessing from an external God for your own benefit. But this is very applicable I think to environmental activism. We all take responsibility for our actions; we do creative actions for ecology." These diverse observations emphasize how the participants connect their traditions to their advocacy, to their ability to muster the will and take action, according to their own interpretations of those traditions—even if their interpretations are not as formally precise as an academic might find them.

Norris and Evagrius thus echo the themes raised by my research participants in their own reflection on the green blues: the damnable role of distraction and the necessary antidote of persistence. Nonetheless, only a heartless automaton would say this is easy, because we do have multiple feelings and obligations. It is very difficult to prioritize only a few key priorities amidst floods of distractions.

Evagrius offers prayer as a way to drive away the thoughts that attempt to tear the beloved, one's authentic priorities, out of the center of one's attention. Prayer restores integrity by rightly prioritizing the passions. Prioritizing addresses the green blues by reducing the unreasonable number of goals to the most important ones. Prioritizing loosens the shackles of feeling overwhelmed and enables people to act even with their "finite pool of worry." One's actions become proportionate to one's abilities and proportionate to the needs of self and others. In this way prioritizing can heal the hidden guilt and unease niggling at even the most dedicated environmentalists, troubling them with the feeling that they are not doing enough.

The Weapon of Focused Prayer

Evagrius's chief weapon for battling mercilessly tormenting thoughts is prayer that displaces bad thoughts once they are labeled correctly. Thoughts must be diagnosed correctly, identifying the kind of demon, or distraction, or temptation involved, and channeling one's thoughts positively through prayer. For Evagrius, prayer is a powerful "skillful means," a practical method for refocusing on the disciple's most essential priority: awareness of God.

Prayer works by displacement and transformation; for Evagrius, prayer displaces the thoughts (or demons) that turn us away from God. Evagrius believed that one can only think one thought at a time. He would agree with Elke Weber from the Center for Research on Environmental Decisions, cited in chapter 2, that people have a mental capacity for anxiety that is limited, a "finite pool of worry." Many healers today continue to recognize that prayer and meditation counter stress.[34] In Evagrius's more poetic visualization, the mind can only host a few demons or thoughts at one time. Evil thoughts can be countered by other thoughts, by prayer, and by perseverance. Thus, focusing prayer drives out the demon, leaving peace of mind. Evagrius advises, "Use good thoughts to dispel bad ones," like sending tormenting worry splashing out of the pool with a tremendous cannonball leap of prayer.

Prayer also transforms and leads the spiritual seeker's thoughts and desires to their highest ends. Marie spoke specifically about the communal form of prayer that sustained her, the Mass. The prayer and ritual of the Mass offered her communion with "a transforming God somehow connected with the Eucharist. I am always looking for transformation, not only for myself but for my family."

The Goal: Seeking Apatheia. While *apatheia* had multiple meanings among non-Christian philosophers, the primary sense of *apatheia* is health, stability, an unassailable form of integrity.[35] Among early Christian writers such as Clement of Alexandria, *apatheia* reflected divine freedom and preserved the disciple from demonic temptation. Clement observed that *apatheia* bore fruit in daily life, inspiriting charitable actions, almsgiving, and good relations with one's neighbor.[36] John Cassian, the fifth-century monk from southern Gaul, considered *apatheia* as both purity and

---

34. Tsakiridis, *Evagrius Ponticus*, 9. For example, see the Benson-Henry Institute for Mind Body Medicine, Massachusetts General Hospital, http://www.massgeneral.org/bhi.

35. Augustine Casiday, *Evagrius Ponticus* (London: Routledge, 2006), 361-62. The classic meaning of "not suffering" makes *apatheia* to be an attribute of God. Here we are discussing its meaning for the disciple.

36. Ibid., 366.

agape.[37] For Evagrius, *apatheia* meant the tranquility and health of the soul. *Apatheia* meant freedom from passion, meaning both self-control that prevents active sins and inner peace. Positively, *apatheia* meant the transformation of distorted emotions to virtues.

Cassian, who interpreted Evagrius for the Latin tradition, speaks of the freedom of a tranquil mind in terms that echo Ricoeur's view of the centrality of the heart, and my contention that conflicted feelings need to be prioritized. "The heart's attention is most tenaciously fastened upon the one and highest good."[38] The monastics at the Big Sur interfaith dialogue shared the observation that the heart is the point of equipoise in the person. The heart refers to the ultimate depth, the balanced, reproportioned loves and action that Ricoeur explored in the mode of *dis*proportion and discord.[39]

What exactly *is* prayer? What are its practices? The almost infinite diversity of forms of prayer and spiritual practices cannot be discussed here. Nor were they the focus of my conversations. As odd as it may seem, prayer was not a frequent topic among my participants. This reflects the guiding questions within our focus groups, which addressed faith and environmental action, not spiritual practices specifically. We had to stop after two hours, which was hard enough in every case, without even exhausting that topic!

As Wilken observes, "Cassian knew that 'prayer' is too general a category to be of much help in teaching someone to pray. Prayer is varied and takes different forms at different times. A person prays one way, he says, when he is happy and another way when burdened

---

37. Hunt, "Doubt and Breakthrough," 174. Regarding the unmovable detachment of Eckhart, and how Benedict related *apatheia* to the progress of humility, see Donald Corcoran, "Benedictine Humility and Confucian 'Sincerity,'" in *Purity of Heart and Contemplation: A Monastic Dialogue between Christian and Asian Tradition*, ed. Bruno Barnhart and Joseph Wong (New York: Continuum, 2001), 228.

38. Casiday, *Evagrius Ponticus*, 385.

39. Corcoran, "Benedictine Humility," 240. For example, the Benedictine Donald Corcoran interprets *apatheia* as an opening of the heart, freeing from obstacles and gaps. Opening the heart creates "an ever-widening capacity for the spirit," which he compares to the Confucian ideal of *jen* (love, compassion).

by a weight of sadness, one way when enjoying spiritual successes and another when oppressed by troubles, one way when begging pardon for sins and another when asking for grace or some virtue."[40]

But indeed prayer served diverse functions, as a few mentions from the participants showed: to meditate and offer praise, as Joel Hunter commented, grateful that his environmental advocacy gave him permission to praise God through the wonder of the turtles in his backyard pond; to seek guidance and direction, as Sarah did through her practice of scripture study; to pray for persistent growth in spiritual integrity, as the Gwich'in chief observed.

Prayer, among its many function, descriptions, and unique characterization, ultimately intends to bring persons closer to God (or their nontheistic spiritual goal). For my participants, being in nature brought them closer to God. The simple, spiritual, natural function of being in nature was bringing them closer to God. It was a form of prayer: natural, spiritual, spontaneous openness to the divine as they sought it. The conscious orientation of that openness into practices and priorities is the formal act of prayer. In a sense, it was the entire function of the discussions we had and their own work in their committees and communities to engage in that conscious prioritizing, discussing, and transforming of habits; in short, practical prayer.

Community Support

In this work, everyone needs the refreshment of hope and support of friends.

> *Elaine (Buddhist): It's easier I think when you have a group that is moving in that direction and you learn from them. If you're by yourself, I don't know, it probably takes a little longer.*

While religious traditions differ about how much human efforts must rely on God to succeed, most emphasize the power of

---

40. Robert Louis Wilken, "Cassian the Monk and John Cassian: The Conferences," *First Things* (November 2000).

communal support. The Christian tradition emphasizes that God's grace heals the struggling will, though different denominations and theologians throughout time have disputed just how depraved or dependent the human will is and have debated the role of human freedom in the soul's transformation. Most Buddhist traditions are best described as nontheistic, and do not affirm a God or dependence on a God. The spiritual seeker progresses by human effort.[41] Nonetheless, the *sangha*, or community, is one of the three Jewels of the tradition. Together with the Buddha and the dharma, or teaching, the *sangha* supports one's progress. Interestingly, some of my Hindu participants expressed theistic views, but did not consider the human will weakened and in need of help from the divine, in distinction to Christian models. For them, humanity was capable of significant moral effort and was responsible to undertake it. Their discussions of habit in chapter 2 reflected this.

And yet, most agree that a life shared in community is critical for spiritual growth precisely to check the limitations and myopia of even the most enthusiastic individual—indeed, perhaps *especially* the most enthusiastic individual.

The persons I met felt that their own hopes were strengthened by joining forces with a community. Congregations support the transformation of good intentions and conscious values into habits. Communal habits of reflection, study, and prayer provide the essential social support needed to encourage the lonely pioneer trying to persevere. Even among secular activists in the virtual age of social media, groups are important.[42]

The struggle is long and slow, but gradually the monastic finds spiritual integrity, the "purity of heart" that brings together body, soul, and spirit. Evagrius lived in a creative tension: an "ascetic vision, integrating concern for cultivating the body, the mind and

---

41. I thank Leo D. Lefebure for noting that much Theravada and Zen Buddhist rhetoric is directed toward human efforts alone.

42. Sociologist Dana Fisher documents the supportive power of working in groups; see Dana R. Fisher and Marije Boekkooi, "Mobilizing Friends and Strangers: Understanding the Role of the Internet in Days of Action," *Information, Communiation & Society* 13, no. 2 (2010): 200.

the heart in pursuit of Christian perfection."[43] Madeleine expressed the support of her community in her struggle to resist the temptation of luscious, out of season raspberries in an earlier chapter. The language of temptation just may not be accidental: she kept saying "what the hell!"

> *Madeleine: Somebody's told me, "These foods have been trucked in; this is not good for the environment." I get to the point where I think, "Oh, what the hell. Throw it in the basket." I hate to keep saying what the hell. But now I've heard Ann's story and I'm telling you, this is leadership because I am going to think, "Well if Ann can do it . . . "*

Community stories like Ann's helped her. Evagrius's teachings belong to a whole genre of community advice from elder monastic to disciple, the sayings of the desert mothers and fathers. With that help, she could aim to make slow progress, in the spirit of one saying from these early monastics: "What do you do in the monastery? We get up and we fall down. We get up and we fall down." Perfection is a risky goal. It is enough to discover the gift of clarity about what one's highest good indeed is and train the heart's attention on it. Such is integrity, struggling for that creative tension between the relative priorities of emotions and values and allowing these values to guide action that confirms one's life in the community. Evagrius's battle to surface operative values confronts head-on the "hidden values" Anna Peterson described as operative values. Confronted with fortitude, the hidden values may yet slink away like a demon caught in the light.

Recall Hardcastle's discussion of addiction and Strasser's view

---

43. Casiday, *Evagrius Ponticus,* 369. Evagrius's critics were many, past and present: Casiday discusses Jerome's scorn for Evagrius's apparent wish to have a soul as immovable as a stone. The model of gradual progress in the spiritual life is cited as the approach of Augustine and Cassian, two monastic founders responsible for community life of spiritual seekers, who engaged *apatheia* for the Latin tradition with the term *impassibilitas* (372). For additional reference, see also Mette Sophia Bocher Rasmussen, "Like a Rock or Like God? The Concept of *Apatheia* in the Monastic Theology of Evagrius of Pontus," *Studia Theologica* 59 (2005): 148.

of habits. One's being as an active subject, someone who chooses to respond to others—one's true humanity—centers in the heart. The heart is the "finite spirit transformed by habit."[44] New dispositions become deeds, and new habits become the undergirding of a new self. Communities support the transformation of conscious values into habits through social support, shared social goals, the reinforcement of ritual, the sacred repetition of tradition, inspiration by leaders, accepting community critiques, discovering new ideas—all the dynamics common to online support groups, book groups, and prayer circles. Knowing becomes a permanently energizing motivation through conversion to new habits.

As described above, early Christian monastic tradition trusts that prayer can release the paralysis of anxiety and strengthen the determined will, especially if prudently guided by accurate knowledge of the demons. But this knowledge, and the transformation to which it leads, depends in large part on the wisdom and support of the community. Spiritual guides, community traditions, others on the journey: these all support the monk—or the religious environmentalist to strengthen the will for action. For the person of faith, prayer accesses an endless pool of hope. In short, prayer, prioritization, social support, and God's help guide the pilgrim forward despite the battling emotions and the chasm of the caring gap.

Holy Companionship: The Gift of the Earth and What Is *Not* Possible

Interrelation is central to Buddhist philosophy, but other traditions reflect on kinship as well. Even the Abrahamic traditions, whose classic Genesis texts have been famously charged with causing the entire earth-dominating master narrative, have foundational symbols that celebrate kinship and unity.[45] Many beautiful Christian kinship theologies have been written, none more beloved than St. Francis's great song of the kinship of creation. Christians and all

---

44. See Andrew Tallon, "The Concept of the Heart in Strasser's *Phenomenology of Feeling*," *American Catholic Philosophical Quarterly* 66, no. 3 (1992): 351.

45. See Introduction, n. 4.

devotees of St. Francis rejoice in their relationship to Brother Sun, Sister Moon, Sister Water, Brother Wolf, and all the creatures.[46]

Central to Jewish interpretations of kinship is the reality of different roles within the relationships. In this section, we look at how Rabbi Soloveitchik, a modern leader of Orthodox Jewish philosophy, examines the roots of the dominion question in the conflicting vocations of the created person. Most of my participants did not feel entitled to dominate nature or struggle to reconcile their advocacy with anthropocentrism. Some did—and Soloveitchik speaks directly to those few. (Some, like one who scoffed at biocentrism, saying, "Yeah, yeah, trees are people too," might not care to listen.) The larger reason for listening to his work is to highlight how perennial and deep-seated are the conflicts related to self-understanding in relation to the earth and to others. The conflicts of the green blues relate to enduring human struggles.

In his book *The Lonely Man of Faith*, Rabbi Soloveitchik confronts the risk that selfishness can taint the fundamental conflict of ascertaining and accepting one's place in the covenant community.[47] Rashi, the great eleventh-century rabbinic commentator, also addressed "mankind's double-edged relationship with nature." He linked the words dominion (*rayda'*) and descent (*y'rida*) within the word *v'yirdu*. He concluded that "if he is worthy, then he will rule over the animal kingdom and if not, he will experience descent before them and the wild animals will rule over him."[48]

What emerges from Rabbi Soloveitchik is a fascinating account of how the apparent scriptural justification of humanity's superior

---

46. Dawn M. Nothwehr, *Ecological Footprints: An Essential Franciscan Guide for Faith and Sustainable Living* (Collegeville, MN: Liturgical Press, 2012).

47. Joseph D. Soloveitchik, *The Lonely Man of Faith* (New York: Doubleday, 1965).

48. Shmuel Simenowitz, "Water Conservation and *Halacha*: An Unorthodox Approach," in *Compendium of Sources in Halacha and the Environment,* ed. Ora Sheinson and Shai Spetgang (New York: Canfei Nesharim, 2005), 48. Rashi is quoting almost verbatim an earlier work, Midrash Genesis Rabbah (c. fourth to sixth century CE) to Genesis 1:28 (7:12). I am indebted to Lawrence Troster for this observation.

status results from an inner conflict in the human person: a primordial green blues in the Garden of Eden.

Various contemporary Jewish views on humanity's role range from anthropocentrism to biocentrism. A leading Conservative Jewish educator expressed a classic view of humanity's special role by telling me, "I don't see how you can sacrifice the hegemony of the human. I don't go with this whole thing about speciesism, whatever it's called, because I don't see how you can be faithful to my tradition and not put special responsibility on human beings for the preservation for the world. No animal has that responsibility and therefore no animal merits the degree of care the human being merits." Here he tapped on his desk for emphasis. Nonetheless, anthropocentrism is contradicted by the baffling and theocentric message of Job. Jewish theologian Jon Levenson points to the speeches of God in chapters 38-41 of the book of Job, "The brunt of that harangue is that creation is a wondrous and mysterious place that baffles human assumptions and expectations because it is not anthropocentric but theocentric." [49]

Reflecting that spirit, a contrasting interpretation of Genesis comes from Rabbi Lawrence Troster. Troster is a Jewish scholar and environmental educator, long associated with the Coalition on the Environment and Jewish Life (COEJL) as well as GreenFaith. Troster has revised this stewardship model in a biocentric emphasis, a holistic view approaching the deep interrelation of Eastern traditions.

Troster proposes a "citizen" ethic to complement the traditional "caretaker" ethic. As citizen, humanity is considered within a more holistic creation perspective. He writes, "Creation theology expresses a model of the natural world in which humans are part of an order in which they do not necessarily have a prime place." [50]

---

49. Jon D. Levenson, *Creation and the Persistence of Evil: The Jewish Drama of Divine Omnipotence* (San Francisco: Harper & Row, 1988), 155-56.

50. Lawrence Troster, "Caretaker or Citizen: Hans Jonas, Aldo Leopold, and the Development of Jewish Environmental Ethics," in *The Legacy of Hans Jonas: Judaism and the Phenomenon of Life*, ed. Hava Tirosh-Samuelson and Christian Wiese (Boston: Brill Academic Press, 2010), 375.

Troster combines Aldo Leopold's land ethic and Hans Jonas's ethic of responsibility to limit human power over the natural world and expands the human ethical concern to the nonhuman world. Leopold's land ethic enlarges the community, including the soils, water, plants, and animals—the land in its entirety. Jonas insists that the "outcry of mute things" must be heeded.[51] With the appeal to the mute things, the contrasting, nonanthropocentric vision of biocentrism appears. Troster points to the universal community vision of Psalm 148, in which an "earthly choir consists of the forces of the nature world, the landscape, animal life (both wild and domesticated) and all kinds of humans."

While a contrast to classic Abrahamic anthropocentrism, biocentric metaphors such as Troster's are not new. Even before our ecological era, Rav Avraham Yitzhak Kook, Ashkenazi Chief Rabbi, expressed his sense of spiritual and ecological unity: "Not the least speck of existence is superfluous, everything is needed, and everything serves its purpose. 'You' are present within everything that is beneath you, and your being is bound up with all that transcends you."[52] This phrase "your being is bound up with all that transcends you" could easily be taken as a Buddhist teaching.

Jewish environmental thinking thus exists in strands that are hierarchical and egalitarian, anthropocentric and biocentric. If all these terms imply some tension between role and relation, how

---

51. Discontinuity comes from the ontological divide that occurs with the appearance of human sentience. For Jonas, this discontinuity does not separate humans from the rest of life; it creates an ethical responsibility to the lower forms of being. The human role may be a unique role, but it requires a response to "outcry of mute things." In modern nihilism the natural world is no longer a divinely created order but a mindless, purposeless process determined by inherent law. Without these values and purposes, modern technology becomes "radically different from previous technology in principle and scope" (Troster, "Caretaker or Citizen," 390). Regarding Psalm 148, see ibid., 384.

52. Orot ha-Kodesh, ed. Rabbi David Cohen, p. 361, cited in David Sears, "Cosmic Consciousness, Man, and the Worm: Ecology and Spirituality in Jewish Tradition," in *Compendium of Sources in Halacha and the Environment* (New York: Canfei Nesharim, 2005), 28. Rav Kook was the first Ashkenazi chief rabbi of the British Mandate in Palestine before the creation of the state of Israel.

does Soloveitchik assess the proper place of the human in nature? What are humanity's roles? Several key points will be made by Soloveitchik, in dialogue with other religious thinkers. First, one must reject selfishness and honor the needs of the community. Second, one must honor the limits of the earth. Three, communities must direct technology with wisdom. And fourth, the covenantal community must remember to wonder at the beauty of creation, thus honoring the creator.

The Complex Vocation of Adam One and Adam Two

Humanity's vocation is complex. For Soloveitchik, the inner conflict that ultimately leads to exploiting creation emerges from a fundamental contradiction in the two created vocations of the human person. The contradictory creation accounts in Genesis indicate more than the historical blending of literary sources. In fact, there is "a real contradiction in the nature of man."[53] Soloveitchik portrays humanity as torn between a dual vocation for technological ingenuity and wonder. He refers to these two vocations as those of "Adam One" and "Adam Two."

Soloveitchik speaks of "a real contradiction in the nature of man," who struggles to realize his humanity. Human creativity and technological capacity concern the uniquely human, *functional* assessment of how the world works. Such creativity contradicts a second, equally human capacity for *wonder*, receptivity, and awe of the world's beauty.

Adam One exists in a practical and functional relationship with nature. His response to nature is not meditative or philosophical. He wants to know how the world works in order to reconstruct his environment.

> To be precise, his question is related not to the genuine functioning of the cosmos in itself but to the possibility of reproducing the dynamics of the Cosmos by employing quantified-mathematized media. . . . Not of an exploratory-cognitive nature [it] is rather nurtured by the *selfish desire* on the part

---

53. Soloveitchik, *Lonely Man of Faith*, 10.

of the Adam to better his own position in his environment (*emphasis added*).[54]

By contrast, Adam Two seeks meaning and purpose. He exists in a living encounter with the world, not in Adam One's conceptual attempt to reduce the world to abstract or scientific representations.

> He looks for the image of God not in the mathematical formula or the natural relational law but in every beam of light, and every bud and blossom, in the morning breeze and the stillness of a starlit evening. . . . His existential "I" experience is interwoven in the awareness of communing with the Great Self whose footprints he discovers along the many tortuous paths of creation.[55]

Part of Adam Two's existential experience is loneliness, a condition that God relieves by providing a human community. Humanity's deep existential loneliness takes new forms in changing social and cultural situations. Today this form of loneliness, a sense of loss and disconnection from nature, has been described by Gardner as being "environmentally orphaned."[56] Many can identify with the phenomenon of the "last child in the woods." Humanity looks for God throughout creation; the pain of being an environmental orphan means one risks becoming a spiritual orphan as well, searching for God where nature's stillness and blooming is overpowered by the grit of civilization. Religious loneliness invades the green blues, prompting Kathy's wish, previously mentioned, that all might experience God in nature.

Selfishness. This deeper conflict sets humans at odds with creation. At stake is how far one may reach to express one's creative activities. This uncertainty is inherent in Adam One's creative nature but is intensified by humanity's capacity to use technology and vitiated by potential selfish disregard for community. Adam's

---

54. Ibid., 14.

55. Ibid., 23-24.

56. Gary T. Gardner, *Inspiring Progress: Religions' Contributions to Sustainable Development* (New York: W.W. Norton & Company, 2006), 156.

selfish desire to better himself warps the originally healthy tendency to re-create and manipulate the world.

Why is this question, this curiosity, described as nurtured by a "selfish desire" to better his own position? God wishes him to subdue nature. Indeed, Soloveitchik next describes Adam One's longing as "legitimate." At the same time, he writes that Adam One claims unlimited power, seeking not sacrifice and humility but convenience.[57]

> Adam the first transcends the limits of reasonable and probable and ventures into the open spaces of the universe. Even this longing for vastness, no matter how adventurous and fantastic, is *legitimate*. Man reaching for the distant stars is acting in harmony with his nature which was created, willed, and directed by his Maker (*emphasis added*).[58]

A longing for vastness is legitimate. Reaching beyond limits of reasonable and probable is consistent with his nature. Yet to better his own position is selfish. This seems to be a paradox not merely within Adam but within God's instructions to humanity. In other words, the conflict stems from two original but distinct capacities: to revere and to use—even by transcending reasonable limits.

Perhaps, Adam One is intended to exercise his transcendent reach without taking more than his share of earth's resources. The problem is not reaching for the stars but selfishly grabbing others' share.

Rabbi Yehudah Levi, a contemporary Orthodox thinker, prompts this answer by emphasizing selfishness as the key to ecological exploitation. "In searching for the sources of the problems of ecological destruction, whether industrial or consumer-centered, we will find that they lie chiefly in people's selfishness." Likewise,

---

57. Ibid., 103. The convenience to which Soloveitchik refers is the pleasant, undemanding satisfaction of an aesthetic religious experience, rather than a religious call to commitment and self-giving. Soloveitchik describes this kind of religion as a "cultural experience," as comfortable and convenient: the characteristics of the action gap.

58. Ibid., 20.

Rabbi David Sears repeats, we are but "cells in the body of the cosmos, symbiotically connected parts of a greater whole ... singing praises of its Creator."[59] Because of this spiritual and ecological unity, binding all in a common future, "our most fundamental attitude should be one of compassion, not acquisitiveness or aggression." Not surprisingly, acquisitiveness and aggression are exactly the traits Ricoeur expected to observe when the human quest for affirmation is distorted by vanity. Acquisitiveness and aggression emerge when the self falsely eliminates the others from its being.

The Gift of Technological Reason Is Not Absolute

If, as Rabbi Soloveitchik suggests, it is selfish of Adam One to better his own position in the environment through technological manipulation, what *are* the moral bounds of technology? Creative use of technology that serves the community is moral, even a blessing. But technology extends the reach of the human person beyond moral limits; it enables her disproportionate grasp to seek even further. Technological power exceeds its moral limit when its power to obtain more exploits the needs of others.

While many philosophers and theologians have addressed the existential meaning of technology today, it is interesting to engage the specific vision of technology within the human vocation as expressed by Pope Emeritus Benedict XVI, because of how intimately his vision blends technology and human dignity. Benedict analyzes technology as a tool that "reveals man and his aspirations; it expresses an inner tension that impels him gradually to overcome material limitations." Technology is not only a tool but a liberating reality: "Technology—it is worth emphasizing—is a profoundly human reality, linked to the autonomy and freedom of man."[60] Technology even promotes contemplation.

---

59. Yehuda Levi, "Ecological Problems: Living on Future Generations' Account," in *Compendium of Sources in Halacha and the Environment* (New York: Canfei Nesharim, 2005), 26; Sears, "Cosmic Consciousness," 29.

60. Benedict XVI, *Caritas in veritate*, www.vatican.va. Benedict writes, "The human spirit, 'increasingly free of its bondage to creatures, can be more easily drawn to the worship and contemplation of the Creator.'" Dignity is

Fundamentally, humanity resists limits, and this is part of the inner conflict between a contemplative and interventionist relationship with nature.

> Technology is highly attractive because it draws us out of our physical limitations and broadens our horizon. But human freedom is authentic only when it responds to the fascination of technology with decisions that are the fruit of moral responsibility.[61]

While enabling humanity to transcend physical limits, technology must respect the limits inherent in things. Power over nature, and especially use of technological power to take nature's common resources, must accord with moral responsibility to serve the needs of the global community. Responsibility must correlate with power, in proportion to the impact of modern technological power.

Again the theme of proportion and disproportion emerges, because modernity has made the gift of rationality more costly for the environment by orders of magnitude. The radical difference in exploitative impact between the gift of plowing created by human ingenuity and the disruption of horizontal hydraulic fracturing, which shears underground layers of rock, saturates water tables with chemicals, and releases methane and benzene besides, is not even comparable. The question of the limits of technology becomes ever more urgent.[62] Thus, even for Benedict, who views technol-

---

expressed in society through action, within the community of work, and so is served by technology. See the extensive discussions of Benedict's environmental ethics in Jame Schaefer and Tobias Winright, eds., *Environmental Justice and Climate Change: Assessing Pope Benedict XVI's Ecological Vision for the Catholic Church in the United States* (Lanham, MD: Lexington Books, 2013).

61. Benedict XVI, *Caritas in veritate*, 70. Jonas similarly insists on the limits of power; see Troster, "Caretaker or Citizen," 387.

62. Sona also addresses the fundamental causes of alienation from nature from his Buddhist perspective. "Our technological society has allowed us to become insulated and therefore alienated from the natural world" (Sona, "Birken," 45). The Muslim scholar Seyyed Hossein Nasr speaks to

ogy as fundamentally liberating, technology must be restrained. Benedict concludes that technology must "serve to reinforce the covenant between human beings and the environment, a covenant that should mirror God's creative love."[63]

Knowing our dependence on the health of the earth, reinforcing the "covenant between human beings and the environment," means refusing to poison it and ourselves. Kinship increases the respect, sense of interrelation, and wonder for all the living that enhances care for oneself and the earth community. At a very real level, these are one reality.

The Earth Is a Gift That Isn't Free

In the covenantal perspective stressed by Jewish teachers, the earth and life itself are given by God with purpose to meet the needs of all the living. Selfishness vaunts the self above all others, robbing the earth's resources from those who need them in the present as well as in the future. In this sense, the earth is a gift that isn't free. Adam and Eve inherited the gift of the garden, but it is a gift with responsibilities.

Liana Stein, an Orthodox Jewish environmentalist, notes that to be placed in the garden (*vayanicheyhu*) is associated with an inheritance (*nachala*) by commentators on Deuteronomy 12:9.

> But an inheritance implies a gift—the wonders of Nature, with all its complexity and diversity of abundant life, were a gift to the first humans and their progeny. It is not a free gift, however; but one that requires responsible handling so that "all the generations of Adam" (Gen 5:1) can benefit.[64]

---

alienation as well, judging that the loss of cosmology in the West, the rise of rationalist philosophy and positivist science have dethroned the mind as the judge of values and allowed rationalist science to be the sole criterion of truth; see Seyyed Hossein Nasr, "Islam, the Contemporary Islamic World, and the Environmental Crisis," in *Islam and Ecology: A Bestowed Trust*, ed. Richard C. Folz, Frederick M. Denny, and Azizan Bahruddin (Cambridge, MA: Harvard University Press, 2003), 88.

63. Benedict XVI, *Caritas in veritate*, 69.

64. Ilana Stein, "*Le'ovda Uleshomra:* Judaism and the Environmental

In her reading, Stein combines several meanings of gift—the expectation and entitlement of an inheritance, which nonetheless is a gift. A gift is a treasure received, but not absolutely without price; the receiver is accountable for it. Responsible handling is required.

Benedict also warns that one must carefully handle "the freedom that seeks to prescind from the limits inherent in things."[65] In other words, there *are* inherent limits in things, even if human creativity reaches in an unlimited way to the stars. Mother Nature can take only so much abuse. The earth needs rest. This is the positive side of finitude: the need and the invitation to rest.

The depth of the gift of possible action includes understanding the limits on what is possible. And in this finite world, everything is subject to limits. Extreme applications of technology must be limited in order to limit individual exploitation of resources, in order to respect the needs of the other and the finite capacity of the earth.

Failure to attend to these limits brings down the judgment of the earth, as much as by God. The philosopher Hans Jonas warns that ecology is issuing its own judgment. "It was once religion which told us that we are all sinners, because of original sin. It is now the ecology of our planet which pronounces us all to be sinners because of the excessive exploits of human inventiveness."[66]

The ancient Jewish tradition that insists the earth lie fallow every seven years recognizes this. The earth needs rest.[67] This tradition existed long before people assaulted the earth with relentless and toxic extractive technologies and intensive petrochemical farming. The end of 2 Chronicles says that the land must rest so it can retrieve its lost Sabbaths (36:21). So it is not only humans who need rest. This truth honored by the biblical teaching to honor the

---

Ethic," in *Compendium of Sources in Halacha and the Environment* (New York: Canfei Nesharim, 2005), 17.

65. *Caritas in veritate*, 70.

66. Troster, "Caretaker or Citizen," 373.

67. The sabbatical year (Exodus 23:10-11; Leviticus 25:20-22) refers to the seven-year rest; in Deuteronomy the remission of all debts is added. The Jubilee is once every 50 years and teaches that land goes back to its original owners.

Sabbath is increasingly raised as a part of environmental spirituality and practice.

What began as a Jewish tradition is increasingly recognized by Christians. For example, Dr. Matthew Sleeth, an evangelical Christian and environmental advocate, has written *24/6* to emphasize how rest and relaxation that doesn't involve shopping can create more sustainable lifestyles.[68] These spiritual practices refresh people to continue on over the action gap. One can shop, work, surf the Internet, travel constantly—the busyness of the rat race need never want. But there is a gap between what one can do and what one ought to do, for personal well-being as well as earth care. As a contemporary Orthodox environmentalist writes, "The halachic mandate to conserve is found dancing a delicate spiritual dance on the high wire which spans the chasm between what we can do and what we should do."[69]

The Vocation for Wonder and Holy Companionship

If created vocations of both the inventor and the contemplative are legitimate, the final message is that Adam One's gift for technical ingenuity risks selfish overextension. He is saved by the complementary presence of Adam One's complementary vocation for wonder, and the companionship and needs of the covenant community.

Belonging to the community teaches the self its legitimate boundaries and offers the comfort of companionship. Humankind may invent, explore, create, innovate, and rejoice in human genius, but remember it is not alone among the world's creatures. All in the covenant community have rights. The earth's goods belong to the family of all the living, and the generations of the future.[70]

---

68. Matthew Sleeth, *24/6: A Prescription for a Healthier, Happier Life* (Carol Stream, IL: Tyndale House Publishers, 2012). The Catholic Coalition for Climate Change also has initiatives to encourage Sabbath rest.

69. Simenowitz, "Water Conservation," 49.

70. This is the meaning of the Catholic teaching of the "universal destination of all goods." God's covenant and blessing of all the living infuse the world with its values and goods. It is to be good for all—the resources are for all—the universal destination of goods. Therein lie the limits. See

God is never outside the covenant community. He joins humanity and shares in his covenantal existence. In Soloveitchik's beautiful phrase, "Finitude and infinity, temporality and eternity, creature and Creator become involved in the same community."

See Christiana Z. Peppard, "Commodifying Creation? Pope Benedict XVI's Vision of the Goods of Creation Intended for All," in *Environmental Justice and Climate Change: Assessing Pope Benedict XVI's Ecological Vision for the Catholic Church in the United States*, ed. Jame Schaefer and Tobias Winright (Lanham, MD: Lexington Books, 2013), 90. Note also the importance of interdependence as phrased in Catholic social teaching. For example, Pope John Paul II stated in his 1987 encyclical *Sollicitudo Rei Socialis* that "the conviction is growing of a radical interdependence and consequently of the need for a solidarity which will take up interdependence and transfer it to the moral plane" (#26).

CHAPTER SIX

Spiritual Community and Shared Self-Giving

The question is, what has made you environmentally unconscious?

Mohamad, a leader of the DC Green Muslims, was convinced that wholeness is impossible if one is divorced from the divine—and from nature. For Mohamad, wholeness includes a sense of kinship with the earth, the awareness of being an organic part of nature, expressed with the traditional term *fitra*.

> *Mohamad: We have this understanding of in Islam something called* fitra, *and it's this state that everybody has, an original wholeness. Everybody has a* fitra, *and this is what they are connected to. And so the question often is about the opposite of* fitra, *ahufla,* which is an unconsciousness. So the question isn't what made you environmentally conscious because we're all so by nature, but what has made you environmentally unconscious?*

Many faith-based environmentalists lament that our natural relationship to the earth has been forgotten, including Pope Francis. "Everything is connected!" This refrain repeats throughout his stunning and inspiring encyclical *Laudato si'*.[1] *Laudato si'* recalls us to our universal kinship with all beings as creatures of one loving

---

1. Francis, Encyclical letter *Laudato si'*, 138, http://w2.vatican.va.

God. All creatures are one family, living on one common home, and caring for creation is an act of love for the neighbor and for ourselves. Humanity cannot continue to exploit and pollute the world without enormous cost to human and ecosystemic health, economic sustainability, and climate stability. Yet the environmental unconsciousness that Mohamad and Rima lamented is widespread: the knowledge, concern, and action gaps have not gone away.

Recovering the unity of earthly kinship is essential to inspire the actions that restore a sustainable relationship with the earth. Seeing our interconnections makes it possible to see even sacrificial action as a creative way of planting seeds for a healthy future. The wisdom traditions consulted in the previous chapter propose that recalling our communal identities helps cross the gaps and counter environmental unconsciousness. Recovering an awareness of kinship, the perspective of prioritizing prayer, and the centering effect of community identity restores balance between one's energies and abilities to respond to the earth. Additionally, Mohamad's Islamic tradition conveys particular insight about the dangers of forgetfulness.

Forgetting one's spiritual identity. Seyyed Hossein Nasr, a well-known scholar of comparative religion and philosophy of science, inspired Mohamad to ponder the crisis of forgetting one's true creaturely identity. According to Nasr, humanity "needs revelation because although a theomorphic being, he is by nature negligent and forgetful; he is by nature imperfect. Therefore he needs to be reminded." One could thus view the knowledge and caring gaps through the lens of Islamic spirituality as the sin of forgetfulness.[2]

Mohamad interpreted forgetfulness as being unconcerned about climate change, and divorced from one's inner relationship to the earth. This divorce is the real crisis. Placing his hand on his heart, he said,

> *The worst kind of impervious surface is the one that can form here. Ecological and social crises are all spiritual crises. There's a world within, and anything that happens in the*

---

2. Seyyed Hossein Nasr, *Ideals and Realities of Islam* (Boston: Beacon Press, 1966), 22.

world without is just a reflection of this inner world. And so if we're saying that we're okay with leaving the tap running, it's something here that's missing.

"Impervious surface" has double meaning for a student of urban engineering like Mohamad. Water runoff from miles of impervious pavement washes water over oily and toxic surfaces, flooding drainage capacities, risking sewage overflow. Seen spiritually, the impervious surface is the heart that doesn't care, isolated from its true communion, its affiliations with the world.

By contrast, sensing these multiple affiliations not only grounded the participants' spirituality of interdependence but led to a feeling of unity. Feeling this unity inspired many to perceive that acting to care for the earth community—one's vaster self—is not, fundamentally, a sacrifice that betrays one's truest well-being. While the limits of human finitude mean that the sacrifices to create sustainable societies do require some cost, restoring our common home also restores our personal and collective well-being. Paradoxically, sacrifice, personal identity, and community identity may be mutually reinforcing.[3]

The oneness of God and creation. That unity is strongly emphasized by Islamic environmental thought. Nasr emphasized that there is a rich body of Islamic doctrine calling for care for the natural world, reverence for the beauty of nature, and sensitivity to the revelation of God through God's signs (*ayat*) throughout the cosmos. As he writes, "Is there a Persian speaker who has not heard the verse of Sa'di in his Gulistan? 'I am joyous in the world of nature for the world of nature is joyous through Him, I am in love with the whole cosmos for the whole cosmos comes from Him.'"[4]

---

3. Erin Lothes Biviano, *The Paradox of Christian Sacrifice: The Loss of Self, the Gift of Self* (New York: Herder & Herder, 2007), esp. chap. 3.

4. Seyyed Hossein Nasr, "Islam, the Contemporary Islamic World, and the Environmental Crisis," in *Islam and Ecology: A Bestowed Trust*, ed. Richard C. Foltz, Frederick M. Denny, and Azizan Baharuddin; Religions of the World and Ecology (Cambridge, MA: Harvard University Press, 2003), 95.

Abdul-Matin, a leading contemporary American Islamic environmentalist, outlines six principles of a "green deen," or way. These core spiritual principles flow from "Islam's commitment to the Oneness of all things" and recover humanity's birthright connection with nature. Abdul-Matin shows that because of that focus on Oneness, environmental concerns and Islam's core principles align naturally. In other words, the core principles of Islam correlate to essential environmental concerns. These principles are

1. Understanding the Oneness of God and His creation (*tawhid*)
2. Seeing signs of God (*ayat*) everywhere
3. Being a steward (*khalifah*) of the earth
4. Honoring the covenant, or trust, we have with God (*amana*) to be protectors of the planet
5. Moving toward justice (*adl*)
6. Living in balance with nature (*mizan*)[5]

All creatures are *islam*, which literally means all are "submitted." Humanity is called to seek sanctity through surrendering oneself to God.[6] Such submission is the ground of ecological peace, which includes surrender to the limits of oneself and the earth.

Many other traditions recognize the need to honor the limited resources of the earth, the excesses of consumerist society, and one's personal limits tested by workaholism. Pope Francis writes very pastorally that we are also "God's gift" to ourselves, gifted with natural structures and a place in the earth that should be respected. Thus, honoring one's own limits, humankind can avoid acting against them.[7] No less must we respect the limits of Mother Earth. That a more balanced, sustainable, and relaxed life is spiri-

---

5. Ibrahim Abdul-Matin, *Green Deen: What Islam Teaches about Protecting the Planet* (San Francisco: Berrett-Koehler, 2010), 5.

6. Regarding the unity of all reality (*tawhid*) and balance of nature (*mizan*), see Adnan Z. Amin, Preface, in *Islam and Ecology: A Bestowed Trust*, ed. Richard C. Foltz, Frederick M. Denny, and Azizan Baharuddin; Religions of the World and Ecology (Cambridge, MA: Harvard University Press, 2003), xxxiii.

7. *Laudato si'*, 115.

tually renewing and ecologically sustainable is affirmed by Christian writers such as David Cloutier and Matthew Sleeth.[8]

Reconciling with finitude. The finitude of the earth and the human person is blessed by our companionship with the divine. The religious imagination, painfully aware of finite limits, searches for what theologian Edward Schillebeeckx calls the depth dimension of salvation. The depth dimension of salvation goes beyond the need for abundant clean water and a sustainable future free of environmental calamity. Drought, hunger, intense weather, and the displacement of climate refugees are challenges enough. Yet a spiritual need for salvation remains to restore the forgotten wholeness and spiritual integrity of the religious seeker. Schillebeeckx teaches that this depth dimension of salvation *is* offered by God; humanity is ultimately accepted by the divine. In his beautiful phrase, the boundary between humanity and God is a boundary that exists only on one side—ours. The human is always finite and dependent, though met by God through a boundary that is on man's side only. Nasr similarly reflects that the "Divine Being is not veiled from us, we are veiled from him, and it is for us to try to rend this veil asunder, to try to know God."[9]

One spirit: grace embracing disproportion. In such unity, grace embraces disproportion; humanity finds acceptance. One of the greatest Christian theologians speaks of the unity that Mohamad mentions in this way. Augustine shows how worship is the properly religious way to coincide in the human state of limited infinitude. The worshiper knows that "the love of God is poured out in our hearts ..." (Romans 5:5). True knowledge, which is worship,

---

8. See again Tim Jackson, *Prosperity without Growth?* (Sustainable Development Commission, 2009), http://www.sd-commission.org.uk; David Cloutier, *Walking God's Earth: The Environment and Catholic Faith* (Collegeville, MN: Liturgical Press, 2014). Also Matthew Sleeth, *24/6: A Prescription for a Healthier, Happier Life* (Carol Stream, IL: Tyndale House Publishers, 2012).

9. Nasr, *Ideals and Realities*, 22. "The boundary between God and us is our boundary, not that of God" (Edward Schillebeeckx, *Interim Report on the Books Jesus and Christ*, trans. John Bowden [New York: Crossroad, 1981], 115).

directs one's attention to the infinite. Worship therefore is appropriate, stable, holy disproportion: the graced union of the human spirit with the Spirit of God.[10]

Worship and contemplation bring the sacred knowledge of unity to the fore. This theological and liturgical truth is pragmatic as well: most participants found worship to be the most successful way to engage their congregation, since worship was the celebration of unity with creation amidst the familiar and beloved traditions of each community.

Augustine considers that a kind of union with the Trinity is possible by sharing in God's wisdom though love. In section 9 of book 6 he writes, "So whoever cleaves to the Lord is one spirit (1 Corinthians 6:17), and yet the Lord does not thereby become bigger, although he who cleaves to him does."

Augustine thus perfectly anticipates the revelation of Dan, one of the evangelical participants, who found in his expanding environmental awareness a "bigger God!" Uniting to others, to the community of life, it seemed that Dan knew of a bigger God, as Dan's heart and mind grew into a new awareness of God's concern for all life. This is the spirit uniting all the faith-based environmentalists who felt themselves part of something larger in the kinship of creation.

---

10. Augustine's *De Trinitate*, like *Fallible Man*, offers a psychological analysis of human interiority. This great text is Augustine's exhortation to the proper prioritization of attention and love. His profound study of memory and consciousness envisions all human processes of knowing, based in memory, understanding, and will, as perfected in the active state of worship. Searching for a model of human consciousness that images the triune God, Augustine considers self-knowledge: "Here we are then with the mind remembering itself, understanding itself, loving itself. If we see this we see a trinity, not yet God of course, but already the image of God" (14.11). However, the priority of consciousness is awareness of God: the true wisdom of worship (14.1) And so true wisdom does not consist in perfect equality. Worship is appropriate, stable, holy disproportion: the graced union of the human spirit with the Spirit of God: "This trinity of the mind is not really the image of God because the mind remembers and understands and loves itself, but because it is also able to remember and understand and love him by whom it was made. And when it does this it becomes wise" (14.15).

Mohamad: And I think somewhere between learning Native American traditions and Muslim tradition I realized that knowing the names of things and realizing that I entered into relationships meant that there were two things, the Native [American] perspective is that they're your brothers and sisters, and the Muslim perspective is they're Muslims. All of creation is Muslim by definition, that is, it's submitted, it's created by the same creator. This is always present for all of us, and it's reconnecting to them that's important.

Sharing in God's spirit increases the freedom to choose new habits, to continue to struggle for sustainability. Accepting that we have a finite ability to act emboldens irresolute commitment by empowering a focus on the gift of the possible rather than shrinking from the overwhelming trap of the impossible. Finding a starting point in love of oneself and coming "little by little" to understand more, there is the hope, as Carmen said, that "because God works with us, everything that is negative is going to change into the positive." Thus, one of the most essential ways to "change the negative into the positive"—sacrifice—becomes itself positive, and possible.

Interexistent Sacrifice: *Shalom*

The participants' consciousness of moral globalization was infused with spiritual visions of interbeing. Struggling to live in peace and justice was the practical way to acknowledge these bonds. Acting sustainably might include choices for simplicity, sacrificial changes to lifestyle, and the most precious gift of time for advocacy and community work.

Angelina, an Episcopal woman, said it most clearly. "What is sacrifice? Sacrifice is making holy, it is not giving up." Sacrifice is prioritization, rebalancing, shifting focus to gain integrity. Sacrifice is the sanctifying of one's highest priorities, a willingness to dispense with trivialities, even good things that are still, nonetheless, less important than the health of the earth.

For the participants who felt the spiritual and ethical interconnection that is expressed in multiple traditions, sacrifice was no longer sacrifice. Their diverse symbols of unity and self-giving invite a weaving together of symbols themselves: connected to all (interexistence), one finds that loving self-giving (sacrifice) is the means to peace (*shalom*).

This convergence of multiple religious symbols affirms how sacrifice is a means to balance. Living simply and accepting sacrifice brings peace. Meaningful and creative self-giving reflects and affirms our interbeing, the connections of our selves to others.

Sacrifice remains an ambiguous spiritual challenge. Like solidarity, it is easily romanticized but always contains conflict. It's *almost* easy. As Sarah said, "I wouldn't characterize it as a sacrifice. I think [it] will actually make me happier, you know, *almost*. So, yeah, I don't see it as a sacrifice at all." And the Unitarian committee hoped that their friends would all remember they voted for 60 degrees in the sanctuary. Their choice was strongly rooted in central Christian symbols of sacrifice, referring to a feast, the banquet of abundance in the Reign of God, the generous availability of the resources of the earth for all. Yet, sacrifice precisely to maintain that abundance for others required renewed commitments.

Carol echoed the spirituality of unity that transforms sacrifice into choice.

> *Carol: When you can broaden your level, your horizon of awareness, and feel interconnected to something that goes beyond you and is more about what's all around you and you can see what poison is for you, it's not sacrifice not to do that thing. It's just common sense. We will be empowered with no problem, working to help each other survive. I think it really isn't a giving up of anything; it's a moving towards something.*

Tim astutely diagnosed one problem with sacrifice as playing into Christian notions of reward and merit. Instead, the changes in one's life are more truly about becoming consonant with one's relationship to the earth.

> *Tim (Baptist): I don't have to say, oh gee, look at poor me, making a sacrifice on behalf of the world to get on the bus. ... No, you begin to say, the religion of my life is that steward-*

ship is important, and it will take a certain amount of time; it will take a certain amount of planning. It will take decisions about what I do and don't do. So it's not about getting extra credit because I've sacrificed. It's that I'm living in concert with the rhythm of the earth.

Thich Nhat Hanh teaches that because of the depth of inter-dependence, one can truly say we are the trees. True reality is our absolute interbeing. Perhaps this is the reason trees seem able to stir up great passion. A Jain participant talked about the original tree huggers, explaining how the fifteenth-century Bishnoi sect origi-nated the term "tree huggers" by protecting trees with their lives five hundred years ago. Sacrifice had a dramatic place in the his-torical legacy of that Hindu Bishnoi community, who literally sac-rificed their lives to save animals and trees from exploitation. The radically extreme tree hugging of the Bishnoi community was a passionate, desperate witness, yet one that inspires ongoing, steady commitments.

It is essential to see the creative and life-restoring aspect of sustainable living, even with its demands that may be sacrificial. Christian insight into the paradox of sacrifice acknowledges that it is cruciform but also a feast of unity. Two major leaders of religious environmentalism point to the power of this vision of sacrifice. As the ethicist Larry Rasmussen writes in his pioneering work of envi-ronmental theology, *Earth Community, Earth Ethics,* a cruciform ecological theology is a resource for hope.[11]

The revelation of a crucified God is the divine intimacy with suffering and acquaintance with the grief of the exploited earth—a God present and witness to its losses. Yet knowing the divine power to oppose this suffering enables hope to rise again.

Ecumenical Patriarch Bartholomew emphasizes that sacri-fice is an expression of communion, a celebration of the commu-nity's highest goods. Christians ideally understand sacrifice as an

---

11. Larry Rasmussen, *Earth Community, Earth Ethics* (Maryknoll, NY: Orbis Books, 1996).

expression of love for the other. In that expression of love, sacrifice is a creative, life-giving choice; it is not a suppression of self, but renews the self's deepest loves.[12]

In Bartholomew's view, science, technology, and policy are tools of social transformation that can create new ways of living sustainably. Sacrifice is not a call to "shiver in the dark." But no technology or policy by itself will have impact without the willingness to change. The gap between ideals and action remains open until decisive action, even sacrifice, is undertaken. Bartholomew asks, "How shall we bridge this tragic gap between theory and practice, between ideas and actuality? There is only one way: through the missing dimension of sacrifice."

Sacrifice is most profoundly an expression of unity and gratitude. "This is surely the distinctive characteristic of ourselves as human beings: humankind is not merely a logical or a political animal, but above all . . . capable of gratitude and endowed with the power to bless God for the gift of creation. Without such thanksgiving we are not truly human."[13] Gratefulness is the faithful receptivity of our created natures that puts finitude in its place in the drama of salvation. Drawing back down into the space, time, commitments, and consumption we can actually handle is a way to thankfully exhale, to reinhabit our limited lives in balance.

The triumphant painter of joyful and unthinkable new futures, Friedensreich Hundertwasser, imagines clothing as a person's second skin, and buildings as a third. The earth is easily imagined as a fourth skin, and one that must be inhabited sustainably to endure. The Hebrew prophet Isaiah anticipated how exploiting resources meant for all will exhaust the earth, our greater garment. "The earth shall wear out, like a garment" (Isaiah 51:6).

If, as Mohamad believed, the conflicts of the hardened heart contribute to ecocide, the philosopher and statesman Václav Havel

---

12. Lothes Biviano, *Paradox of Christian Sacrifice*, esp. chap. 5.

13. Ecumenical Patriarch Bartholomew, "Sacrifice: The Missing Dimension," *Address at the Closing Ceremony of the Fourth International Environmental Symposium*, (2001), http://www.ec-patr.org.

agrees that renewing the human spirit creates hope for restoring our ecology and economy. "If a better economic and political model is to be created, then perhaps more than ever it must derive from profound existential and moral changes in society . . . it must above all be an expression of life in the process of transforming itself."[14] How can life find the way to transform itself?

Shonto, the Navajo artist and activist, knew that only hopefulness kept him looking ahead.

> *Shonto: I have to be hopeful. It would be hard to be gloomy and seeing everything just hopeless. Then you affect your own environmental spirituality, and you introduce a little bit of hopelessness in that. That's not good. So always be hopeful. I look forward ... the Native people, when we talk about saving the earth or saving the land or saving a grove of trees or saving something, it's always not for us, or it's always seven generations from now.*

> *Erin: That's a long time. If we can do that, we'd be in good shape.*

> *Shonto: That's how we keep the hope.*

American society continues to look to religious traditions for moral guidance, but more than guidelines are required to overcome the barriers that keep our society from making life-giving choices for the earth. The creative faith-based leaders I was privileged to meet drew on the power of spirituality to empower creative and lasting commitments to the earth despite the gaps they struggled with and the ambiguity of moral discernment and resolve. Honestly confronting the green blues, they searched for the sources of green hope, finding that renewal of hope and energy in their communities, their traditions of meaning, faith, and celebration. The invitation comes now to us to take on the challenge facing the earth.

---

14. Václav Havel, "The Power of the Powerless," in *The Power of the Powerless: Citizens against the State in Central-Eastern Europe*, by Václav Havel, John Keane, et al. (Armonk, NY: Sharpe, 1985), 30.

Pope Francis summons us to hope in stirring fashion. If "people no longer seem to believe in a happy future . . . Let us refuse to be resigned to this, and continue to wonder about the purpose and meaning of everything!"[15]

These inspiring words will be followed in years to come by the new generations who renew our ways of living sustainably, finding peace in the beauty of the earth in the cool of the evening. Today is always the day in which we can plant seeds for action.

---

15. *Laudato si'*, 113.

Afterword

I began this project with a deep case of the green blues, a fascination for Ricoeur's *Fallible Man*, and a modest plan to interview six environmentally active congregations in New Jersey. As time went on, I reached out to other groups . . . and other groups. . . and others. I could have conducted focus groups without end, to keep up the conversations with hundreds more exciting leaders. The conversations were so engaging, inspiring, and enlightening. I have often thought I should simply publish the entire transcripts of all the meetings, to share the flame of earth-loving passion these gifted environmental leaders shared with me.

Here is a closing wish. Being in nature is a simple, irreplaceable source for renewing spirituality, faith, and the energy to care for the good earth. I hope you find a day to rest in the place where you belong most in God's good earth. If not a moment of rest every day, or a day of rest each week (and why not?), let there be some time you honor to be at home in nature. I hope you find peace there, as well as the inspiration to work to let nature continue to be a beautiful, healthy, beloved and holy home for you, a common home for us all.

Research Design and Methods

My research method was designed to provide a theological and interdisciplinary analysis of *the green blues*. As discussed in the introduction, the green blues are a mélange of ambiguity, conviction, and discouragement experienced by faith-based environmentalists amid their persistent efforts for sustainable living. The green blues are documented by my ethnographic research with faith-based environmentalists through 29 focus groups and interviews. Their statements provide the starting point for my analytic method, which incorporates grounded theory and liberation theology methods to generate a theory of the green blues. Because the green blues evoke inner conflicts about motivation and action, this ethnographic data is complemented by Ricoeur's phenomenology of fallibility. These two sources, ethnography and phenomenology, are interpreted with classic religious texts and environmental decision theory.

This section describes the method more fully.

Summary Description of Method

As a liberation theology generated with grounded-theory methodology, green blues theory moves in a hermeneutical circle. The ethnographic data generate the central concepts of the knowledge, caring, and action gaps. Those concepts correlate with Ricoeur's phenomenology of fallibility and thus gain deeper meaning from Ricoeur's philosophical reflection. Continuing in this hermeneutical circle, the analysis further engages insights from world religions on inner conflicts to interpret the gaps. Finally, the circle offers a "green possibility theory"—the response of intellectual hospitality, prioritized values, and empowered action.

Theoretical Sources of Method

The methodological sources are (1) liberation theology as model and inspiration; and (2) grounded theory as a method committed to authenticity and relevance to lived experience. The content sources are (3) my ethnographic data; and (4) Paul Ricoeur's phenomenological scholarship. The interpretive sources are (5) classic texts from several world religions; and (6) environmental decision theory with its complementary quantitative rigor. These interpretive sources are brought to bear on the ethnographic data and phenomenological scholarship.

Influences

Three main influences have shaped my development of this liberation theology based on grounded theory. First, my own discipline of theology, which in turn draws from hermeneutics, phenomenology, the study of texts, critical theory, ecological theology, religion and ecology, and feminist scholarship. Second, my personal engagement with interfaith advocacy, at parish, regional, and national levels through organizations such as GreenFaith and the Forum on Religion and Ecology. Third, my experience with interdisciplinary studies as an Earth Institute fellow at Columbia University, with the Center for the Study of Science and Religion and the Center for Research on Environmental Decisions.

Coherence of Green Blues Method with Grounded Theory

Glaser and Strauss, the formulators of grounded theory, argue that theory generated from data that is systematically obtained from social research is more relevant and useful than theory generated "by logical deduction from *a priori* assumptions."[1] Theory fundamentally provides conceptual categories for describing and explaining behavior.[2] Theory also predicts behavior, leads to prac-

---

1. Barry Glaser and Anselm L. Strauss, *The Discovery of Grounded Theory; Strategies for Qualitative Research* (Chicago: Aldine, 1967), xv.

2. Glaser and Strauss argue that the adequacy of a theory will relate to the

tical applications, advances other sociological theories, and guides future research. The purpose of data is to generate these conceptual categories for describing human experience that are interpretive and predictive.[3]

Therefore, in terms of grounded theory, my aim is to purposefully and systematically generate from the data of ethnography and phenomenology a theory about the green blues that analyzes the values and conflicts present in environmental decisions. Specifically, as a scholar of faith-based environmentalists, I am analyzing the factors that inspire or block the motivation to act among faith-based environmentalists. The key conceptual categories I develop to interpret the green blues are the "gaps": the knowledge gap, the caring gap, and the action gap.

Why do I, as a theologian, gravitate toward a grounded theory method in order to analyze the green blues? At this stage of its development, the movement of faith-based environmentalism needs a more targeted analysis of *what inspires and blocks personal action* in order to accelerate the movement's effectiveness. This analysis requires a focused, relevant, data-grounded study to build on the foundations of ecological theology, the scholarship of religion and ecology, and the pastoral and official teachings on religious obligation to care for the environment.

Correlation of Grounded Theory and Liberation Theology Method

The aims, tasks, and process-based model of grounded theory, detailed by Glaser and Strauss, complement the methods of liberation theology as outlined by Juan Luis Segundo. Both insist on reading current reality in a relevant and deeply probing way.

The aims of grounded theory cohere with the aims of liberation theology because both are methodologically rigorous, experience-based investigations that revise old views, create new understand-

---

process by which it was generated. Adequacy is assessed by consistency, clarity, parsimony, density, scope, and integration (ibid., 5).

3. Ibid., 23.

ings of reality, and promote the ongoing generation of theory. Liberation theology seeks to discover "a deeper or rich layer of reality";[4] grounded theory seeks relevant and descriptive conceptual categories for describing human experience.[5]

Both methods insist that the tasks of research and reflection begin with the particular situation: the "commitment and partiality" of liberation theology, and the particular, committed, or grounded questions advocated by grounded theory. Insisting on relevant questions enables powerful explanations that serve the future. The future orientation of liberation theology is seen in the renewal of theology through the continuation of the hermeneutical circle. The future orientation of grounded theory drives its own cyclic process: comparative analysis yielding data and theory, the replication and validation of the data, predictions and ongoing revision to theory.

Both emphasize theory as process. Glaser and Strauss explain that the strategy of comparative analysis "puts a high emphasis on *theory as process*; that is, theory as an ever-developing entity, not

---

4. Juan Luis Segundo, *Liberation of Theology* (Maryknoll, NY: Orbis Books, 1976), 23.

5. Glaser and Strauss, *The Discovery of Grounded Theory,* 23. Unlayering the depths of experience is a recurring methodological aim that also parallels hermeneutics and phenomenology, and further validates my use of Ricoeur. Don Ihde describes phenomenology as "a version of a comparativist strategy and as a means of 'recovering the intentionalities of symbolic expressions,' i.e., of unlayering the experiential significations of these expressions" (Don Ihde, *Hermeneutical Phenomenology: The Philosophy of Paul Ricoeur* [Evanston, IL: Northwestern University Press, 1971], xv). All these methods avoid deductive and idealist reasoning. Rather than explicitly pursuing the connections with Ricoeur's broader project of hermeneutics, or with the emerging field of environmental hermeneutics, I refer the reader to excellent collections such as Forrest Clingerman, Brian Treanor, Martin Drenthan, and David Utsler, eds., *Interpreting Nature: The Emerging Field of Environmental Hermeneutics*, Groundworks: Ecological Issues in Philosophy and Theology (New York: Fordham University Press, 2014). While my project has similar approaches, I target the nexus of grounded theory and Segundo's liberation theology methodologically, and focus on Ricoeur's topical analysis of fallibility as a content source.

as a perfected product."[6] Similarly, Segundo writes, "It is my feeling that the most progressive theology in Latin America is more interested in being liberative than in talking about liberation. In other words, liberation deals not so much with content as with the method used to theologize in the face of our real-life situation."[7] To emphasize process is to seek a method of analysis that will yield concepts that are relevant and responsive to reality.

I emphasize method and process to clarify that this research is a constructive analysis. It is not a report on pastoral-ecological activity, nor a guideline for how to begin environmental ministry. These are critical projects, and I hope this work increases their effectiveness.[8] But this research further seeks to clarify the experience of inspiration and conflict and the process of rediscovering and interpreting one's ethical commitment to the earth. Restating Marx's famous salvo, the conflict must be understood in order to resolve it. Precisely because ecological theologies and religious statements have not galvanized the movement as robustly as is desirable, a new question is needed, and a more direct and grounded method is required.

Inspired Sustainability analyzes the conflict of the green blues, the self-interpretation of faith-based environmentalists, *with the suspicion that the conflict is revelatory.* This core insight is a methodological key borrowed from liberation theology, grounded theory, and feminist scholarship: the trust that *experience is revelatory.* Here, I claim that the green blues are revelatory. The green blues are a source for theologizing about ourselves, our relationship with our earth, and the conflicts therein.

---

6. Glaser and Strauss, *The Discovery of Grounded Theory,* 32, emphasis original.

7. Segundo, *Liberation of Theology,* 9. Incidentally, both methods have had to defend against charges of naiveté or lack of rigor; see Segundo, *Liberation of Theology,* 5.

8. Many excellent models exist, as documented by Roger Gottlieb, *A Greener Faith: Religious Environmentalism and Our Planet's Future* (New York: Oxford University Press: 2006). See also Sarah McFarland Taylor, *Green Sisters: A Spiritual Ecology* (Cambridge, MA: Harvard University Press, 2007).

Having outlined the coherence of the aims, tasks, and process of grounded theory and liberation theology (both seeking to generate theory/unlayered reality), I will now detail the steps of the hermeneutical circle interpreting the green blues.

Developing Green Blues Method as a Liberation Theology

For Segundo, liberation theology begins with *questions* from the present situation that are profound enough to compel theology to reinterpretation. He represents this relationship of questioning and reinterpreting as a hermeneutical circle with four steps.[9] Briefly, (1) an experience of reality leads to (2) suspicion of the dominant ideological worldview (he speaks of a "superstructure"). This ideological suspicion leads to (3) a new experience of theology along with a commitment to a different way of doing theology (an "exegetical suspicion"). Finally, (4) the exegetical suspicion, or new way of doing theology, leads to a new interpretation of faith. The new experience of faith, reality, and questioning continues the circle of interpretation. Segundo also developed his theory out of concern for the poor, the marginalized, and the vulnerable—concerns that also drive ecological theology.

My particular experience of reality is the apprehension of the ecological crisis as *ecocide*. Ecocide is an ugly and shocking sacrilege, a dissonant absurdity destroying the abundance and beauty of creation. Ecocide lacks even commercial justification, as its short-term profit contradicts humanity's fundamental self-interest. To experience current reality as ecocide is to wince from the pain of the green blues.

Recognizing ecocide leads to the second step, an ideological suspicion that *religious statements about the environment and ecological theologies are not enough.* They are an essential and rich foundation for new worldviews and a significant contribution to a new scholarly field of religion and ecology. But to accelerate the effectiveness of the faith-based environmentalist movement, new approaches are needed. This very need for new approaches is itself

---

9. Segundo, *Liberation of Theology*, 9.

a tribute to the success of the field of religion and ecology and its development into multiple subfields.

Ecocide calls for a new, more compelling experience of theological reality—specifically, for a new theological anthropology: a new interpretation of inner conflict about action in the face of ecocide. This is the third step, Segundo's "exegetical suspicion" that vital sources of data are not taken into account. A radical examination of self-reported descriptions of the green blues is needed. In short, it is critical to listen to people; the struggles of the green blues need to be heard.[10]

Therefore, I have chosen an ethnographic strategy. Taking participant statements as starting point, I attempt to bracket presuppositions about the moral influence and effectiveness of official religious statements. A new vital question of what exactly drives faith-based environmentalism arises—the question of the dynamics of motivation.

The ultimacy of this question emerges in that all of us are conflicted about fully living out our values, even beyond the context of the environment. We are all challenged by the blues of fallibility and imperfect integrity. The study of inspiration and conflict has universal implications beyond ecological theology since conflict and ambiguity are part of the human condition; this is a particular study of fallibility in an ecological key. To borrow Segundo's comparison, this project is less about the *content* of faith-based environmentalism (as he describes Gustavo Gutiérrez analyzing the content of liberation) than about an *epistemic method* that brings new tools to the analysis of conflict and motivation.

The fourth step, the new interpretation of faith, is green blues theory (emerging in chapters 4 and 5), with its core concepts of the knowledge, caring, and action gaps. What will finally emerge are the outlines of a theology of green possibility: a more hospitable and interdependent view of the world, the peace to release the overwhelming challenge of the impossible by attending to true priorities, and collaborating and acting even within our limits.

---

10. Ada María Isasi-Díaz, *En la Lucha/In the Struggle: Elaborating a Mujerista Theology* (Minneapolis: Augsburg Fortress Publishers, 1993).

Intersection with Environmental Decision Theory

Liberation theology acknowledges the essential need to use the disciplines that help explain the present at every step. Environmental decision theory is one set of explanatory disciplines. As developed by the Center for Research into Environmental Decisions, this is not a single theory but a coordinated set of investigations drawing on behavioral psychology, economics and decision science, social affiliation theory, anthropology and field research, focus groups, cognitive psychology and laboratory experiments, etc.[11]

So, to discover "what the green blues reveal?" we must ask, What is the data of the green blues?

The Framework of the Study

I sought to understand how active faith-based environmentalists understood the inspiration for their advocacy and how they understood the barriers to fully committing to that advocacy.

Research Participants (See Appendix B)

Participants were chosen from mainstream congregational sustainability committees and included some individual interviews.[12] These participants, who initiated or joined faith-based sustainability or "creation care" committees, were chosen because they insisted on mainstreaming "green faith" by bringing it to their faith communities; they did not relegate environmentalism to a hobby compartmentalized from their congregational life.[13] Leaders of

---

11. See CRED website for review of their research projects: http://cred. columbia.edu/research/. See also the Yale Project on Climate Change Communication at http://environment.yale.edu and the George Mason University Center for Climate Change Communication at http://www.climatemaryland. org.

12. The research took place during a 2007–2009 Earth Institute Fellowship at the Center for the Study of Science and Religion, Columbia University, approved by the Columbia Institutional Review Board. All participants agreed to be identified by name and tradition or authorized a pseudonym.

13. Selecting homogenous groups fosters freer discussion among participants and surfaces differences in perspectives within the group; in this case, a

regional and national faith-based environmental coalitions (such as GreenFaith and the National Religious Partnership for the Environment) identified local leaders or congregations.

Twenty-nine focus groups were held with over one hundred participants. These included Baptists (Washington), Buddhists (New Jersey), Catholics (suburban New Jersey, urban New York, rural Washington), Conservative Jews (New York), Episcopalians (suburban and urban New Jersey), megachurch Christian evangelicals (Florida), Hindus (New Jersey), Jains (New Jersey), Muslims (Washing, DC), Native Americans (Navajo and Gwich'in—Arizona), Reconstructionist Jews (Illinois), Reformed Christians (New Jersey), Reform Jews (Arizona), Presbyterians/PCUSA (Maryland), Unitarian-Universalists (New Jersey), migrant workers (Washington), southern pastors (North Carolina), urban environmental justice advocates (New York), and self-identified agnostics and atheists (New York).

The empirical research reported here was conducted while I was an Earth Institute fellow, Columbia University (2007–2010), and was approved by the Columbia University Institutional Review Board. All participants completed Institutional Review Board–approved consent forms.

Comparative analysis. Comparative analysis is a method of grounded theory that generate evidences and validates it. Multiple groups enable the replication of evidence, by which I mean that in multiple conversations, similar topics are raised again and again. Such replication validates the meaningfulness of participant statements. I am using the term "validation" qualitatively. When a topic recurs, that suggests interest and importance to many people; this recurrence validates its significance qualitatively. Of course, a single powerful insight may also have great significance. Recognizing significance, whether widely attested or through a unique insight, belongs to my interpretive task as a researcher.

My chief aim was to surface the similarities within American faith-based environmentalists *across traditions* as regards the

---

single faith community. See David L. Morgan, *Focus Groups as Qualitative Research* (London: Sage Publications, 1997), 35.

factors that motivated, inspired, or challenged their advocacy. It is my presupposition that individual views, beliefs, and spiritualities vary widely within every faith community. My Baptist group unanimously affirmed this variety as a theological good, as "soul freedom." Thus I affirm the heterogeneity within each group, and also across the faith groups.

Nonetheless, I wished to see if common factors in motivation could be identified. Thus, a large number of focus groups are needed to reach data saturation.[14] "Data saturation" means that answers begin to recur in recognizable patterns. The recurrence establishes that a topic is of common interest and that more research isn't needed to demonstrate that. "Using groups that are segmented by background ... has the cost of requiring more groups because it takes a certain minimum number of groups within each category to observe that category's range of responses to a topic."[15] The number of focus groups was set by a desire to sample a range of traditions and denominations, recognizing the impossibility of capturing the incredible diversity of American religious experience. The temptation to continue conducting the focus groups forever was reined in by recognizing the point of reasonable data saturation.

Strategies

I chose to explore the factors that drive motivation via the particular strategies of *ethnography* and *focus groups*.

Ethnography

Ethnography is a type of social research characterized by participant observation.[16] Ethnographic accounts are written from the

---

14. See ibid., 44.

15. Ibid., 37.

16. Mary Clark Moschella, *Ethnography as a Pastoral Practice: An Introduction* (Cleveland: Pilgrim Press, 2008), 25-29. Moschella discusses ethnography as a pastoral theological tool, a means to understand a congregation, assess its needs, and determine how ministries might develop; see p. 5. Pastoral ethnography can "hear people into speech," honoring their stories and uncovering hidden insights (141). As a transient listener, my project did not

researcher's perspective, and so are not exact and objective. Ethnographic accounts describe culture, meaning, and behavior, entities that are themselves inherently varied and perspectival. Thus ethnographic accounts are narrative interpretations, reflecting both the diversity of multiple observed experiences and the interpretive style and interests of the researcher. Anthropologists call this kaleidoscopic perspective the "multivocalic voice."[17]

By listening to others in the focus groups, I sought a body of empirical data on the problem of the green blues. But the values and assumption of the researcher are not absent. My concerns emerge in my fundamental suspicion: that regarding the environmental crisis, inaction is wrong, cultural apathy is destructive, and the green blues reported by my research participants are themselves revelatory of the crisis, of their self-interpretation as environmental advocates, and of a way forward. Nonetheless, interpretations need not be wholly subjective. Rigorous analysis and construction of theory emerge through strategies for increasing objective assessment of the data, which are described below.

The Advantage of Focus Groups

Focus group data reflect the concern of liberation theology and grounded theology for *process*. The transcribed discussions—the data generated by focus groups—are not sets of answers to lists of questions. Rather, the essence of this kind of qualitative data is the interaction within the group. "The hallmark of focus groups is their explicit use of group interaction to produce data and insights that would be less accessible without the interaction found in a group."[18]

---

intend to be a pastoral ethnography in this sense. Yet those dynamics of discovery and healing were evident, as persons observed that connections were made and values affirmed through the discussion that had not had a forum before.

17. Jeanette Rodriguez, *Our Lady of Guadalupe: Faith and Empowerment among Mexican-American Women* (Austin: University of Texas Press, 1994), xx.

18. Focus groups and participant interviews are the two main ways to collect *qualitative* data in the social sciences. Morgan, *Focus Groups*, 2, 7.

It is especially fruitful to employ focus groups to research questions of attitudes and decision making, because social interaction is especially relevant to such topics in social psychology.

When conducting the focus groups, I responded to participant statements, probed for further clarity, and raised tangential issues. The discussions were "semi-structured"—I used standard questions but allowed the dialogue to flow and cover new areas if of particular interest to any one in the group. Semi-structured focus groups surface both similarities and differences in how congregations respond to the environmental crisis, though these may be keyed to institutional patterns of interpretation.

This back and forth (the "semi" in semi-structured questions) provides "direct evidence about similarities and differences in the participants' opinions and experiences as opposed to reaching such conclusions from *post hoc* analyses of separate statements."[19] Most suggestively, focus groups are peculiarly able to elicit unexpected insights into habitual actions or unexamined attitudes. Participants may even be unaware of their attitudes until asked to explain and justify commitments or assumptions of which they themselves were not aware. The focus group methodology allows people in the same religious tradition who nonetheless have various spiritualities, worldviews, and priorities to react to one another and evokes the full range of responses and possible dimensions of each issue. The comparisons participants themselves make provide insight into complex motivations.

I have chosen to do semi-structured focus groups because I am interested in similarities and differences in how congregations respond to the environmental crisis. Therefore I asked similar questions of each congregation, to see what similar dynamics are part of the responses of religious communities in general (see Appendix A). At the same time I tailored some questions to tap into unique aspects of each congregation's teachings, symbols, and values. In a few cases I have conducted interviews that were a cross between semi-structured interviews and oral history.

As a result, this methodology surfaced a wide range of personal-

---

19. Ibid., 10.

ized religious beliefs that exist even within the same faith tradition. I transcribed all discussions (over 600 pages of transcripts) and coded the transcripts both inductively (assigning a code to every statement to capture all themes) and deductively (looking for particular themes associated with religious environmentalism). I used NVivo 8 content analysis software (QSR Software, Melbourne) to sort, compare, and rank the coded responses (see Appendix C).

Strategies for Increasing Objective Assessment of the Data

Any narrative interpretation will be somewhat subjective. But in the attempt to limit my subjective susceptibility to a priori theoretical presuppositions, I chose an inductive as well as deductive approach.

Coding inductively (from the data) allowed participant statements to provide the primary data as the starting point for analysis. Emphasizing an inductive method sought to be true to the reality of religious environmental experience as described by the research participants. Taking their statements as primary data to guide further reflection and research was my strategy for limiting the imposition of theoretical presuppositions. This inductive approach allowed me to avoid rehashing "the usual suspects"—my own expectations about what would be significant concerns and issues.

Coding deductively (from my questions) was also important. At times I am interested in their interpretation; at others I need to understand certain direct topics and have specific questions to explore. Coding deductively allowed me to identify, code, and further investigate the recurrence and meaning of issues that were important to me as the researcher.

Questions. I asked questions about congregational activity, personal motivations, how beliefs developed and behavior changed, and employed semi-structured questions to permit systematic comparison and analysis. I ordered the questions to begin with a friendly warm-up question that grounds the participants in a positive and self-owned view of their identity in their tradition. I then move to their understanding of why programs succeeded or failed. That practical and concrete reflection prepares for more theological questions, and then questions about patterns in environmental behavior in the broader society. I end with personal stories and an opportunity to add things they feel are important that have not been raised. See Appendix A.

Verification

Glaser and Strauss argue that a researcher may legitimately choose an emphasis in verifying or generating theory, while both are important and mutually enriching tasks. Generally, verification is a task for future research on established theories, to revise, enlarge, or reject this theory.[20] My emphasis is on generation of a theory to explain the green blues, not verify it.

Validation primarily occurs by recognizing data saturation and recurring themes. By addressing standard questions to multiple groups, replicability and systematic analysis were sought. Multiple discussions refine the questions and redefine gaps in knowledge until "data saturation" is reached, meaning that answers begin to recur and to indicate characteristics that are unique to Christians, to religious environmentalists in general, or indicate other commonalities.

A note about validity in a theological sense: one may think of the difference between searching for replicable results in a laboratory and searching for consistent evidence in a trial. If the fundamental tenet of scientific method is accurate observation and replicability, the comparable approach in listening to personal accounts is careful hearing and resonance—the echoes of similar themes that establish a level of confidence. Such a test is not quantifiable, replicable data but a cumulative account of repeated themes in human experience. This compares to the validity of evidence presented in court by multiple witnesses. Paul Ricoeur's retrieval of testimony as a category for human wisdom complements the scientific use of data that are replicable. Despite use of standard questions, the interview is cocreated by respondents, based on their interpretation of the question, their interpretive selection of themes, and the stories brought forth in their responses.

---

20. Glaser and Strauss, *The Discovery of Grounded Theory*, 28.

Hearing all people tell the same story means something; it points to a cohort or institutional effect. There is an additional qualitative meaning in the consistency, if not unanimity. This also reflects the theological teaching about the value of listening to the consensus of the faithful, the *sensus fidelium*. Evidence always contains variety. Its usefulness derives not from unanimity but from the ability to generate theory.

The risk exists that some participants may retreat to conformity or that others might express more polarized opinions.[21] With a large data set, I was able to code, group, and rank the number of similar statements; this also reduces the risk that outlier statements about topics that do not occur often will be taken as representing broad consensus. Statements that are true outliers fall to the bottom of the NVivo coding ranks.[22]

Justification for Strategy of Ranking Codes

The ranking of codes by highest frequency is, I suggest, a qualitative measure of the significance of the theme represented by the code. It is a nonstatistical form of validation (not verification). It is difficult even to define what "verification" might mean in relationship to the attempt to establish the relative importance of themes. Such verification is perhaps impossible, as the attitudes and statements persons express are almost infinitely variable. Still, the usefulness of a theory based on the conceptual categories is open to further validation and a measure of quantitative verification. Quantitative studies can be derived from these concepts to test their recurrence in other groups (for example, climate refugees, or rescue workers, etc.). Such studies may verify the recurrence of the codes I have found to be most common or identify variant forms of my conceptual categories. Such studies would indicate the robustness and explanatory power of the theory based on the concept of the gap and continue the process of developing grounded theory.

---

21. Morgan, *Focus Groups*, 15, 27.
22. One does not presume that mountains of evidence make for theory by itself (Glaser and Strauss, *The Discovery of Grounded Theory*, 28).

Glaser and Strauss recommend a flexible, cyclic process of explicating coding, analyzing the codes, theorizing their relationships, and refining those theories by continuing to code and analyze evidence. This comparative method aims to generate a theory that is "integrated, consistent, plausible, [and] close to the data."[23] Frequency summoned my attention to dominant concerns of the participants. At the same time I listened closely to particular insights, and these also shaped my analysis.[24] (See Appendix C: Association of Codes by Theme.)

Methods Not Used

Many important disciplines are not examined in this study. To be clear, I did not primarily seek to compare one faith group's unique approach to another faith group's approach. This project could clearly be extended in a more comparative direction. Future projects with a goal of verification could also conduct more groups within each faith tradition, and particularly within other-than-Christian traditions.

Nor does this study contrast persons formally unaffiliated with faith traditions to faith-based environmentalists. This is a very important question but one beyond the scope of this study. These factors may or may not be generalizable to persons who are not faith-based. Those comparisons are not explicitly addressed here and remain a question for future research.

In order to focus on understanding decisions, commitments, actions, and barriers to action as perceived by the participants themselves, as an aspect of their self-interpretation as moral agents and as members of faith communities, I have not extensively explored the sociological study of environmentalists. Chief topics in that study include the systematic exploration of the impact of political affiliation, class, and economic background on advocacy.[25]

---

23. Ibid., 103.

24. "A single case can indicate a general conceptual category or property" (ibid., 30).

25. See the Pew Forum, "Faith in Flux: Changes in Religious Affiliation in the United States," http://www.pewforum.org/2009/04/27/faith-in-

The fields of environmental psychology and ecopsychology are not engaged. Rich dialogue is occurring in these fields by scholars such as Clingermann, David Utsler, Thomashow, and Robert Melchior Figueroa.[26] My work has similarities with the emerging field of eco-hermeneutics, which also builds on Ricoeur's phenomenology. However, my work was developed independently. These similarities are a desire to avoid deductive reasoning and limit presuppositions, to describe human experience, and to seek general interpretive categories, while conscious of the postmodern suspicion of essential structures.[27] This legitimate caution especially mandates a grounded method to gather data and establish validity through search for cumulative and repeated themes that reach data saturation.

Additionally, a specific question I am *not* addressing is whether anthropocentric theologies are a driving source of the ecological crisis. That question has been thoroughly researched. Also, there are active environmentalists whose worldview remains anthropocentric. Again, it may be that doctrines are not the primary driving motivating factors at all. Finally, I did develop several hypotheses that were not explicitly raised as questions in a systematic way, but indicate the complex of issues in my mind as I guided the discussions. See Appendix D.

---

flux. Anthony Leiserowitz and Karen Akerlof, *Race, Ethnicity and Public Responses to Climate Change* (New Haven, CT: Yale University Press, 2010). See also Dana R. Fisher, "On Social Networks and Social Protest: Understanding the Role of Social and Personal Ties in Large-Scale Protest Events," *Research in Social Movements, Conflicts, and Change* 30 (2010): 115.

26. Clingermann et al., eds., *Interpreting Nature.*

27. The aim of hermeneutic phenomenology, a field exemplified by Paul Ricoeur, is to liberate awareness from unexamined presuppositions or uncritical preconceptions that narrow one's awareness of phenomena. Eco-hermeneutics addresses one's self-interpretation in relationship to the environment. More generally, phenomenology seeks to describe human experience, avoiding deduction from rationality, but intuiting directly the phenomenon of immediate experience. This study emphasizes the intentional structures of consciousness and aims for insight into essential structures behind a variety of phenomena. See "Phenomenology of Religion," in *Encyclopedia of Religion,* 2nd ed. (New York: Thomas Gale, 2005), 7086-7101.

Summary

My theoretical framework, a liberation-grounded-ethnography-phenomenology is an interdisciplinary method, a net to catch the bird that sings the green blues. If Gutiérrez simply stated his method as "sing and set free," the song of green blues theory may be "sing and mend, sing and repair, sing and renew." Through the hermeneutical circle, listening to many inspired and struggling environmental advocates, the green blues reveals a way to green possibility as well.

List of Appendices

Appendix A.
Focus Group Questions

Appendix B.
Research Participants

Appendix B.1
Clergy Consent Form

Appendix B.2
Participant Consent Form

Appendix B.3
List of Focus Groups and Research Participants

Appendix C.1
Comprehensive Chart of All Topics Discussed by Participants,
Organized by Theme

Appendix C.2
Selective Chart of Topics with Highest Number of References
by Participants

Appendix C.3
Thematic Charts of Interrelated Topics

Table 1.1 Topics Relevant to Green Spirituality
Table 1.2 Topics Relevant to Leadership

Appendix D. Hypotheses

Note: The ethnographic data that generates green blues theory, with its central concepts of the knowledge, caring, and action gaps, are presented in illustrative fashion throughout the text. The complete ethnographic data are not presented in their entirety in any final appendix; such an appendix would be 600 pages long.

APPENDIX A

Focus Group Questions

Opening Question
- What is your favorite thing about being Christian/Jewish/Hindu, etc.?

Action
- I've learned about your environmental programs. What aspects of this work were most successful and why did they succeed?
- What other aspects of your activities were more challenging?
- Are there specific values, traditions, or moral teachings that have inspired your actions?
  - ◊ What are the beliefs that make you get up and do something? What really moved you?
  - ◊ Were traditional teachings effective in gaining support for these measures?
- Has lifestyle change been a focus?
  - ◊ What approaches encouraged others to begin changes in energy use or recycling or other lifestyle habits?
- Have you made changes as a consumer? What was hardest? Do you feel sacrifices are necessary?
- What are the biggest barriers to making commitments to sustainability in your community?
  - ◊ In the bigger picture, what are the main reasons people as individuals don't act to make changes to protect the environment? (What makes it hard to live a more sustainable life?)
  - ◊ Is it a struggle to live green and if so, how do you interpret this spiritually?

Let me switch to background issues ...

Attitudes
- Did your attitude toward the environment change at any point, and if so, what caused the change?
- Can you recall a moment, event, statement, or image that changed how you felt about the environment?
- What about that changed how you acted?
  - ◊ What did you hope would be the outcome of your actions? (Did you feel you could make a difference?)

Theology
- Has the environmental crisis made you look differently at aspects of your faith or religious teaching?
  - ◊ In what ways, if any, has focusing on the environment changed how you think about yourself or your relationship to others, or God?
  - ◊ How do you interpret your responsibility as humans?
  - ◊ What is your definition of stewardship (subdue earth vs. tend and protect it)?
  - ◊ In general, how do you view the tension of biocentrism and anthropocentrism?

- Are there aspects of your religious tradition that might make it *less* likely to focus on the environment?
  - ◊ In what ways have you seen these to be influential?
  - ◊ How does official religious leadership influence your thinking on environment? In what way does formal organized religious life relate to your commitments?
- In your view, are there religious grounds for saying people must act to protect the environment? In other words, is changing to a sustainable lifestyle an optional expression of one's personal spirituality or a moral claim on everyone?
  - ◊ How would you express this in the language of your tradition?
  - ◊ Do you feel there is a mandate from God, or is this an individual choice of one's "issue," one's responsibility?
  - ◊ Is it relevant to speak of unsustainable practices as bad deeds, or sins?

What is the distinctive contribution of your tradition to the environmental crisis?

Science
- How do people's views on science relate to environmental concern?
- How does modern environmentalism contrast with traditional resource conservation? Is there a different mindset in the global-warming era?
- What is the influence of politics on environmental concern or action?
- How does being American interact with environmental concerns?
  ◊ Does being green conflict with patriotism, with support for the American way of politics, or economics?
  ◊ Does the environmental crisis require a political solution?
  ◊ How do your religious or environmental views affect your political choices or voting?
- Globally, what are the most pressing problems to overcome? What are the most serious problems that the environment crisis might bring?
- What would be the best outcome of all the environmental work that is going on? What would be the signs that the work is done? (Probe for concern for ecosystems/animals/plants vs. hungry people.)

Personal
- How do childhood experiences or family influences play a part in your attitudes toward the environment?
- What emotions come up when you think about the environment?
  ◊ Have these changed?
  ◊ What is encouraging or discouraging in your past experience with environmental work?

Final Summary: Any Other Thoughts (Community, Creation, Covenant? Future generations? Image of God? Are particular environmental themes often encountered in your traditions?)

◊ Do you see a distinctive green meaning to traditional rituals and symbols?

◊ How do you test out a new idea or new problem, especially if it requires changing how things are usually done at home, at church, in society, in the workplace or in our economy?

◊ What lessons would you propose for other faith communities based on your experience?

◊ What about your congregation or its history or members supports this kind of work?

APPENDIX B

Research Participants

B.1 Clergy Consent Form

Dear Dr. Lothes,

Thank you for your invitation to participate in your research regarding religious congregations and environmental concern. As pastor of _____, we are committed to environmental advocacy as an expression of our faith and justice ministries. There are also many members of the congregation who share this interest and have been leaders in our environmental ministry. Having read the information you provided, I understand the purpose and goals of your research. Our church would be interested in participating in the focus groups you described in your letter, and I give consent for you to list us among your study participants and begin to schedule a discussion group.

B.2 Participant Consent Form

Environment and Religious Attitudes Research
Erin Lothes, Ph.D.
Center for the Study of Science and Religion,
Columbia University

As you know, the consent forms signed by you or the group representative/clergyperson before the focus group gave me permission to record the conversation, list the group as a participant in the study, and use the transcript for my research and paraphrasing your words.

The second purpose of this note is to give you options about the level of anonymity you prefer and how your comments will be acknowledged in case they are used in the final book or other future articles or reports. The ability to cite the transcript in whole or in part is an invaluable resource that also ensures the record reflects as closely as possible your own expressions without mediation from me.

Please feel free to contact me with any questions.

> I understand that analysis based on this research will be published in a book or other future reports and articles. If my exact remarks are cited, in whole or in part, I understand that a pseudonym chosen by Dr. Lothes will be used.

Signature: _____
Print Name: _____

I wish to choose my own pseudonym: _____
(indicate a first name).

OR I give permission to use my real first name

OR I give permission to use my real first name and last name.

B.3 *List of Focus Groups and Research Participants*

Christian
  1. Towson Presbyterian Church Earth Corps, Towson, MD: Charles Conklin, Mary McGibbon, Madeleine Mysko, Carole, Barbara, Ann Rudd, and Barrett Rudd.
  2. Presbytery of Baltimore Creation Care Task Group, MD: William Breakey, Pat Collins, Julie Erickson, Dan McConaughy, Cheryl Thurber, and Branch Warfield.
  3. Unitarian-Universalist Congregation of Monmouth County, NJ: Jim McCorkel, Irene Gibson, John, Anne, Roshan, Bob Guenther, Richard Held, Lynn Dash, Richard Muise.

4. St. Mary's Catholic Church—Environmental Committee, NJ: Stephen, Ann, Judith Major, Marie Savoia, Michael Savoia, Kathleen Mogensen, William Mogensen, Elaine Carroll.
5. Reformed Church of Highland Park, NJ: Seth Kaper-Dale, David Day, Marc Laurano, Patricia Ruff, Jean Stockdale, Monica, and Wendy.
6. University Baptist Church, Seattle, WA: Eric, Erika, Ralph, Pete, Martha Bean, and Tim.
7. Catholic pesticide educators and agricultural workers, Mattawa, WA: Rafael, Pablo, Carmen, Maria.
8. Church of the Atonement (Episcopal), Tenafly, NJ: Angie, Carole, Judy, Alison, Guy.
9. Medicine and Ministry Christian leadership conference, NC: Anne Edwards, Nancy Hobe, Richard Hobe, George Kinnivan, Susan Lefler, Charles Lefler, Patrick McAleney, Wendy McCain, John McCormick, Donna McCormick, Jack Nietert, and Chris Nietert.
10. St. Pascal Baylon Catholic Church, Queens, NY: Mercedes Asemota, Benson Asemota, Bruce Brown, Gladys Brown, Edith Gallmon, and Arthurine DeSola.
11. St. Elizabeth's Episcopal Church, Elizabeth, NJ: Anthony Davis, Barbara Davis, Helen Gamova, Patricia Davis Adams, Corine Shillingford Judah, Asha Brown, Barbara Camacho, Shoan Davis, Karen Tanner-Oliphant, Burnett Davis, Veronica Funderberk, and Eugene Wilson.
12. Northland, A Church Distributed (evangelical)—Creation Care Task Force, FL: Bob Giguere, Amber Hoffmann, Sarah, Dan, Paul Rahill, and Raymond Randall.
13. Rev. Dr. Joel Hunter, pastor, Northland, A Church Distributed, FL (interview).

Jewish
1. Jewish Reconstructionist Congregation, Chicago, IL: Jerry, Julie, Carole, Sybil, and Howard.
2. Garrett Rosenblatt, (Reform tradition) environmental advocate, AZ (interview).

3. (Conservative tradition) Jewish Theological Seminary, NY (anonymous interview).

Native American
1. Shonto Begay, Navajo artist, AZ (interview).
2. Tony Skrelunas, Navajo sustainable economic development leader, AZ (interview).
3. Gordon Isaac, Navajo, KEYA Earth, AZ (interview).
4. Gabriel Yaiva, Navajo/ Hopi, KEYA Earth, AZ (interview).
5. Evon Peters, Gw'ichin chief (Arctic Circle; interviewed in AZ).

Other World Religions
1. Buddhist focus group, NJ: Jason Davis, Katrina Fossas-Durante, Elaine Held, Ellen Lichtig, and Dick Muise.
2. Hindu focus group, NJ: Madhav, Ved Chaudhary, Piyush Desai, Veena Desai, Satya Dosapati, Sunanda Dosapati, Lata Phadke, Madhav, Lata Swamy, Uma, and Ramesh.
3. Jain focus group, NJ: Naresh Jain, Rahul Garg, Vinay Garg, Aridaman Jain, Poonam Garg, Alok Jain, and Neelam. (Note: The Buddhist, Hindu, and Jain focus groups were organized by members of the Monmouth Center for World Religions and Ethical Thought.)
4. D.C. Green Muslims, Washington, DC: Sanjana Ahmad, Mohamad Chakaki, Sarah Jawaid, and Rima Kharuf.

Environmental Advocates; Religious Affiliation Unspecified
1. Jorge Lobos, migrant worker advocate, Yakima, WA.
2. Tito Rodriguez, migrant worker advocate, Yakima, WA.
3. Charles Callaway, urban environmental advocate, NY.
4. Focus group of self-described atheists and agnostics, NY: Andrew Burrell, Kate Detwiler, Eleni Nikitopoulos, SuJen Roberts, Eliza, Jonathan.

Participants' last names are included according to their preferences.

APPENDIX C

C.1. Comprehensive Chart of All Topics
Discussed by Participants, Organized by Theme

Italicized topics had the highest number of references (see Appendix C.2).

Favorite Aspect of Tradition
freedom of inquiry
sense of community
small community
shared values
other

New Ways of Looking at Faith
doctrines applied to environment
doctrines revisioned in light of earth
anthropocentrism
supernatural themes

Sources of Motivation for Environmental Action
knowledge
knowledge gap
recognizing interdependence
  ecological
  spiritual
  economic
  globalization/ social
influences (books, lectures, etc.)
grandchildren
future time span

frugal
interest
concern harm
economics
social justice
health
neighbor
religious obligation
stewardship
act virtuously regardless of hope
experiences in nature

Leadership

persistence
set example
peer pressure
pioneers
respond to friend's invitation
respect

Community Factors That Were Obstacles

complicit in societal disengagement
politics as divisive
zealotry
the tree hugger perception
earth issues were a "hard sell"

Community Factors That Created Success

clergy
interfaith collaboration
sense of mission
community support/an "easy sell"
celebration and worship
economically practical
practical
radical change or simple steps
youth
guidance from national governance

Social Barriers or Obstacles to Environmental Action
  industry lobbies and misinformation
  action gap
  consumerism and waste
  caring gap
  convenience
  progress
  busy
  unsustainable habits
  lazy, could do more
  doubt actions made a difference
  economically costly
  overwhelmed
  affect and emotions
  hardest thing done/sacrifice

C.2. Selective Chart of Topics with
Highest Number of References by Participants

These topics were discussed most frequently (at least 30 references). The numbers following each topic show the total number of references to the topic, inclusive of all conversations.

Theme	*Number of References*	*In How Many Conversations*
Knowledge	79	23
Sense of spiritual interdependence	75	23
Doctrines applied to environment	65	18
Industry lobbies and misinformation	57	17
Social justice	55	17
Knowledge gap	50	16
Action gap (caring but not taking action)	49	15

Consumerism/waste	49	18
Aware of social interdependence	47	20
Influence of books, lectures, movies, media	40	15
Religious obligation	44	19
Freedom of inquiry as favorite aspect of faith	40	13
Community as favorite aspect of faith	39	15
Interfaith collaboration	39	19
Congregations' complicity in societal denial	39	10
Environmental mission as congregation	39	12
Politics as divisive	38	15
Health concerns as a motivator	38	14
Leadership	36	14
Experiences in nature	35	12
Aware of ecological interdependence	34	17
Caring gap (understanding but not caring)	32	13
Doctrines revisioned in light of environment	32	14

C.3. Thematic Charts of Interrelated Topics

Tables of Data Relevant to Chapter 1

Table 1.1 Topics Relevant to Green Spirituality		
Topic given a separate code in NVivo	*Number of References*	*In How Many Conversations*
Knowledge about the environment, climate change	79	23
Sense of spiritual interdependence	75	23
Concern for social justice	55	17
Experiences in nature	53	13
Knowledge gap	50	16
Aware of social globalization (cultures, politics)	50	16
Religious obligation	44	19
Interfaith sensibility	46	18
Aware of ecological interdependence	40	15
Free inquiry as favorite aspect of faith identity	40	13
Community as favorite aspect of faith identity	39	15
Emotional connection to environment	28	10
Desire to protect the gift of the earth	27	10
Sense of future time span	26	12
Experiencing reverence in nature	25	13
Commitment to stewardship	20	6
Act despite lack of hope	19	12
Being habitually frugal	17	10
Concern for grandchildren	17	8
Acting for economic savings	2	9
Longstanding interest in nature	14	7

Table 1.2 Topics Relevant to Leadership		
Topic Given a Separate Code in NVivo	*Number of References*	*In How Many Conversations*
Leadership in general	36	14
Persistence	26	11
Setting an example	17	11
Peer pressure	11	5
Ability to be a pioneer	6	5
Inviting friends to join initiatives	5	5
Having community respect	2	2

Tables of Data Relevant to Chapter 2

Table 2.1. Topics Generating the Knowledge Gap Construct		
Topic given a separate code in NVivo	*Number of References*	*In How Many Conversations*
Knowledge about the environment, climate change	79	23
Industry lobbies	57	17
Knowledge gap	50	16
Influence of books, lectures, movies, media	40	15

Table 2.2. Topics Generating the Caring Gap Construct (*"I know, but … "*)		
Topic given a separate code in NVivo	*Number of References*	*In How Many Conversations*
Caring gap (remarks about knowing but not caring)	32	13
Consumerism/waste	49	18
Lifestyle progress entails resource use (paper towels represent advancement over a rag bag)	26	13
Distracted? Disinterest?		

Table 2.3. Topics Generating the Action Gap Construct ("*I care, but ...* ")		
Topic given a separate code in NVivo	*Number of References*	*In How Many Conversations*
Action gap (expressed in general terms)	49	15
Unsustainable habits, unintentional harm to environment	26	11
Convenience	23	10
Poor societal options (lack of public transit, fuel efficient cars)	23	9
Lazy, I could do more	22	12
Busy	19	13
Overwhelmed	18	8
Comfortable	17	6
Doubt can make a difference	6	4

Tables of Data Relevant to Chapter 3

Table 3.1. Topics Related to Successful Initiatives		
Topic given a separate code in NVivo	*Number of References*	*In How Many Conversations*
Strong support for initiatives, "easy sell"	36	16
Involve young people	29	14
Discuss impact of radical changes or simple steps	27	10
Successful because of cost savings	20	14
Successful because practical	15	9
Celebration and worship	15	8
Initiatives involved education	14	8

Table 3.2. Topics Expressing Obstacles to Community Engagement		
Topic given a separate code in NVivo	*Number of References*	*In How Many Conversations*
Congregations' complicity in societal denial	39	10
Politics as divisive	38	15
Costs of environmental initiatives were a barrier	23	12
Environmental "zealotry" is counterproductive	9	6
Tree-hugger stereotype turns off people	6	5
Earth issues were a "hard sell"	5	4
Needed guidance	4	1

APPENDIX D

Hypotheses

This is a partial list of some of the questions that guided my initial research.

If it is true that major steps have been taken beyond privatized, anthropocentric, otherworldly theologies, what steps are needed to take these *beyond individual beliefs into public action*?

Is the starting point for most people environmentalism, brought back to faith, or faith, finding that God is green?

If religious values do not automatically translate into action, do religious values translate into action under certain circumstances?

Religious values correlate with/are determined by/are strongly shaped by political and social values.

How does understanding religious motivations help inspire other religious people?

Theology has focused on demonstrating coherence of care for earth with core religious values: one should care and act. Religious scholars have explored background worldviews: the nature of the cosmos, the nature of the human. The question remains, does one care and act?

What causes religious people to accept that caring for earth is a religious value incumbent on them, and further act on their values?

The existence of official theological teaching affirming care of the earth as a moral responsibility does not by itself cause careful behavior. (1) People must know and accept these teachings. (2) People must then be motivated to act on them. Why do active religious environmentalists actualize these values?

How does environmental advocacy compare to other forms of moral leadership? For example, poverty advocacy, compassion for sick, mentoring, etc.—these are commonly taught values that are differently prioritized.

How can advocates nurture and identify the roots of faith-based care for the earth?

What can religious authority ask? Activism? Sacrifice? Following the Golden Rule?

Index